Unity Game Develo Blueprints

CW00969527

Explore the various enticing features of Unity and learn how to develop awesome games

John P. Doran

BIRMINGHAM - MUMBAI

Unity Game Development Blueprints

Copyright © 2014 Packt Publishing

All rights reserved. No part of this book may be reproduced, stored in a retrieval system, or transmitted in any form or by any means, without the prior written permission of the publisher, except in the case of brief quotations embedded in critical articles or reviews.

Every effort has been made in the preparation of this book to ensure the accuracy of the information presented. However, the information contained in this book is sold without warranty, either express or implied. Neither the author, nor Packt Publishing, and its dealers and distributors will be held liable for any damages caused or alleged to be caused directly or indirectly by this book.

Packt Publishing has endeavored to provide trademark information about all of the companies and products mentioned in this book by the appropriate use of capitals. However, Packt Publishing cannot guarantee the accuracy of this information.

First published: November 2014

Production reference: 1041114

Published by Packt Publishing Ltd.
Livery Place
35 Livery Street
Birmingham B3 2PB, UK.

ISBN 978-1-78355-365-5

www.packtpub.com

Credits

Author

John P. Doran

Reviewers

James King

Gary Riches

Adam Single

Jacquelyn Soh

Kerrie Woollhouse

Commissioning Editor

Akram Hussain

Acquisition Editor

Harsha Bharwani

Content Development Editor

Ruchita Bhansali

Technical Editors

Shiny Poojary

Sebastian Rodrigues

Copy Editors

Roshni Banerjee

Sarang Chari

Adithi Shetty

Project Coordinator

Kranti Berde

Proofreaders

Simran Bhogal

Lucy Rowland

Jonathan Todd

Indexers

Hemangini Bari

Tejal Soni

Production Coordinator

Aparna Bhagat

Cover Work

Aparna Bhagat

About the Author

John P. Doran is a technical game designer who has been creating games for over 10 years. He has worked on an assortment of games in teams with members ranging from just himself to over 70, in student, mod, and professional projects.

He previously worked at LucasArts on *Star Wars: 1313* as a game design intern; the only junior designer on a team of seniors. He was also the lead instructor of DigiPen-Ubisoft Campus Game Programming Program, instructing graduate-level students in an intensive, advanced-level game programming curriculum.

John is currently a technical designer in DigiPen's Research and Development department. In addition to that, he also tutors and assists students on various subjects while giving lectures on game development, including C++, Unreal, Flash, Unity, and more.

In addition to this title, he has authored *Getting Started with UDK* and *Mastering UDK Game Development*, and co-authored *UDK iOS Game Development Beginner's Guide*; he is also the author of the *UDK Game Development* video—all available from Packt Publishing.

I want to thank my brother, Chris, and my wife, Hannah, for being supportive and patient with me as I spent my free time and weekends away from them to work on this book.

On that same note, as always, I also want to thank Samir Abou Samra and Elie Hosry for their support and encouragement while working on this book as well as the rest of the DigiPen Singapore staff.

Last but not least, I'd love to thank my family as well as my parents, Joseph and Sandra, who took me seriously when I told them I wanted to make games.

About the Reviewers

Gary Riches is a senior software engineer and long-standing member of the iOS developer community. He has a keen interest in emerging technologies and is currently exploring what's possible with virtual reality.

Having worked as a software engineer for 16 years, he has had the opportunity to present his work worldwide at technology events, such as CES, Electronica, and Apps World.

He is the author of *Ouya Unity Game Development, Packt Publishing* and co-author of *You can make an APP, Future Publishing*.

When not building apps for clients, he also creates games and educational experiences for his own company, Bouncing Ball Games. The titles so far include *Aztec Antics, Amazed*, and *Nursery Rhymes: Volumes 1, 2, and 3*.

Adam Single is a husband, father, professional developer, indie developer, lover of music, and gamer. He's the coder for 7bit Hero; a programmer on the tech team at Real Serious Games in Brisbane, Australia; cofounder, programmer, and codesigner at Sly Budgie; and co-organizer of the Game Technology Brisbane meetup.

Since entering the professional game development industry in 2011, Adam has worked on numerous mobile games, including the Android hit Photon and a pre-installed game for specific Disney Japan handsets. He's been the programmer on a team that created a huge, interactive display at Queensland University of Technology's amazing multitouch screen installation, The Cube, as a part of Australia's first Digital Writing Residency and worked on a team at Real Serious Games creating large-scale, interactive simulations for the mining and construction industries. All of this has been done using the Unity game engine.

Adam has a passion for the unique and engaging possibilities inherent in modern technology. When he's not working on exciting new game mechanics for Sly Budgie, he's experimenting with "homemade VR" using mobile phone technology and pushing the exciting ideas behind 7bit Hero's live music/multiplayer game interaction down whichever fascinating path it may lead.

Jacquelyn Soh is a game developer who has been creating games for over 7 years. She is proficient in multiple aspects of game development, including programming, game designing, producing, and even art development. She is skilled in multiple languages and engines, including C, C++, C#, JavaScript, ActionScript, Python, HTML, CSS, Unity, Scirra Construct, Microsoft XNA, and several others.

Jacquelyn began her programming career in Flash, working on an online virtual world. Unsatisfied with her knowledge, she joined DigiPen Institute of Technology and graduated with a Bachelor's degree in Computer Science and Game Design with a Mathematics Minor.

Jacquelyn has since worked on a variety of games including virtual worlds, indie games, serious games, and various professional projects. Some game titles she has worked on include *Tiny Dice Dungeon, Wiglington and Wenks*, and *Lord of the Guardians*. She is currently working as a software engineer and an indie developer. She can be found online at www.jacquelynsoh.com and can be contacted at jacquelyn.soh@gmail.com.

Kerrie Woollhouse is a very creative and artistic individual with 7 years of experience in game development, web development, art, and photography. She has also recently enjoyed being a technical reviewer for Packt Publishing Unity books, including *Learning Unity 2D Game Development by Example*.

Kerrie continues to follow her passions with the highest ambitions and looks forward to expanding on current and future projects.

I would like to say a special thank you to my wife for all her love and continuous support.

www.PacktPub.com

Support files, eBooks, discount offers, and more

You might want to visit www.PacktPub.com for support files and downloads related to your book.

Did you know that Packt offers eBook versions of every book published, with PDF and ePub files available? You can upgrade to the eBook version at www.PacktPub.com and as a print book customer, you are entitled to a discount on the eBook copy. Get in touch with us at service@packtpub.com for more details.

At www.PacktPub.com, you can also read a collection of free technical articles, sign up for a range of free newsletters and receive exclusive discounts and offers on Packt books and eBooks.

http://PacktLib.PacktPub.com

Do you need instant solutions to your IT questions? PacktLib is Packt's online digital book library. Here, you can access, read and search across Packt's entire library of books.

Why subscribe?

- Fully searchable across every book published by Packt
- Copy and paste, print and bookmark content
- On demand and accessible via web browser

Free access for Packt account holders

If you have an account with Packt at www.PacktPub.com, you can use this to access PacktLib today and view nine entirely free books. Simply use your login credentials for immediate access.

Table of Contents

Preface

Unity, available in free and pro versions, is one of the most popular third-party game engines available. It is a cross-platform game engine, making it easy to write your game once and then port it to PC, consoles, and even the Web, which makes it a great choice for both indie and AAA developers.

Unity Game Development Blueprints takes readers on an exploration into using Unity to the fullest extent, working on 3D and 2D titles, exploring how to create GUIs, and publishing the game for the world to see. Using this book, you will be able to create a 2D twin-stick shooter, a side-scrolling platformer with an in-game level editor, a first-person survival horror shooter game, and a GUI menu system to use in all your future titles. In addition, you will learn how to publish your game with an installer to make your title look really polished and stand out from the crowd.

Each chapter either pushes your skills in Unity into new areas or pushes them to the very limits of what they can be used for. Finally, we will also explore Unity's new GUI system, which is currently in beta, showing examples while discussing the advantages and disadvantages of using it.

What this book covers

Chapter 1, 2D Twin-stick Shooter, shows us how to create a 2D multidirectional shooter game. In this game, the player controls a ship that can move around the screen using the keyboard and shoot projectiles in the direction the mouse is pointing at. Enemies and obstacles will spawn towards the player, and the player will avoid/shoot them. This chapter will also serve as a refresher on a lot of the concepts of working in Unity and give an overview of the recent addition of native 2D tools to Unity.

Chapter 2, Creating GUIs, will expand on our twin-stick shooter game, adding additional UI elements, including a main menu as well as a pause menu and options menu, and will give us the ability to restart our project.

Chapter 3, Side-scrolling Platformer, shows us how to create a side-scrolling platformer. We will learn the similarities between working in 2D and 3D and the differences, in particular, when it comes to Physics.

Chapter 4, First Person Shooter Part 1 – Creating Exterior Environments, discusses the role of a level designer who has been tasked to create an outdoor environment while learning about mesh placement. In addition, we will also learn some beginner-level design.

Chapter 5, First Person Shooter Part 2 – Creating Interior Environments, discusses the role of a level designer who has been tasked to create an interior environment using assets already provided to us by the environment artist.

Chapter 6, First Person Shooter Part 3 – Implementing Gameplay and AI, shows how we are going to be adding in interactivity in the form of adding in enemies, shooting behaviors, and the gameplay to make our game truly shine. In addition, we'll also learn how to use an Xbox 360 Controller to accept input in our game.

Chapter 7, Creating Save Files in Unity, talks about how to add in functionality to some of our previously created games, adding in high scores and even an in-game level editor that can be used for future projects.

Chapter 8, Finishing Touches, talks about exporting our game from Unity and then creating an installer so that we can give it to all of our friends, family, and prospective customers!

Chapter 9, Creating GUIs Part 2 – Unity's New GUI System, explores Unity's new GUI system, including creating health bars that move with characters, with text. We will also learn how to work with buttons using the new system, while also having elements scale correctly to work with any resolution.

What you need for this book

Throughout this book, we will work within the Unity 3D game engine, which you can download from `http://unity3d.com/unity/download/`. The projects were created using Version 4.5.3, but the project should work with minimal changes, with differences between this version and the 4.6 beta being pointed out when they occur. In *Chapter 9, Creating GUIs Part 2 – Unity's New GUI System*, since we are using the new GUI system, we will be using the Unity beta version, which can be downloaded from `http://unity3d.com/unity/beta/4.6`.

For the sake of simplicity, we will assume that you are working on a Windows-powered computer. Though Unity allows you to code in either C#, Boo, or UnityScript; for this book, we will be using C#.

Who this book is for

This book is for those who want to do more with Unity and have a series of completed projects by the end of the book. Readers who are familiar with the basics of how to create things in Unity will have an easier time.

Conventions

In this book, you will find a number of text styles that distinguish between different kinds of information. Here are some examples of these styles and an explanation of their meaning.

Code words in text, database table names, folder names, filenames, file extensions, pathnames, dummy URLs, user input, and Twitter handles are shown as follows: "Once inside, go to your operating system's browser window, open up the Chapter 1/Assets folder that we provided, and drag the playerShip.png file into the folder to move it into our project."

A block of code is set as follows:

```
// Add game's title to the screen, above our button
GUI.Label( new Rect(buttonX + 2.5f ,
            buttonY - 50,
            110.0f, 20.0f),
  "Twinstick Shooter", titleStyle );
```

When we wish to draw your attention to a particular part of a code block, the relevant lines or items are set in bold:

```
// Add game's title to the screen, above our button
GUI.Label( new Rect(buttonX + 2.5f ,
                buttonY - 50,
                110.0f, 20.0f),
  "Twinstick Shooter", titleStyle );
```

New terms and **important words** are shown in bold. Words that you see on the screen, in menus or dialog boxes, appear in the text like this: "From there, click on **Folder**, and you'll notice that a new folder has been created inside of your **Assets** folder."

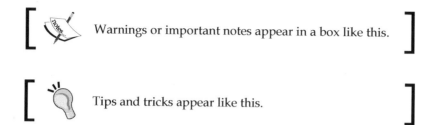

Reader feedback

Feedback from our readers is always welcome. Let us know what you think about this book—what you liked or may have disliked. Reader feedback is important for us as it helps us develop titles that you really get the most out of.

To send us general feedback, simply e-mail feedback@packtpub.com, and mention the book's title in the subject of your message.

If there is a topic that you have expertise in and you are interested in either writing or contributing to a book, see our author guide at www.packtpub.com/authors.

Customer support

Now that you are the proud owner of a Packt book, we have a number of things to help you to get the most from your purchase.

Downloading the example code

You can download the example code files from your account at http://www.packtpub.com for all the Packt Publishing books you have purchased. If you purchased this book elsewhere, you can visit http://www.packtpub.com/support and register to have the files e-mailed directly to you.

Downloading the color images of this book

We also provide you with a PDF file that has color images of the screenshots/diagrams used in this book. The color images will help you better understand the changes in the output. You can download this file from: https://www.packtpub.com/sites/default/files/downloads/3655OT_Graphics.pdf.

Errata

Although we have taken every care to ensure the accuracy of our content, mistakes do happen. If you find a mistake in one of our books—maybe a mistake in the text or the code—we would be grateful if you would report this to us. By doing so, you can save other readers from frustration and help us improve subsequent versions of this book. If you find any errata, please report them by visiting `http://www.packtpub.com/submit-errata`, selecting your book, clicking on the **errata submission form** link, and entering the details of your errata. Once your errata are verified, your submission will be accepted and the errata will be uploaded to our website or added to any list of existing errata under the **Errata** section of that title. To view the previously submitted errata, go to `https://www.packtpub.com/books/content/support` and enter the name of the book in the search field. The required information will appear under the Errata section.

Piracy

Piracy of copyrighted material on the Internet is an ongoing problem across all media. At Packt, we take the protection of our copyright and licenses very seriously. If you come across any illegal copies of our works in any form on the Internet, please provide us with the location address or website name immediately so that we can pursue a remedy.

Please contact us at `copyright@packtpub.com` with a link to the suspected pirated material.

We appreciate your help in protecting our authors and our ability to bring you valuable content.

Questions

If you have a problem with any aspect of this book, you can contact us at `questions@packtpub.com`, and we will do our best to address the problem.

1
2D Twin-stick Shooter

The *shoot 'em up* genre of games is one of the earliest kinds of games. In shoot 'em ups, the player character is a single entity fighting a large number of enemies. They are typically played with a top-down perspective, which is perfect for 2D games. Shoot 'em up games also exist with many categories, based upon their design elements.

Elements of a shoot 'em up were first seen in the 1961 *Spacewar!* game. However, the concept wasn't popularized until 1978 with *Space Invaders*. The genre was quite popular throughout the 1980s and 1990s and went in many different directions, including *bullet hell* games, such as the titles of the Touhou Project. The genre has recently gone through a resurgence in recent years with games such as Bizarre Creations' *Geometry Wars: Retro Evolved*, which is more famously known as a twin-stick shooter.

Project overview

Over the course of this chapter, we will be creating a 2D multidirectional shooter game similar to *Geometry Wars*.

In this game, the player controls a ship. This ship can move around the screen using the keyboard and shoot projectiles in the direction that the mouse points at. Enemies and obstacles will spawn toward the player, and the player will avoid/shoot them. This chapter will also serve as a refresher on a lot of the concepts of working in Unity and give an overview of the recent addition of native 2D tools into Unity.

Your objectives

This project will be split into a number of tasks. It will be a simple step-by-step process from beginning to end. Here is the outline of our tasks:

- Setting up the project
- Creating our scene

- Adding in player movement
- Adding in shooting functionality
- Creating enemies
- Adding GameController to spawn enemy waves
- Particle systems
- Adding in audio
- Adding in points, score, and wave numbers
- Publishing the game

Prerequisites

Before we start, we will need to get the latest Unity version, which you can always get by going to http://unity3d.com/unity/download/ and downloading it there:

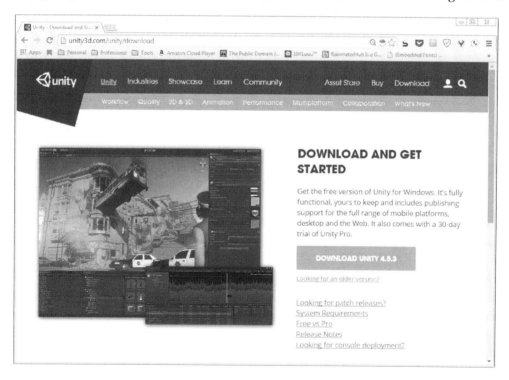

At the time of writing this book, the version is 4.5.3, but this project should work in future versions with minimal changes.

We will also need some graphical assets for use in our project. These can be downloaded from the example code provided for this book on Packt Publishing's website (`http://www.PacktPub.com`).

Navigate to the preceding URL, and download the `Chapter1.zip` package and unzip it. Inside the `Chapter1` folder, there are a number of things, including an `Assets` folder, which will have the art, sound, and font files you'll need for the project as well as the `Chapter_1_Completed.unitypackage` (this is the complete chapter package that includes the entire project for you to work with). I've also added in the complete game exported (`TwinstickShooter Exported`) as well as the entire project zipped up in the `TwinstickShooter Project.zip` file.

Setting up the project

At this point, I have assumed that you have Unity freshly installed and have started it up.

1. With Unity started, go to **File | New Project**. Select **Project Location** of your choice somewhere on your hard drive, and ensure you have **Setup defaults for** set to 2D. Once completed, select **Create**. At this point, we will not need to import any packages, as we'll be making everything from scratch. It should look like the following screenshot:

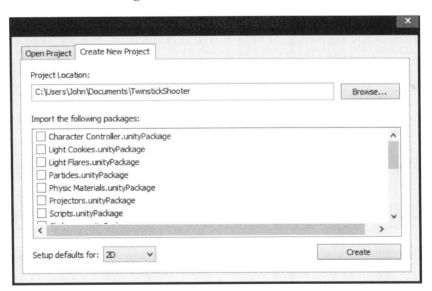

2. From there, if you see the **Welcome to Unity** pop up, feel free to close it out as we won't be using it. At this point, you will be brought to the general Unity layout, as follows:

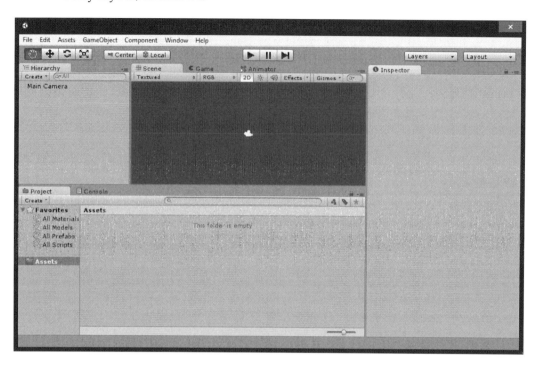

 Again, I'm assuming you have some familiarity with Unity before reading this book; if you would like more information on the interface, please visit http://docs.unity3d.com/Documentation/Manual/LearningtheInterface.html.

Keeping your Unity project organized is incredibly important. As your project moves from a small prototype to a full game, more and more files will be introduced to your project. If you don't start organizing from the beginning, you'll keep planning to tidy it up later on, but as deadlines keep coming, things may get quite out of hand.

This organization becomes even more vital when you're working as part of a team, especially if your team is telecommuting. Differing project structures across different coders/artists/designers is an awful mess to find yourself in.

Setting up a project structure at the start and sticking to it will save you countless minutes of time in the long run and only takes a few seconds, which is what we'll be doing now. Perform the following steps:

1. Click on the **Create** drop-down menu below the **Project** tab in the bottom-left side of the screen.

2. From there, click on **Folder**, and you'll notice that a new folder has been created inside your **Assets** folder.

3. After the folder is created, you can type in the name for your folder. Once done, press *Enter* for the folder to be created. We need to create folders for the following directories:

    ° Animations

    ° Prefabs

    ° Scenes

    ° Scripts

    ° Sprites

If you happen to create a folder inside another folder, you can simply drag-and-drop it from the left-hand side toolbar. If you need to rename a folder, simply click on it once and wait, and you'll be able to edit it again.

You can also use *Ctrl + D* to duplicate a folder if it is selected.

4. Once you're done with the aforementioned steps, your project should look something like this:

Creating our scene

Now that we have our project set up, let's get started with creating our player:

1. Double-click on the `Sprites` folder. Once inside, go to your operating system's browser window, open up the `Chapter 1/Assets` folder that we provided, and drag the `playerShip.png` file into the folder to move it into our project. Once added, confirm that the image is **Sprite** by clicking on it and confirming from the **Inspector** tab that **Texture Type** is `Sprite` (Sprite (2D and UI) in 4.6). If it isn't, simply change it to that, and then click on the **Apply** button. Have a look at the following screenshot:

 If you do not want to drag-and-drop the files, you can also right-click within the folder in the **Project Browser** (bottom-left corner) and select **Import New Asset** to select a file from a folder to bring it in.

 The art assets used for this tutorial were provided by Kenney. To see more of their work, please check out www.kenney.nl.

2. Next, drag-and-drop the ship into the **Scene** tab (the center part that's currently dark gray). Once completed, set the position of the sprite to the center of the **Screen** (0, 0) by right-clicking on the **Transform** component and then selecting **Reset Position**. Have a look at the following screenshot:

3. Now, with the player in the world, let's add in a background. Drag-and-drop the `background.png` file into your **Sprites** folder. After that, drag-and-drop a copy into the scene.

   If you put the background on top of the ship, you'll notice that currently the background is in front of the player (Unity puts newly added objects on top of previously created ones if their position on the Z axis is the same; this is commonly referred to as the **z-order**), so let's fix that.

Objects on the same Z axis without sorting layer are considered to be equal in terms of draw order; so just because a scene looks a certain way this time, when you reload the level it may look different. In order to guarantee that an object is in front of another one in 2D space is by having different Z values or using sorting layers.

4. Select your background object, and go to the **Sprite Renderer** component from the **Inspector** tab. Under **Sorting Layer**, select **Add Sorting Layer**. After that, click on the **+** icon for **Sorting Layers**, and then give **Layer 1** a name, Background. Now, create a sorting layer for Foreground and GUI. Have a look at the following screenshot:

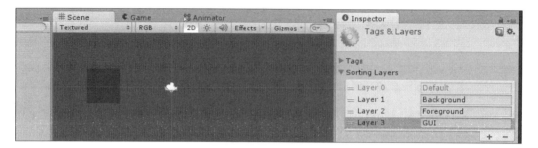

5. Now, place the player ship on the foreground and the background by selecting the object once again and then setting the **Sorting Layer** property via the drop-down menu. Now, if you play the game, you'll see that the ship is in front of the background, as follows:

At this point, we can just duplicate our background a number of times to create our full background by selecting the object in the **Hierarchy**, but that is tedious and time-consuming. Instead, we can create all the duplicates by either using code or creating a tileable texture. For our purposes, we'll just create a texture.

6. Delete the background sprite by left-clicking on the background object in the **Hierarchy** tab on the left-hand side and then pressing the *Delete* key. Then select the background sprite in the **Project** tab, change **Texture Type** in the **Inspector** tab to **Texture**, and click on **Apply**.

7. Now let's create a 3D cube by selecting **Game Object | Create Other | Cube** from the top toolbar. Change the object's name from **Cube** to Background. In the **Transform** component, change the **Position** to (0, 0, 1) and the **Scale** to (100, 100, 1).

> If you are using Unity 4.6 you will need to go to
> **Game Object | 3D Object | Cube** to create the cube.

Since our camera is at 0, 0, -10 and the player is at 0, 0, 0, putting the object at position 0, 0, 1 will put it behind all of our sprites. By creating a 3D object and scaling it, we are making it really large, much larger than the player's monitor. If we scaled a sprite, it would be one really large image with pixelation, which would look really bad. By using a 3D object, the texture that is applied to the faces of the 3D object is repeated, and since the image is tileable, it looks like one big continuous image.

8. Remove **Box Collider** by right-clicking on it and selecting **Remove Component**.

9. Next, we will need to create a material for our background to use. To do so, under the **Project** tab, select **Create | Material**, and name the material as BackgroundMaterial. Under the **Shader** property, click on the drop-down menu, and select **Unlit | Texture**. Click on the **Texture** box on the right-hand side, and select the background texture. Once completed, set the **Tiling** property's **x** and **y** to 25. Have a look at the following screenshot:

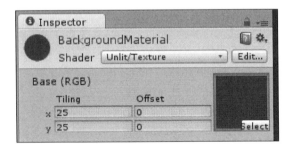

> In addition to just selecting from the menu, you can also drag-and-drop the background texture directly onto the **Texture** box, and it will set the property.
>
> Tiling tells Unity how many times the image should repeat in the **x** and **y** positions, respectively.

10. Finally, go back to the Background object in Hierarchy. Under the **Mesh Renderer** component, open up **Materials** by left-clicking on the arrow, and change **Element 0** to our **BackgroundMaterial** material. Consider the following screenshot:

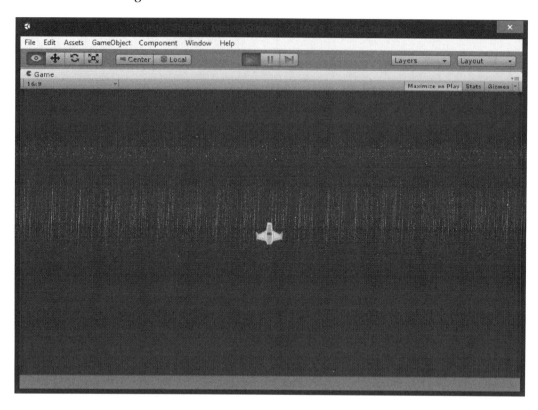

Now, when we play the game, you'll see that we now have a complete background that tiles properly.

Scripting 101

In Unity, the behavior of game objects is controlled by the different components that are attached to them in a form of association called **composition**. These components are things that we can add and remove at any time to create much more complex objects. If you want to do anything that isn't already provided by Unity, you'll have to write it on your own through a process we call **scripting**. Scripting is an essential element in all but the simplest of video games.

Unity allows you to code in either C#, Boo, or UnityScript, a language designed specifically for use with Unity and modelled after JavaScript. For this book, we will use C#.

C# is an object-oriented programming language—an industry-standard language similar to Java or C++. The majority of plugins from Asset Store are written in C#, and code written in C# can port to other platforms, such as mobile, with very minimal code changes. C# is also a strongly-typed language, which means that if there is any issue with the code, it will be identified within Unity and will stop you from running the game until it's fixed. This may seem like a hindrance, but when working with code, I very much prefer to write correct code and solve problems before they escalate to something much worse.

Implementing player movement

Now, at this point, we have a great-looking game, but nothing at all happens. Let's change that now using our player. Perform the following steps:

1. Right-click on the **Scripts** folder you created earlier, click on **Create**, and select the **C# Script** label. Once you click on it, a script will appear in the **Scripts** folder, and it should already have focus and should be asking you to type a name for the script—call it `PlayerBehaviour`.

2. Double-click on the script in Unity, and it will open **MonoDevelop**, which is an open source integrated development environment (IDE) that is included with your Unity installation.

After MonoDevelop has loaded, you will be presented with the C# stub code that was created automatically for you by Unity when you created the C# script.

Let's break down what's currently there before we replace some of it with new code. At the top, you will see two lines:

```
using UnityEngine;
using System.Collections;
```

Downloading the example code

You can download the example code files for all Packt Publishing books you have purchased from your account at http://www.packtpub.com. If you purchased this book elsewhere, you can visit http://www.packtpub.com/support and register to have the files e-mailed directly to you.

The engine knows that if we refer to a class that isn't located inside this file, then it has to reference the files within these namespaces for the referenced class before giving an error. We are currently using two namespaces.

The `UnityEngine` namespace contains interfaces and class definitions that let MonoDevelop know about all the addressable objects inside Unity.

The `System.Collections` namespace contains interfaces and classes that define various collections of objects, such as lists, queues, bit arrays, hash tables, and dictionaries.

We will be using a list, so we will change the line to the following:

```
using System.Collections.Generic;
```

The next line you'll see is:

```
public class PlayerBehaviour : MonoBehaviour {
```

You can think of a class as a kind of blueprint for creating a new component type that can be attached to `GameObjects`, the objects inside our scenes that start out with just a `Transform` and then have components added to them. When Unity created our C# stub code, it took care of that; we can see the result, as our file is called `PlayerBehaviour` and the class is also called `PlayerBehaviour`. Make sure that your `.cs` file and the name of the class match, as they must be the same to enable the script component to be attached to a game object. Next up is the : `MonoBehaviour` section of the code. The : symbol signifies that we inherit from a particular class; in this case, we'll use `MonoBehaviour`. All behavior scripts must inherit from `MonoBehaviour` directly or indirectly by being derived from it.

Inheritance is the idea of having an object to be based on another object or class using the same implementation. With this in mind, all the functions and variables that existed inside the `MonoBehaviour` class will also exist in the `PlayerBehaviour` class, because `PlayerBehaviour` is `MonoBehaviour`.

For more information on the `MonoBehaviour` class and all the functions and properties it has, check out `http://docs.unity3d.com/ScriptReference/MonoBehaviour.html`. Directly after this line, we will want to add some variables to help us with the project. Variables are pieces of data that we wish to hold on to for one reason or another, typically because they will change over the course of a program, and we will do different things based on their values.

Add the following code under the class definition:

```
// Movement modifier applied to directional movement.
public float playerSpeed = 2.0f;

// What the current speed of our player is
private float currentSpeed = 0.0f;

/*
 * Allows us to have multiple inputs and supports keyboard,
 * joystick, etc.
 */
public List<KeyCode> upButton;
public List<KeyCode> downButton;
public List<KeyCode> leftButton;
public List<KeyCode> rightButton;

// The last movement that we've made
private Vector3 lastMovement = new Vector3();
```

Between the variable definitions, you will notice comments to explain what each variable is and how we'll use it. To write a comment, you can simply add a // to the beginning of a line and everything after that is commented upon so that the compiler/interpreter won't see it. If you want to write something that is longer than one line, you can use /* to start a comment, and everything inside will be commented until you write */ to close it. It's always a good idea to do this in your own coding endeavors for anything that doesn't make sense at first glance.

For those of you working on your own projects in teams, there is an additional form of commenting that Unity supports, which may make your life much nicer: XML comments. They take up more space than the comments we are using, but also document your code for you. For a nice tutorial about that, check out http://unitypatterns.com/xml-comments/.

In our game, the player may want to move up using either the arrow keys or the *W* key. You may even want to use something else. Rather than restricting the player to just having one button, we will store all the possible ways to go up, down, left, or right in their own container. To do this, we are going to use a list, which is a holder for multiple objects that we can add or remove while the game is being played.

For more information on lists, check out `http://msdn.microsoft.com/en-us/library/6sh2ey19(v=vs.110).aspx`

One of the things you'll notice is the `public` and `private` keywords before the variable type. These are access modifiers that dictate who can and cannot use these variables. The `public` keyword means that any other class can access that property, while `private` means that only this class will be able to access this variable. Here, `currentSpeed` is private because we want our current speed not to be modified or set anywhere else. But, you'll notice something interesting with the `public` variables that we've created. Save your script by pressing **Ctrl + S** and then go back into the Unity project and drag-and-drop the `PlayerBehaviour` script onto the `playerShip` object. Before going back to the Unity project though, make sure that you save your `PlayerBehaviour` script. Not saving is a very common mistake made by people working with `MonoDevelop`. Have a look at the following screenshot:

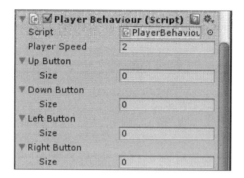

You'll notice now that the `public` variables that we created are located inside **Inspector** for the component. This means that we can actually set those variables inside **Inspector** without having to modify the code, allowing us to tweak values in our code very easily, which is a godsend for many game designers. You may also notice that the names have changed to be more readable. This is because of the naming convention that we are using with each word starting with a capital letter. This convention is called CamelCase (more specifically headlessCamelCase).

Now change the **Size** of each of the **Button** variables to 2, and fill in the **Element 0** value with the appropriate arrow and **Element 1** with w for up, A for left, S for down, and D for right. When this is done, it should look something like the following screenshot:

Now that we have our variables set, go back to MonoDevelop for us to work on the script some more.

The line after that is a function definition for a method called Start; it isn't a user method but one that belongs to MonoBehaviour. Where variables are data, functions are the things that modify and/or use that data. Functions are self-contained modules of code (enclosed within braces, { and }) that accomplish a certain task. The nice thing about using a function is that once a function is written, it can be used over and over again. Functions can be called from inside other functions:

```
void Start () {

}
```

Start is only called once in the lifetime of the behavior when the game starts and is typically used to initialize data.

> If you're used to other programming languages, you may be surprised that initialization of an object is not done using a constructor function. This is because the construction of objects is handled by the editor and does not take place at the start of gameplay as you might expect. If you attempt to define a constructor for a script component, it will interfere with the normal operation of Unity and can cause major problems with the project.

However, for this behavior, we will not need to use the `Start` function. Perform the following steps:

1. Delete the `Start` function and its contents.

   The next function that we see included is the `Update` function. Also inherited from `MonoBehaviour`, this function is called for every frame that the component exists in and for each object that it's attached to. We want to update our player ship's rotation and movement every turn.

2. Inside the `Update` function (between { and }), put the following lines of code:

   ```
   // Rotate player to face mouse
   Rotation();
   // Move the player's body
   Movement();
   ```

   Here, I called two functions, but these functions do not exist, because we haven't created them yet, which is why the text shows up as Red inside of MonoDevelop. Let's do that now!

3. Below the `Update` function and before } that closes the class at the end of the file, put the following function to close the class:

   ```
   // Will rotate the ship to face the mouse.
   void Rotation()
   {
       // We need to tell where the mouse is relative to the
       // player
       Vector3 worldPos = Input.mousePosition;
       worldPos = Camera.main.ScreenToWorldPoint(worldPos);

       /*
        * Get the differences from each axis (stands for
        * deltaX and deltaY)
        */
       float dx = this.transform.position.x - worldPos.x;
       float dy = this.transform.position.y - worldPos.y;
   ```

```
// Get the angle between the two objects
float angle = Mathf.Atan2(dy, dx) * Mathf.Rad2Deg;

/*
  * The transform's rotation property uses a Quaternion,
  * so we need to convert the angle in a Vector
  * (The Z axis is for rotation for 2D).
*/
Quaternion rot = Quaternion.Euler(new Vector3(0, 0, angle +
90));

// Assign the ship's rotation
this.transform.rotation = rot;
}
```

Now if you comment out the Movement line and run the game, you'll notice that the ship will rotate in the direction in which the mouse is. Have a look at the following screenshot:

4. Below the Rotation function, we now need to add in our Movement function the following code. Uncomment the Movement function call if you commented it out earlier:

```
// Will move the player based off of keys pressed
void Movement()
{
  // The movement that needs to occur this frame
  Vector3 movement = new Vector3();

  // Check for input
  movement += MoveIfPressed(upButton, Vector3.up);
  movement += MoveIfPressed(downButton, Vector3.down);
  movement += MoveIfPressed(leftButton, Vector3.left);
  movement += MoveIfPressed(rightButton, Vector3.right);

  /*
    * If we pressed multiple buttons, make sure we're only
    * moving the same length.
```

```
*/
movement.Normalize ();

// Check if we pressed anything
if(movement.magnitude > 0)
{
    // If we did, move in that direction
    currentSpeed = playerSpeed;
    this.transform.Translate(movement * Time.deltaTime *
                            playerSpeed, Space.World);
    lastMovement = movement;
}
else
{
    // Otherwise, move in the direction we were going
    this.transform.Translate(lastMovement * Time.deltaTime *
                            currentSpeed, Space.World);
    // Slow down over time
    currentSpeed *= .9f;
}
}
```

Now inside this function I've created another function called MoveIfPressed, so we'll need to add that in as well.

5.   Below this function, add in the following function as well:

```
/*
 * Will return the movement if any of the keys are pressed,
 * otherwise it will return (0,0,0)
*/
Vector3 MoveIfPressed( List<KeyCode> keyList, Vector3 Movement)
{
    // Check each key in our list
    foreach (KeyCode element in keyList)
    {
        if(Input.GetKey(element))
        {
            /*
             * It was pressed so we leave the function
             * with the movement applied.
            */
            return Movement;
        }
    }
```

```
    // None of the keys were pressed, so don't need to move
    return Vector3.zero;
}
```

6. Now, save your file and move back into Unity. Save your current scene as `Chapter_1.unity` by going to **File | Save Scene**. Make sure to save the scene to our `Scenes` folder we created earlier.

7. Run the game by pressing the play button. Have a look at the following screenshot:

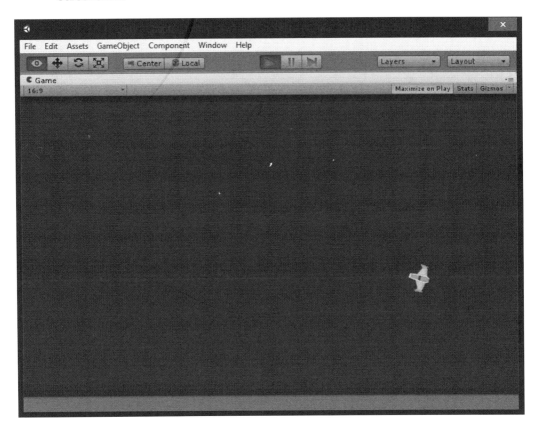

Now you'll see that we can move using the arrow keys or the $W A S D$ keys, and our ship will rotate to face the mouse. Great!

Shooting behavior

The next thing we will do is give our player the ability to shoot:

1. Open up the `PlayerBehaviour` script. In the top section where the other variables are present, we need to add some additional ones that we'll use:

    ```
    // The laser we will be shooting
    public Transform laser;

    // How far from the center of the ship should the laser be
    public float laserDistance = .2f;

    // How much time (in seconds) we should wait before
    // we can fire again
    public   float    timeBetweenFires = .3f;

    // If value is less than or equal 0, we can fire
    private float timeTilNextFire = 0.0f;

    // The buttons that we can use to shoot lasers
    public List<KeyCode> shootButton;
    ```

    One thing you may have noticed is that we have a `laser` variable that is of the type `Transform`. This is the laser we'll fire, which we will create shortly.

2. Inside our `Update` function, we will need to add some additional code, which is as follows:

    ```
    // a foreach loop will go through each item inside of
    // shootButton and do whatever we placed in {}s using the
    // element variable to hold the item
    foreach (KeyCode element in shootButton)
    {
      if(Input.GetKey(element) && timeTilNextFire < 0)
      {
        timeTilNextFire = timeBetweenFires;
        ShootLaser();
        break;
      }
    }

    timeTilNextFire -= Time.deltaTime;
    ```

In a manner very similar to what we did before with the player movement, we check each of the keys we allow the player to shoot with (such as the spacebar and *Enter* keys). If they press any of these keys and can fire again, then we will reset our timer and shoot a laser. However, we haven't made the ShootLaser function. Let's do that now.

3. Underneath the functions, add the following function:

```
// Creates a laser and gives it an initial position in front
// of the ship.
void ShootLaser()
{
  // calculate the position right in front of the ship's
  // position lazerDistance units away
  float posX = this.transform.position.x +
              (Mathf.Cos((transform.localEulerAngles.z - 90) *
               Mathf.Deg2Rad) * -laserDistance);
  float posY = this.transform.position.y + (Mathf.Sin((transform.
              localEulerAngles.z - 90) * Mathf.Deg2Rad) *
              -laserDistance);

  Instantiate(laser, new Vector3 (posX, posY, 0), this.transform.
rotation);
}
```

4. Save your file, and go back into Unity. You'll now see a number of additional variables that we can now set. Be sure to set the **Shoot Button** variable in the same manner that we did the movement buttons, changing the **Size** to 2 and setting **Element 0** to **Mouse0** and **Element 1** to **Space**.

 If, for some reason, your **Inspector** window doesn't update, save your project, and restart Unity. Upon reset, it should be updated.

5. Next, we will need to create our laser. Go back into our Assets folder from the example code, and move the laser.png file into our **Project** tab's Sprites folder.

6. Following that, drag-and-drop it into your scene from the **Scene** tab to place it in the level.

7. Right-click the Scripts folder you created earlier, click on **Create**, and select the **C# Script** label. Call this new script LaserBehaviour. Go into MonoDevelop, and use the following code:

```
using UnityEngine;
using System.Collections;
```

```
public class LaserBehaviour : MonoBehaviour
{
  // How long the laser will live
  public float lifetime = 2.0f;

  // How fast will the laser move
  public float speed = 5.0f;


  // How much damage will this laser do if we hit an enemy
  public int damage = 1;

  // Use this for initialization
  void Start ()
  {
    // The game object that contains this component will be
    // destroyed after lifetime seconds have passed
    Destroy(gameObject, lifetime);
  }

  // Update is called once per frame
  void Update ()
  {
    transform.Translate(Vector3.up * Time.deltaTime * speed);
  }
}
```

8. Attach LaserBehaviour to the laser object. Finally, add a **Box Collider** component by first selecting the laser object and then going to **Component | Physics 2D | Box Collider 2D**. The collision box, by default, will be the size of the image, but I want to shrink it to fit what is visually seen of it. To do that, we will change the **Size** attribute's **X** property to .06 and **Y** to .5.

    Now, the laser will move in the direction that it's facing and die after a period of 2 seconds! Next, let's make it so that the player can shoot them.

9. In the **Project** tab, go to the **Assets | Prefabs** folder, and drag-and-drop the laser object from our **Hierarchy** tab into it. You'll notice that the object **Hierarchy** will turn blue to show that it is a prefab.

Prefabs or prefabricated objects are the objects that we set aside to make copies during runtime, such as our bullets and eventually enemies that we'll spawn into the world, and we can create as many as we want. When you add a prefab to a scene, you create an instance of it. All of these instances are clones of the object located in our `Assets`. Whenever you change something in the prefab located in our `Prefab` folder, those changes are applied to all the objects that are already inside of your scene. For example, if you add a new component to `Prefab`, all the other objects we have in the scene will instantly contain the component as well. We can also apply any of the ones in our scene to be the blueprint for the others as well, which we will do later on. However, it is also possible to change the properties of a single instance while keeping the link intact. Simply change any property of a prefab instance inside your scene, and that particular value will become bolded to show that the value is overridden, and they will not be affected by changes in the source prefab. This allows you to modify prefab instances to make them different (unique) from their source prefabs without breaking the prefab link.

Have a look at the following screenshot:

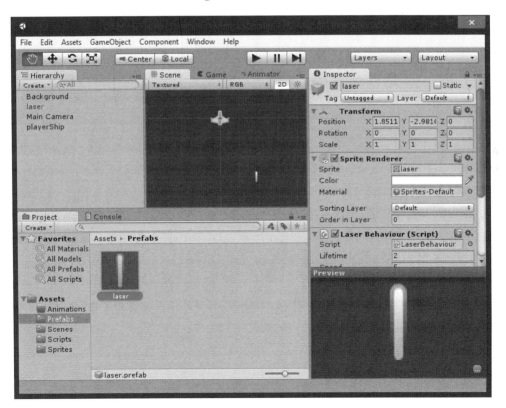

10. Now, delete the `laser` object from our scene, and then go to the `playerShip` object. Drag-and-drop the `laser` prefab into the **Laser** property of the `PlayerBehavior` component.

11. Finally, add a circle collider to our ship by going to **Component | Physics 2D | Circle Collider 2D.** Change the **Radius** property to `.3`.

Generally, in games, we want to be as efficient as possible toward calculations. Polygon collision is the most accurate collision, but it is much slower than using a box or a circle. In this case, I wanted to use a circle, because not only is it more efficient but it also allows the player some leeway in how close they can get to enemies without being hurt. Players will always think it's their skill if they get away, but if the collider is too big they will think the game is broken, which we want to avoid.

Have a look at the following screenshot:

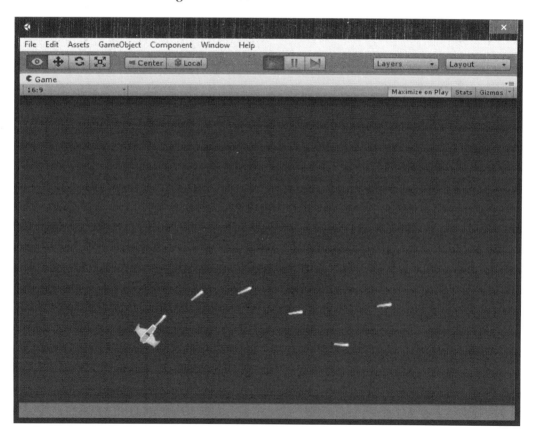

Now, our ship can shoot in the direction that the mouse is currently facing.

Creating enemies

Now, it's really cool that we have a player, but it'll get really boring if all we can do is move around and shoot some lasers in the dark. Next, we'll introduce some simple enemies that will move toward the player that we'll be able to shoot later. Perform the following steps:

1. Exit the game and access our example code's `Assets` folder; move the `enemy.png` file into our `Sprites` folder.

2. Following that, drag-and-drop it into your scene from the **Scene** tab to place it in the level.

3. Right-click on the **Scripts** folder you created earlier, click on **Create**, and select the **C# Script** label. Call this new script `MoveTowardsPlayer`. Go to `MonoDevelop` and use the following code:

```
using UnityEngine;
using System.Collections;

public class MoveTowardsPlayer : MonoBehaviour
{
  private Transform player;
  public float speed = 2.0f;

  // Use this for initialization
  void Start ()
  {
    player = GameObject.Find("playerShip").transform;
  }

  // Update is called once per frame
  void Update ()
  {
    Vector3 delta = player.position - transform.position;
    delta.Normalize();
    float moveSpeed = speed * Time.deltaTime;
    transform.position = transform.position + (delta * moveSpeed);
  }
}
```

In the beginning of the game, I find the player ship and get his transform component. Then, in every frame of the project, we move the enemy from where it currently is to the direction where the player is at.

 If you ever want to have objects run away from the player, use a negative value for the speed variable.

4. Drag-and-drop this newly added behavior onto our enemy object.

5. Next, add a circle collider to our enemy by going to **Component | Physics 2D | Circle Collider 2D**. Change the **Radius** property to .455, and run the game. Have a look at the following screenshot:

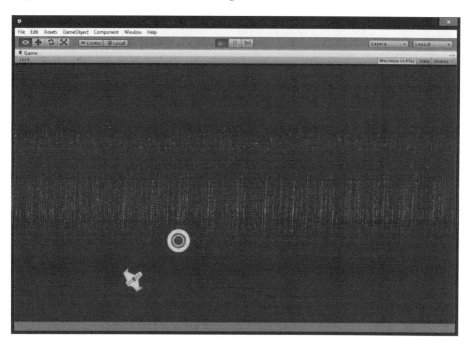

Now, you'll see that the enemy will always move toward you! But if we shoot it, nothing happens. Let's fix that as follows.

1. Right-click on the **Scripts** folder you created earlier, click on **Create**, and select the **C# Script** label. Call this new script EnemyBehaviour. Go to MonoDevelop, and use the following code:

```csharp
using UnityEngine; // MonoBehaviour

public class EnemyBehaviour : MonoBehaviour
{

    // How many times should I be hit before I die
    public int health = 2;

    void OnCollisionEnter2D(Collision2D theCollision)
    {
        // Uncomment this line to check for collision
        //Debug.Log("Hit"+ theCollision.gameObject.name);
```

```
    // this line looks for "laser" in the names of
    // anything collided.
    if(theCollision.gameObject.name.Contains("laser"))
    {
       LaserBehaviour laser = theCollision.gameObject.
GetComponent("LaserBehaviour") as LaserBehaviour;
       health -= laser.damage;
       Destroy (theCollision.gameObject);
    }

    if (health <= 0)
    {
       Destroy (this.gameObject);
    }
  }
}
```

Now, you will notice that we have commented a line of code calling the function Debug.Log. This function will print something onto your console, which may help you when debugging your own code in the future.

2. Save the file, and then go back into Unity. Attach the EnemyBehaviour behavior to your enemy object. For collision events to register we need to add a Rigidbody 2D component to our enemy by going to **Component | Physics 2D | Rigidbody 2D**. Change the **Gravity Scale to 0** so it will not fall. Have a look at the following screenshot:

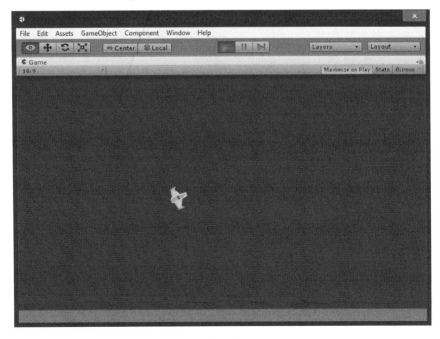

OnCollisionEnter2D is a function that will trigger when two objects with 2D colliders collide. It is important to note collision events are only sent if one of the colliders also has a non-kinematic rigidbody attached (which we just did).

For more info on OnCollisionEnter2D check out http://docs.unity3d.com/ScriptReference/Collider2D.OnCollisionEnter2D.html.

Now, whenever we hit the enemy with our bullets twice, it will die. Nice!

Adding GameController to spawn enemy waves

We have all the mechanics of our game completed at this point. Now, we need to actually create the game or manage what happens in the game. This game controller would be required to run our game, keep track of and display the game's score, and finally end the game whenever the player dies. Later on, we'll discuss a game state manager, which we can use for larger projects with multiple states, but for the sake of this simple project, we will create a single game controller. That's what we'll do now:

1. First, create an empty game object by going to **GameObject | Create Empty**. From there, with the object selected, go to **Inspector** and set its name to GameController, and optionally, for neatness sake, set its **Position** to (0, 0, 0).

2. Underneath the name, you'll see the **Tag** property. Change it from **Untagged** to **GameController**.

A **Tag** is a way to link to one or more game objects in a collected group. For instance, you might use **Player** and **Enemy** tags for players and enemies respectively; a **Collectable** tag could be defined for power-ups or coins that are placed in the scene; and so on. This could also have been used with **EnemyBehaviour** to check whether something was a bullet or not. One thing to note is the fact that **GameObject** can only have one tag assigned to it. Tags do nothing to the scene but are a way to identify game objects for scripting purposes.

3. Next, select **Add Component | New Script**, and once you are brought to the next menu, change the language to C# (C Sharp), and set the name of the script to GameController. Then press *Enter* or click on **Create** and **Add**.

4. Select the newly created script in the `Assets` folder of the **Project** tab, and move it to the `Assets\Scripts` folder. Go to **MonoDevelop** by double-clicking on the script file.

   While our game does many things, the most important thing is the spawning of enemies, which is what we'll be adding in first. Let's create a variable to store our enemy.

5. Inside of the class definition, add the following variable and then save the file:

```
// Our enemy to spawn
public Transform enemy;
```

6. Now, we can set the enemy that we currently have in the scene, but we should instead make the enemy a prefab and use it. To do so, drag the enemy from **Hierarchy** into your `Assets\Prefabs` folder. Once we've created the prefab, we can remove the enemy object from our scene by deleting it.

7. Next, drag-and-drop the enemy prefab into the **Enemy** variable in the **GameController** component.

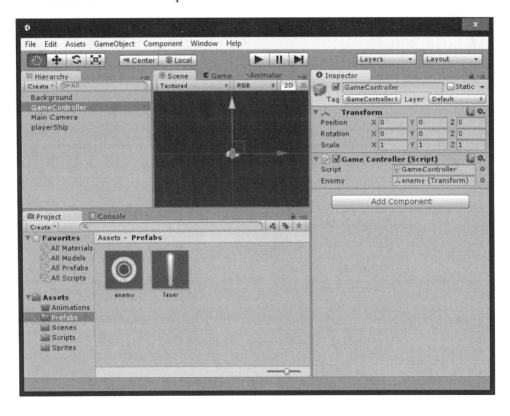

8. Next, go back into our `GameController` script by double-clicking it to go into **MonoDevelop**. Add the following additional variables to the component:

```
// We want to delay our code at certain times
public float timeBeforeSpawning = 1.5f;
public float timeBetweenEnemies = .25f;
public float timeBeforeWaves = 2.0f;

public    int enemiesPerWave = 10;
private int currentNumberOfEnemies = 0;
```

We now need a function to spawn enemies; let's call it `SpawnEnemies`. We don't want to spawn all the enemies at once. What we want is a steady stream of enemies to come to the player over the course of the game. However, in C#, to have a function pause the gameplay without having to stop the entire game, we need to use a coroutine that looks different from all the code that we've used so far.

9. Inside the `Start` method, add the following line:

```
StartCoroutine(SpawnEnemies());
```

A coroutine is like a function that has the ability to pause execution and continue where it left off after a period of time. By default, a coroutine is resumed on the frame after we start to `yield`, but it is also possible to introduce a time delay using the `WaitForSeconds` function for how long you want to wait before it's called again.

10. Now that we are already using the function, let's add in the `SpawnEnemies` function as follows:

```
// Coroutine used to spawn enemies
IEnumerator SpawnEnemies()
{
    // Give the player time before we start the game
    yield return new WaitForSeconds(timeBeforeSpawning);

    // After timeBeforeSpawning has elapsed, we will enter this loop
    while(true)
    {
        // Don't spawn anything new until all the previous
        // wave's enemies are dead
        if(currentNumberOfEnemies <= 0)
        {
            float randDirection;
            float randDistance;
```

```
        //Spawn 10 enemies in a random position
        for (int i = 0; i < enemiesPerWave; i++)
        {
          // We want the enemies to be off screen
          // (Random.Range gives us a number between the
          // first and second parameter)
          randDistance = Random.Range(10, 25);

          // Enemies can come from any direction
          randDirection = Random.Range(0, 360);

          // Using the distance and direction we set the position
          float posX = this.transform.position.x + (Mathf.
  Cos((randDirection) * Mathf.Deg2Rad) * randDistance);
          float posY = this.transform.position.y + (Mathf.
  Sin((randDirection) * Mathf.Deg2Rad) * randDistance);

          // Spawn the enemy and increment the number of
          // enemies spawned
          // (Instantiate Makes a clone of the first parameter
          // and places it at the second with a rotation of
          // the third.)
          Instantiate(enemy, new Vector3 (posX, posY, 0), this.
  transform.rotation);
          currentNumberOfEnemies++;
          yield return new WaitForSeconds(timeBetweenEnemies);
        }
      }
      // How much time to wait before checking if we need to
      // spawn another wave
      yield return new WaitForSeconds(timeBeforeWaves);
    }
  }
```

11. Now, when we destroy an enemy, we want to decrement the number of
    currentNumberOfEnemies, but it's a private variable, which means that it
    can only be changed inside the GameController class or one of the methods
    inside of the class. Simple enough? Now let's add a new function in our
    GameController class:

```
// Allows classes outside of GameController to say when we killed
// an enemy.
public void KilledEnemy()
{
  currentNumberOfEnemies--;
}
```

12. Finally, let's go back into our `EnemyBehaviour` class. Inside the
    `OnCollisionEnter2D` function under the Destroy function call, add the
    following two lines:

```
GameController controller = GameObject.FindGameObjectWithTag("Game
Controller").GetComponent("GameController") as GameController;
controller.KilledEnemy();
```

The preceding line gets the script `GameController` with the tag
`GameController`. The as keyword casts the object to a `GameController`
object. Casting basically tells the computer, "Even though the code says
it's some class, I'm telling you that it's another one."

This will call the `KilledEnemy` function from `GameController`, onto which
we set the `GameController` tag in step 2.

13. With all those changes, save both script files and run the game! Have a look
    at the following screenshot:

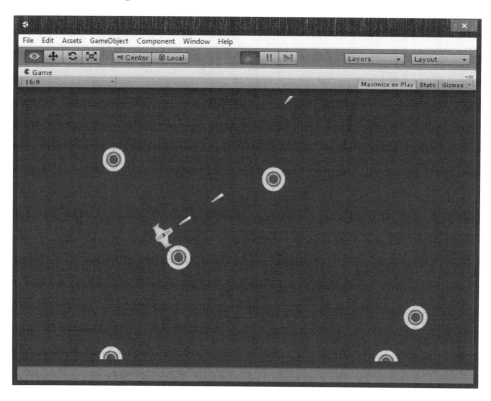

We now have waves of enemies that will now move toward the player! When we
kill all the enemies inside a wave, we will spawn the next wave. In such a short
period of time, we already have so much going on!

Particle systems for enemy explosion

Now that we have the basis for our game, let's spend some time to make the project look nicer. Particle systems are one of my go-to things to add juiciness to a game project and helps to set your project apart from others. Particles systems are composed of two separate parts: a particle and the thing that emits it. A particle is a small object that stores properties; generally we try to make these objects as simple as possible, as we want to spawn a large number of them. The emitter's job is to spawn a number of these and initialize their properties. Thankfully, Unity has a fully featured particle editor that's included with the engine, and we're going to use it in this section. Perform the following steps:

1. Create a new particle system by going to **GameObject | Create Other | Particle System**. Have a look at the following screenshot:

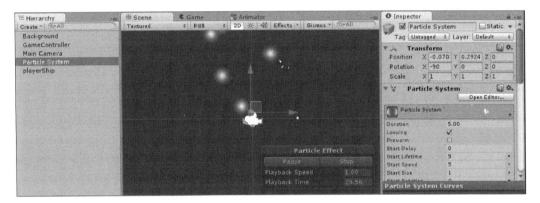

 If you are using Unity 4.6 use **GameObject | Particle System** to create the particle system.

Once you do this, you should see a default particle system show up. Do note that the system will only animate if it is the object selected and Unity is the active window.

2. Change the object's name to Explosion. First, under the **Particle System** tab, change **Duration** to 1.00, and then uncheck **Looping**.

3. Click on the downwards-facing arrow on the right-hand side of **Start Lifetime**, and change the values to be **Random Between Two Constants**. Change those values to 0 and 1. Do the same with **Start Speed**. Make **Start Size** use random values between 0 and .5.

4. Next, we will set the object's **Start Color** value to the same color as the UFO ship (you can use the eyedropper tool or set it to 210, 224, 230) and an **Alpha** value of 125. Have a look at the following screenshot:

5. Open the **Emission** tab, and change **Rate** to 200. This is how many particles are spawned at a time.

6. Open the **Shape** tab, change the **Shape** property to **Sphere**, and then set **Radius** to .35 to fit the rim of the ship. Enable the **Random Direction** option.

7. Back in the **Explosion** section, change the **Simulation Space** to **World**; that way, if this object moves, the already-spawned particles will not move.

8. Now, make this object a prefab by dragging-and-dropping it into the Prefabs folder. After that, delete the Explosion object in your **Hierarchy** object.

9. Go back to your EnemyBehaviour script file. We will first want to add in a new variable for us to use to spawn this explosion when it dies:

```
// When the enemy dies, we play an explosion
public Transform explosion;
```

10. Back in **Inspector**, drag-and-drop your new explosion prefab to fill in the explosion variable slot in our enemy prefab.

11. Coming back to the `EnemyBehaviour` script, let's spawn an explosion whenever we die. Inside your `if(health <= 0)` section of `CollisionEnter2D`, add in the following lines:

```
// Check if explosion was set
if(explosion)
{
  GameObject exploder = ((Transform)Instantiate(explosion, this.transform.position, this.transform.rotation)).gameObject;
  Destroy(exploder, 2.0f);
}
```

12. Save your script and scene files, and run your project! Have a look at the following screenshot:

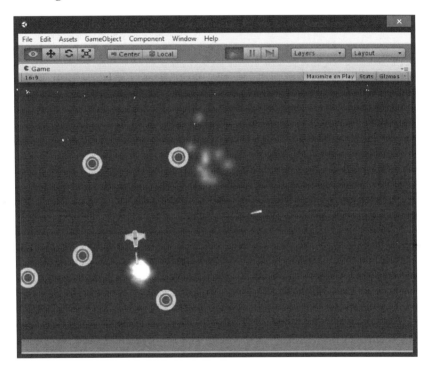

And now, whenever an enemy dies, it will spawn an explosion for us to see!

Adding in sound effects/music

Another thing that we can do to give the project a little more polish is add in sound effects and background music. Let's do that now. Perform the following steps:

1. Select your enemy prefab, and add an **Audio Source** component to it by selecting **Component | Audio | Audio Source**. An audio source lets the audio listener into Main Camera knowing that this is an object that can play sounds. Once you create the Audio Source, open the **3D Sound Settings** and change the **Min Distance** of the **Volume Rolloff** to 10. Unity will attempt to alter the volume and pan sounds to make the project sound nicer, but for this project, it just makes everything much softer, so we're going to undo the effect unless it's far away.

2. After this, let's go into our `EnemyBehaviour` script! As usual, we'll need to add in a new variable for us to use to play whenever we're hit:

   ```
   // What sound to play when we're hit
   public AudioClip hitSound;
   ```

3. Next, go into the `CollisionEnter2D` function. After the `Destroy(theCollision.gameObject)` line, add the following code:

   ```
   // Plays a sound from this object's AudioSource
   audio.PlayOneShot(hitSound);
   ```

> For more information about the `PlayOneShot` function, check out http://docs.unity3d.com/ScriptReference/AudioSource.PlayOneShot.html.
>
> For more information on the **Audio Source** component (audio), check out http://docs.unity3d.com/ScriptReference/AudioSource.html.

Now, we need some actual sounds to play. I've set aside a folder of assets for you in the `Example Code` folder, so drag-and-drop the `Sounds` folder into your project's `Assets` folder:

1. Back in the inspector for our enemy, let's set the `Hit Sound` variable in the `EnemyBehaviour` script to the hit sound that we've imported by using drag-and-drop. Now if we play the game, when we hit an enemy, the sound will be played! Now, let's have a sound if we destroy the enemy!

2. Go to the **Explosion** prefab, and add an **Audio Source** component in the same way we did in step 1. Once you create the audio source, open up the **3D Sound Settings**, and change the **Min Distance** of the **Volume Rolloff** to 10. After this, set the **Audio Clip** property in the component to the `explode` sound.

3. Now, going back to our `EnemyBehaviour` script, go to the line after we instantiate the `exploder` object, and add the following line before we destroy the exploder:

```
exploder.audio.Play();
```

Now, if you play the game, hitting the object will play one sound, and when the object is destroyed, the explosion will play a sound. Because the sound is in the **Audio Clip** property, we can just call the `Play` function. However, if you want an object to play multiple sounds, it's better to have separate `AudioClip` variables just as we did with `EnemyBehaviour`.

4. Finally, I want to play a sound whenever we fire a shot. To do that, let's go to `playerShip` and add an audio source. Once you create the audio source, open **3D Sound Settings**, and change the **Min Distance** of **Volume Rolloff** to 10.

5. Next, go into `PlayerBehaviour`, and add in a new variable, as follows:

```
// What sound to play when we're shooting
public AudioClip shootSound;
```

6. After this, whenever we shoot a bullet, let's play the new sound at the beginning of the `ShootLasers` function:

```
audio.PlayOneShot(shootSound);
```

7. Coming back to **Inspector**, set the **Shoot Sound** property in the `PlayerBehaviour` component to the `shoot` sound effect.

8. Finally, let's add in our background music. Go to your **Main Camera** object in **Hierarchy**. Add an **Audio Source** component. There's no need to set **Min Distance** in this case, because this object is where the audio listener is. Change **Audio Clip** to **bgm**, check the **Loop** option, and set the **Volume** to .25.

> The background music is provided for this project by Stratkat (Kyle Smith). If you are interested in more of his work, check out his website at http://daydreamanatomy.bandcamp.com/.

9. Save everything, and run the game!

While we won't see any changes at this point for those of you actually running the game, you'll notice quite a change when the game is started. It's already feeling much more like a game.

> If you don't want to deal with the 3D settings, you can also select the sound files and uncheck the 3D sound option, but this will give you less control.

Adding in points, score, and wave numbers

One of the most important things to do in a game is reward the player and give them a sense of progression. For now, let's reward the player with a score we will display for them and also let the player know exactly which wave he is on. Perform the following steps:

1. Create a new **GUI Text** object by going to the **Hierarchy** tab and selecting **Create | GUI Text**.

> If you are using the Unity 4.6 beta or higher versions, instead of creating the object in this way, you will need to select **GameObject | Create Empty** to create an empty object. Once you've done that with the object selected, then click on **Component | Rendering | GUIText** to add the component there.

2. After this, switch to the **Game** tab, as you will be unable to see **GUI Text** in the **Scene** view. Note that the game should still not be started as yet, so don't hit the **Play** button. Have a look at the following screenshot:

3. Change the **GUI Text** object's name to Score Counter. Under the **GUI Text** component, change the **Text** to Score: 0. After that, change the **Position** of **Transform** to (0, 1, 0) to put it on the left-hand side of the screen.

   GUI elements are placed in viewport space, which means that the space of the GUI is a value from (0,0) in the bottom-left corner to (1,1) in the top-right corner.

4. Though this is technically fine, it would be nice to have some space so that the text isn't completely off the screen. To give us a bit of padding, let's set the **Pixel Offset** property to (10, -10) to move it 10 pixels toward the right-hand side and 10 pixels down. Note that **Pixel Offset** uses pixel space. Have a look at the following screenshot:

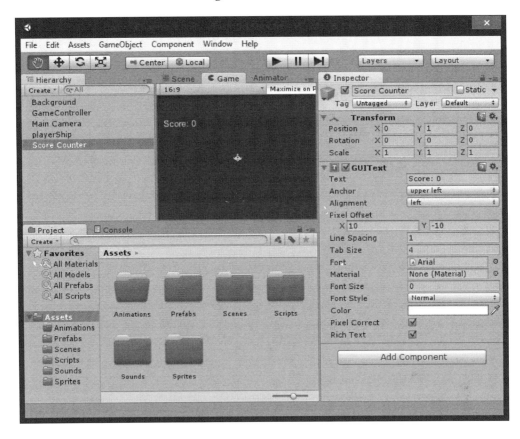

5. Now that we have the text set up, let's set the font. Drag-and-drop the **Font** folder into your project. Then set **Font** to OSP-DIN and **Font Size** to 25.

 The font used in this project was created by the OSP Foundry. For more information about their stuff check out http://ospublish. constantvzw.org/foundry/.

6. Next, duplicate the **Score Counter** object by right-clicking and selecting **Duplicate**. Set this duplicate's name to Waves Counter, and change its text to Wave: 0.

7. Set the **Waves Counter** object's **Position** to (1, 1, 0). Then set **Anchor** to upper right and **Pixel Offset** to (-10, -10). Have a look at the following screenshot:

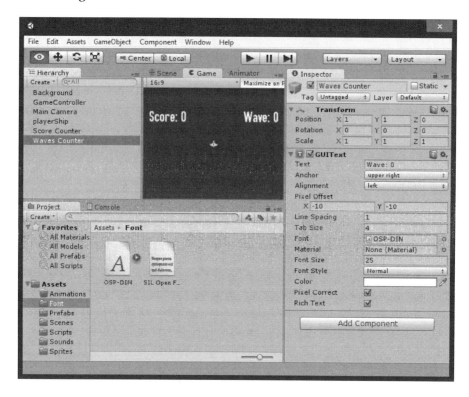

8. Now that we have our text files created, let's now have them function correctly! First, let's go into the GameController class. Inside, we need to create some new variables as follows:

```
// The values we'll be printing
private int score = 0;
private int waveNumber = 0;

// The actual GUI text
public GUIText scoreText;
public GUIText waveText;
```

9. Next, we will need to add a function to call whenever our score increases, as follows:

```
public void IncreaseScore(int increase)
{
    score += increase;
```

```
    scoreText.text = "Score: " + score;
}
```

The += operator will take the current value and add the right-hand side's value to it.

10. Then, we'll need to call this function inside our `EnemyBehaviour` component. After the `controller.KilledEnemy()` line, add the following line:

```
controller.IncreaseScore(10);
```

11. Finally, whenever we increase the wave number we need to change its text as well. Back in the `GameController` class after the `if(currentNumberOfEnemies <= 0)` line, add the following lines:

```
waveNumber++;
waveText.text = "Wave: " + waveNumber;
```

The ++ operator will take the current value of a number and increment it by 1.

12. Save all the script files, go back to **Inspector**, and set the **Score Text** and **Wave Text** objects to the proper variables. After that, run the game. Have a look at the following screenshot:

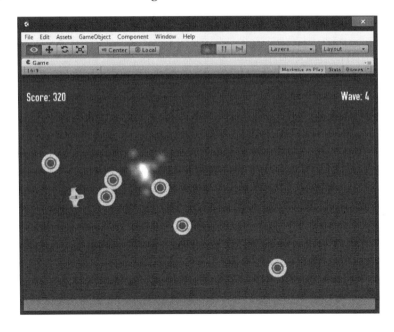

And with that, you can see that everything is working together, killing enemies rewards points, and killing all the enemies in a wave triggers the next wave to start!

Publishing the game

The final thing that we are going to touch on for the project is actually publishing it:

1. Go to **File | Build Settings**. From here, you can decide which platforms and/or scenes to include with your project.

2. Click on the **Add Current...** button to add our current scene to the game, as follows:

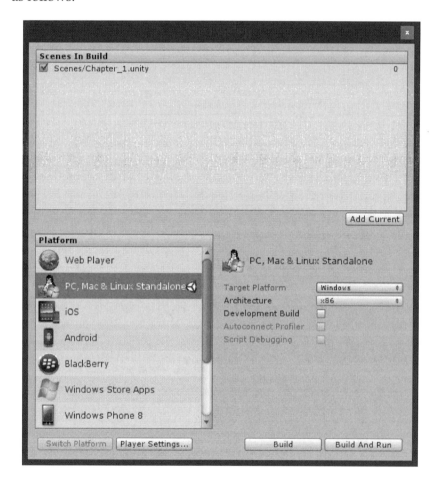

3. After that, since we are just publishing to our current platform, confirm that the settings are correct, and click on the **Build and Run** button.

4. Once you press the button, you'll be brought to a menu to name your application that you are going to save. Give it a name, save it, and wait. If all goes well, you should be brought to a menu allowing you to set some options before the game starts:

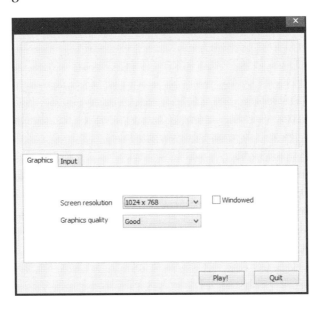

5. After that, click on the **Play!** button to see your completed project. Have a look at the following screenshot:

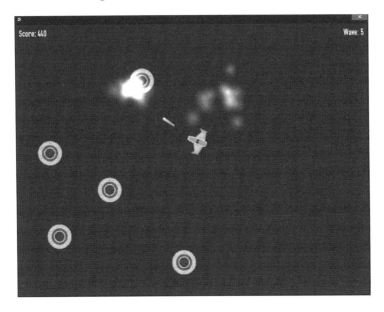

Summary

And there we have it! Within this first chapter, you've already completed an entire game project and learned how to publish it. Moving on, in the next chapter, we will tackle more advanced game types, learn additional things about Unity, and do more to push Unity to do as much as possible.

Challenges

For those of you who want to do more with this project, there are still plenty of things you can do, especially after finishing the rest of this book. Here are some ideas to get your mind thinking:

- Add in feedback whenever the player hits an enemy — perhaps an animation or a change of sprites.

- Give the player lives, and each time he is hit by an enemy, have him lose one life. Add a GUI Text to display lives as well.

- Once you learn how to use a **Game State Manager**, create a main menu, pause screen, and restart button.

- Add in Xbox control and mobile touch support.

- As a learning experiment, convert the player shooting behaviour code to use co-routines to enable/disable being able to shoot. Discuss the advantages/disadvantages towards this method.

2
Creating GUIs

A **Graphical User Interface (GUI)** is way the players interact with your games. You've actually been using a GUI in the previous chapter (the Unity Editor) and also when interacting with your operating system. Without a GUI of some sort, the only way you'd be able to interact with a computer is a command prompt such as DOS or UNIX.

When working on GUIs, we want them to be as intuitive as possible and only contain the information that is pertinent to the player at any given time. There are people whose main job is programming and/or designing user interfaces and there are college degrees on the subject as well. So, while we won't talk about everything that we have to work with on GUIs, I do want to touch on the aspects that should be quite helpful when working on your own projects in the future.

Project overview

Over the course of this chapter, we will be expanding on our twin-stick shooter by adding additional UI elements that will include a main menu, a pause menu, and an options menu and will give us the ability to restart our project. This chapter uses the UnityGUI system that existed before Unity 4.6. Even though the new system does have its advantages, the old system is still quite useful to learn. It's still the only way to create UI elements for the Unity Editor (which you can use to create plugins that you can sell on the Asset Store), and it has a much larger amount of documentation out there to help new users.

If you are interested in learning specifically about the new GUI system, please check out *Chapter 9, Creating GUIs Part 2 – Unity's New GUI System*, where I talk about specific cases in which you'd want to use the new system.

Your objectives

This project will be split into a number of tasks. It will be a simple step-by-step process from beginning to end. Here is the outline of our tasks:

- Creating a main menu
- Customizing the GUI
- Implementing a pause menu
- Restarting the game
- Adding an **Options** screen

Prerequisites

This chapter assumes that you have completed the previous chapter and are working with that project. If you have not completed the project yet, please take the Chapter_1_Completed.unitypackage file and import it to a blank project in Unity.

We will also need some graphical assets for use in our project. These can be downloaded from the example code provided for this book on the Packt Publishing website at https://www.packtpub.com/books/content/support.

Browse through the code files and download the Chapter2.zip package and unzip it. Inside the Chapter2 folder there are a number of things, including an Assets folder that will have the art, sound, and font files that you'll need for the project as well as the Chapter_2_Completed.unitypackage (this is the completed chapter package that includes the entire project for you to work with). I've also added in the completed game exported (TwinstickShooter GUI Exported) as well as the entire project zipped up in the GUI TwinstickShooter Project.zip file.

Project setup

At this point, I have assumed that you have a fresh installation of Unity, and have started it up. You need to perform the following steps:

1. Open the previous project. Now, let's first create a new scene by navigating to **File | New Scene**. With the new scene created, save it by navigating to **File | Save Scene**. Name it Main_Menu.unity and save it inside your Scenes folder.

2. Let's first grab the background from our previous level so that we do not need to create it once again. To do that, double-click on the scene you created in the first chapter. Left-click on the **Background** object in the **Hierarchy** view and navigate to **Edit | Copy**. Go back to your Main_Menu scene and paste it into the world by navigating to **Edit | Paste**:

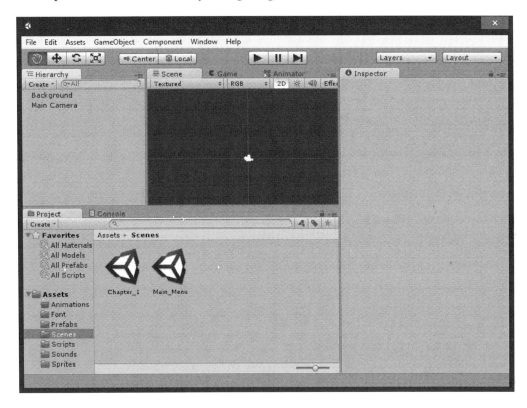

Unity has an inbuilt GUI functionality through the UnityGUI system that allows us to create interfaces through scripts.

 Unless you are using Unity 4.6 or later, Unity doesn't have an included visual GUI development system, but you can find tools on the Unity Asset Store that can be used to create your GUI in a **What You See Is What You Get (WYSIWYG)** fashion. Otherwise, you can also use Autodesk's popular Scaleform system, which allows you to create your GUIs in Adobe Flash for an additional cost.

This system uses a function called OnGUI, which is similar to the Update function we used previously in the way that it gets called every frame that the component is enabled on a game object within the scene. All of your rendering of the GUI controls should be performed inside this function or in a function called inside of the OnGUI function.

3. The first thing we're going to do is add a start button to our game. Right-click on the **Scripts** folder you created earlier, and then click on **Create** and select the **C# Script** label. Call this new script MainMenuGUI. Open MonoDevelop and use the following code:

```csharp
using UnityEngine;
using System.Collections;

public class MainMenuGUI : MonoBehaviour {
  public int buttonWidth = 100;
  public int buttonHeight = 30;
  void OnGUI()
  {
    //Get the center of our screen
    float buttonX = ( Screen.width - buttonWidth ) / 2.0f;
    float buttonY = ( Screen.height - buttonHeight ) /
2.0f;

    //Show button on the screen and check if clicked
    if ( GUI.Button( new Rect( buttonX, buttonY,
                        buttonWidth, buttonHeight ),
              "Start Game" ) )
    {
      // If button clicked, load the game level
      Application.LoadLevel("Chapter_1");
    }

    // Add game's title to the screen, above our button
    GUI.Label( new Rect(buttonX + 2.5f , buttonY - 50,
                  110.0f, 20.0f),
            "Twinstick Shooter" );
  }

}
```

What this code basically does is place a title and button on our screen. Whenever we click on the button, the next level will be loaded. Now, this code may look quite different from what we've done before, so I will explain it after we see exactly what this code does.

4. After saving the code, attach the `MainMenuGUI` script to the **Main Camera** object by dragging the script onto the object in the **Hierarchy** view. Once you complete that, save everything and start up the game! The following screenshot shows what we've created:

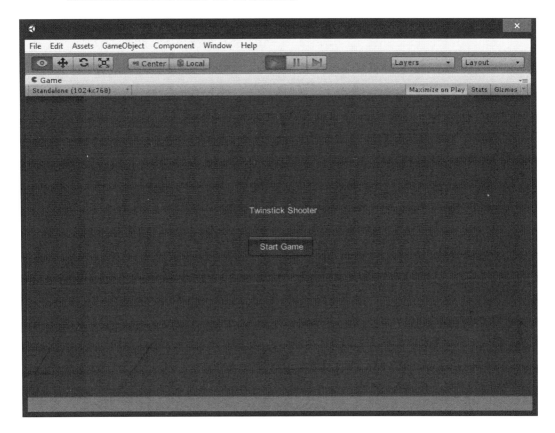

At this point, you should have a very simple main menu screen. Now when we click on the **Start Game** button, we will move on to our game!

 If you are not able to load the game level, make sure that your **Scene** from the last chapter is named `Chapter_1` and it is included in the **Build Settings**.

The anatomy of a GUI control

The most important concepts to grasp first are the `GUI.Button` and `GUI.Label` functions. Both of these functions are what we refer to as a **GUI control**, and there are many others which we will be using in the future. So, to clear up any confusion, let's talk about them now.

Creating any GUI control consists of the following:

```
ControlType(Position, Content)
```

The parts of the preceding line of code are explained in the following sections.

ControlType

The `ControlType` function is a function that exists in Unity's GUI class, and is the name of the element that you want to create in the world. In the preceding code, we used `GUI.Button` and `GUI.Label`, but there are many more.

> For more information on all the different kinds of controls, there are additional definitions for the functions. You can check them out at `https://docs.unity3d.com/Documentation/Components/gui-Controls.html`.

Position

The `Position` parameter is where you want to place the object in the screen space. In the previous chapter, we talked about viewport and screen space (pixel space). When working with the GUI class like we are in this example, we have to manually position each element that we place on the screen based on the screen space in pixels. To do that, we want to know the position (x, y) that we want to place the object at, and the size (width, height) of that object. These are the four parameters of the `Rect` structure, which itself is the first parameter that we provide to many of the GUI class functions.

Since we want this code to work on as many projects as possible, I don't want to hardcode what the middle of the screen is. Thankfully, the `Screen.width` and `Screen.height` properties can be used to let me know the current dimensions of the screen in pixels, no matter what screen size the game is on.

The first thing I need to know is how large I want my displayed objects to be. The constructor of the `Rect` class takes in four floats, so I need to use floating point numbers (add `.0f` to whole number values to use them as floats).

For my button, I'm creating two variables, `buttonWidth` and `buttonHeight`, to fill in values for the third and fourth parameters of the `Rect` variable.

By setting the `buttonX` and `buttonY` values inside the `OnGUI` function, if at any time during the game we change the resolution of the game or port our game to other places, the GUI will work without any modifications, which is pretty great. For the title of our screen, I'll just put in some values to show that we do not need to create variables for this.

The X and the Y position set the top-left of our object, which is great if we're putting something on the top-left. However, if we just set the middle of the screen, it will be a tad offset. So, we'll need to move our position to fit the size of our buttons as well.

Content

The second and final argument for the control is the actual content that we want to display with the ControlType we are using. Right now, we're just passing in a string to display, but we can also display images and other content as well, including other controls. We will talk about other pieces of content that we can add in later.

GUI.Button

One of the most common UI elements is the `Button` control. This function is used to render a clickable object. If you look at the code from the `MainMenuGUI` script, you'll notice that the button is cased inside of an `if` statement. This is because if the button is clicked on, then the function will return `true` when the button is released. If this is true, we will load the level we created in the previous chapter.

GUI.Label

The `Label` control is used to display static data on the screen that the player will not be able to interact with. This is quite similar to the `GUIText` objects that we created in the previous chapter. Labels can contain text, textures, or both. In our case, we are just displaying some text.

Customizing the GUI

While it is great that Unity provides us with all of this functionality to save us time in creating elements, the actual aesthetics leaves a little to be desired. Thankfully, UnityGUI allows us to customize the appearance of our controls by making use of GUIStyle, which is an optional third parameter to our control functions. If we do not specify a GUIStyle parameter, Unity's default will be used, which is what we experienced last time. This can work fine while testing something out. However, since we're trying to create a polished and complete project, we're going to create one of our own by performing the following steps:

1. Open up the MainMenuGUI script file and modify the function to accommodate the changes in bold:

    ```
    using UnityEngine;
    using System.Collections;

    public class MainMenuGUI : MonoBehaviour {
      public int buttonWidth = 100;
      public int buttonHeight = 30;
      public GUIStyle titleStyle;
      public GUIStyle buttonStyle;

      void OnGUI()
      {
        //Get the center of our screen
        float buttonX = ( Screen.width - buttonWidth ) / 2.0f;
        float buttonY = ( Screen.height - buttonHeight ) /
    2.0f;

        //Show button on the screen and check if clicked
        if ( GUI.Button( new Rect( buttonX, buttonY,
                          buttonWidth, buttonHeight ),
              "Start Game", buttonStyle ) )
        {
          // If button clicked, load the game level
          Application.LoadLevel("Chapter_1");
        }

        // Add game's title to the screen, above our button
        GUI.Label( new Rect(buttonX + 2.5f , buttonY - 50,
                      110.0f, 20.0f),
              "Twinstick Shooter", titleStyle );
      }

    }
    ```

2. Once finished, save the file into your `Scripts` folder and then move back into Unity. You should see the two variables showing up in the **Inspector** section:

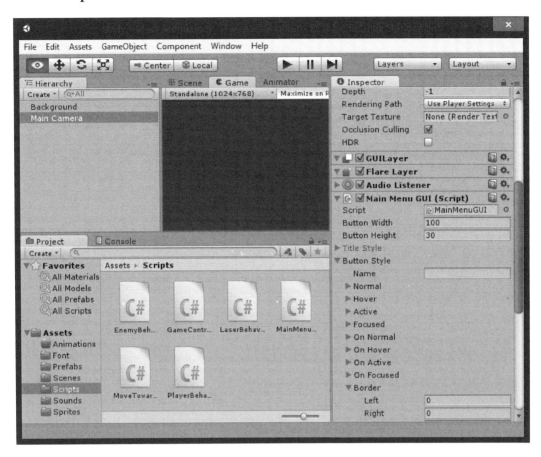

3. For the **Title Style** option, navigate to **Normal | Text Color** and put in white. Change the **Font** option to the **OSP-DIN** font we added in the previous chapter, the **Font Size** option to 42, and the **Alignment** option to **Middle Center**:

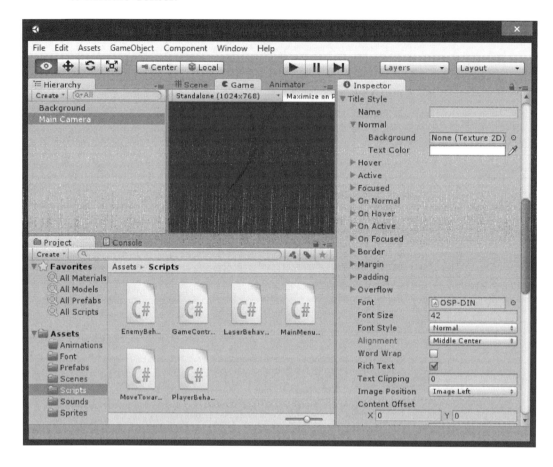

4. Now, for the buttonStyle variable (**Button Style** in the inspector), we're first going to need some additional images for our buttons. So, go into your Chapter 2/Assets location, which you should have obtained from Packt Publishing's website, and drag-and-drop the new images into our Sprites folder.

5. Once that's finished, set the **Normal**, **Hover**, and **Active Background** properties to the blue, yellow, and green buttons, respectively. Next, set the **Border** property to 10 in each of the four directions. Setting the border will make sure that the background images do not exceed those many pixels in each of those directions. This is great for objects that can be different sizes, such as buttons and text fields. Finally, set the **Font** option to **OSP-DIN** and the **Alignment** option to **Middle Center**:

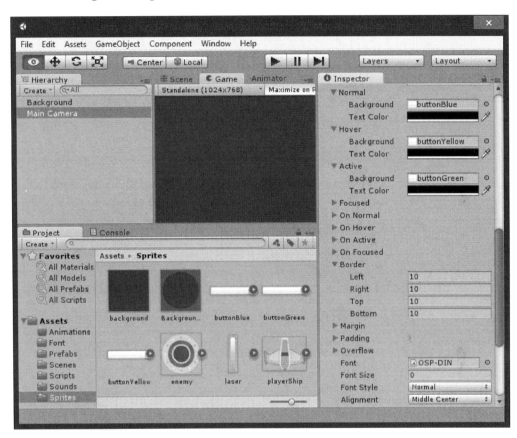

6. With all of that done, save your scene and run the game as shown in the following screenshot:

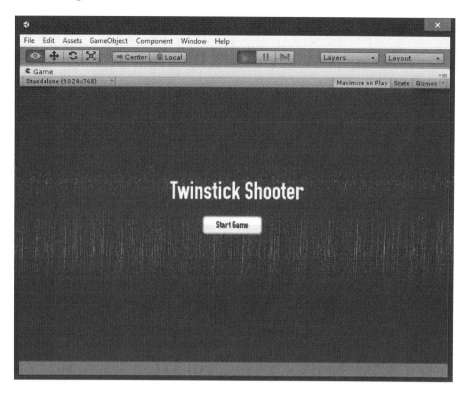

We now have something that already looks a lot better than what we had before, and you learned how to work with different styles!

Pausing the game

Now that we have started on our main menu, let's add some additional GUI functionality to our game, adding in the ability to pause our game and restart it. However, before we do that, let's take a look at some stuff we can do to make our lives easier when it comes to customization:

1. We also want to make these buttons have the same appearance as the stuff we've done previously. However, instead of having to set these properties every single time, we can use something called a **GUISkin** to change what the default controls will appear like by setting the GUI.skin property to a new one.

2. Create a GUISkin by navigating to **Project | Create | GUI Skin,** and rename the skin to GUISkin. Open up the **Button** tab, and you should notice it looks exactly the same as the previous section. Do those same changes that we did previously here, but change the **Text Color** property to black by clicking on the current color and then selecting black from the color cube that pops up. Alternatively, you can set the R (red), G (green), and B (blue) values to 0 and the A (alpha, which is the transparency) to 255 in the slider section.

RGBA colors use values between 0 and 255, with 0 being no color and 255 being full color. Unlike in painting where if you keep adding colors, it'll get darker on the computer, the colors will get brighter and the screen lighter. All the colors on your computer monitor can be represented in this way.

3. Also, change the **Font** property to **OSP-DIN** so that our fonts will not change anywhere. Finally, for the **Label** section, change **Alignment** option to **Upper Center**.

4. Now that we have a basic knowledge of GUISkins, let's actually implement the pause menu. Right-click on the Scripts folder you created earlier and then click on **Create** and then select the **C# Script** label. Call this new script PauseMenu. Open the MonoDevelop IDE and use the following code:

```
using UnityEngine;
using System.Collections;

public class PauseMenu : MonoBehaviour
{
  public static bool isPaused;
  public float windowWidth = 256;
  public float windowHeight = 100;

  public GUISkin newSkin;

  void Start()
  {
    //We don't want the game paused when it starts and/or resets
    isPaused = false;
  }

  void OnGUI()
  {
```

```
    // Set the GUI's default skin to the one we set here
    GUI.skin = newSkin;
    if(isPaused)
    {
        // First, we pause the game
        Time.timeScale = 0.0f;

        // Then we need to display the pause menu
        ShowPauseMenu();

    }
    else
    {
        // Make the game run like normal
        Time.timeScale = 1.0f;
    }
}

void ShowPauseMenu()
{
    // Then we need to display the pause menu
    float windowX = ( Screen.width - windowWidth ) / 2;
    float windowY = ( Screen.height - windowHeight ) / 2;

    GUILayout.BeginArea(new Rect( windowX, windowY,
                                  windowWidth, windowHeight ));

    if (GUILayout.Button ("Resume"))
    {
        //resume the game
        isPaused = false;
    }
    if (GUILayout.Button ("Main Menu"))
    {
        Application.LoadLevel ("Main_Menu");
    }
    if (GUILayout.Button ("Exit Game"))
    {
        // Only works when published
        Application.Quit();
    }

    GUILayout.EndArea();
}
}
```

This script uses a Boolean (`true`/`false`) value to determine if the game is paused or not. If the game is paused, we set the `Time.timeScale` property to `0`, which means that nothing can move because time has frozen. The `Time.timeScale` property changes the scale time. For example, if we set it to `0.5f`, then time will run two times slower than normal (`1.0f`). This will freeze the normal objects, but GUI buttons will still work. In addition, I also called the `ShowPauseMenu` function, which will display a series of buttons that will let the player resume, go to the main menu, or quit the game.

GUILayout

Another thing you may have noticed is the fact that I am using the `GUILayout` class instead of the `GUI` class that we used in the *Adding in points, score, and wave numbers* section in *Chapter 1, 2D Twin-stick Shooter* without writing code. Using the `GUI` class is great if you want to have precise control on where and how things are drawn. However, if you do not want to manually specify a position and are okay with Unity automatically modifying the size and position of controls, you can use the `GUILayout` class.

By default, the `GUILayout` class will just put the buttons up at the top-left side, but I want our pause menu to be on the center of the screen. So, I specify an area that I want the menu to be in using the `BeginArea` function. Anything I place before I call the `EndArea` function will be inside that area, and `GUILayout` will attempt to place it in a pleasing way for me. You need to perform the following steps:

1. With the script written, add the behavior to the **Main Camera** object by dragging and dropping. Set the **New Skin** property to the GUISkin we created previously.

    When working on larger projects, it may be a good idea to use a GUISkin instead of GUIStyles to skin everything, by default, to something else. For more information on GUISkins, check out https://docs.unity3d.com/Documentation/Components/class-GUISkin.html.

2. Now, we need to configure the game such that the player can pause the game when he/she presses the *Esc* key. Also, if the game is paused, no one can move but the player can still rotate and shoot, which we don't want. To fix this, we will need to modify the player behavior script; specifically, we need to modify the `Update` function to support pausing:

   ```
   void Update ()
   {
     if(Input.GetKeyUp("escape"))
   ```

```
{
  // If false becomes true and vice versa
  PauseMenu.isPaused = !PauseMenu.isPaused;
}

if(!PauseMenu.isPaused)
{
  // Rotate player to face mouse
  Rotation();
  // Move the player's body
  Movement();

  foreach (KeyCode element in shootButton)
  {
    if(Input.GetKey(element) && timeTilNextFire < 0)
    {
      timeTilNextFire = timeBetweenFires;
      ShootLaser();
      break;
    }
  }

  timeTilNextFire -= Time.deltaTime;
}
}
```

Normally, we'd need a component to be attached to an object to use it. However, since the `PauseMenu.isPaused` variable is both public and static, anyone can modify it.

3. Now, navigate to **File | Build Settings** and add both the **Main Menu** and **Game (Chapter_1)** scenes to your **Scenes In Build** property if you haven't already. Afterward, make sure that the **Main Menu** scene is in the 0 place. If it is not, feel free to drag it up there via the mouse.

4. Save your files and start up the game once again, as shown in the following screenshot:

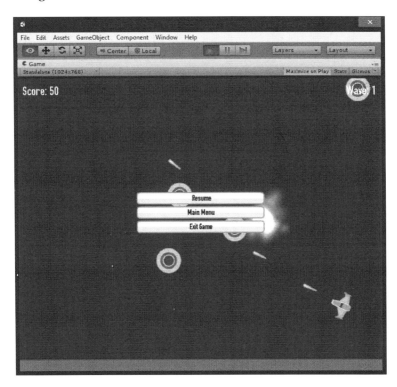

Now, we have a fully functional pause menu that will allow us to press the *Esc* key and leave what we're doing in the project. We've also made it incredibly easy for us to draw buttons in the style that we created for other sections.

Restarting the game

There may come a time in a game when a player makes a mistake and would like to restart the level in the game they're currently playing. If you prepared your project ahead of time like we have, it's actually quite easy to get this functionality placed into your game. With that being said, let's implement that functionality now! We will perform the following steps:

1. Open up the `PauseMenu` script and add the following highlighted code:

```
GUILayout.BeginHorizontal();

    if (GUILayout.Button ("Resume"))
    {
```

```
  //resume the game
  isPaused = false;
}


if (GUILayout.Button ("Restart"))
{
  Application.LoadLevel(Application.loadedLevelName);
}
GUILayout.EndHorizontal();
```

2. Once finished, save your file and move back into Unity and play the game! The following screenshot depicts the game screen:

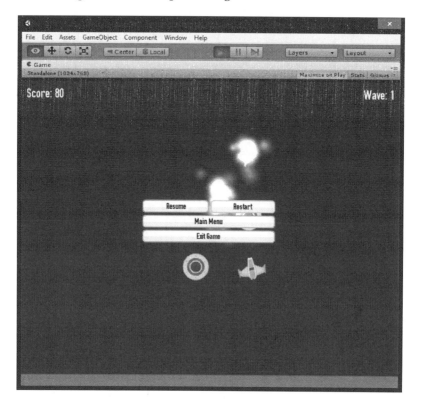

Simple enough! We've now added a new button to our menu and when we click on it, we load the currently loaded level.

 If you use this implementation in your own projects, be sure to initialize all static variables inside your Start function unless you want them to be consistent between run-throughs.

More on the GUILayout class

By default, when you use the `GUILayout` class, controls will appear one after another, from top to bottom, by default. However, there will be times in which you'd like to have more control over what's going on without wanting to hardcode the positions of each element. Some of the various options available to you is horizontal and vertical groups.

Just like we called `GUILayout.BeginArea` and `GUILayout.EndArea` previously, you will need to call functions to start or end these groups, such as the `GUILayout.BeginVertical` and `GUILayout.EndVertical` methods we used in the preceding example.

Any controls placed inside a horizontal group will always be laid out horizontally. Any controls inside a vertical group will always be laid out vertically. This sounds simple enough, and it is. However, when you realize that we can use these groups inside each other, it gives us the ability to create whatever you can imagine for the UI.

 For more information on the `GUILayout` class, check out `http://docs.unity3d.com/ScriptReference/GUILayout.html`.

Creating an Options menu

Something that many games also need is an **Options** menu, so let's create it by performing the following steps:

1. Go back into our `PauseMenu` script.

   The first thing we're going to want to do is add an additional variable, but we can't use a Boolean value (`true`/`false`) because we want an option of one of three constant things. We could create an integer and do something if the value is `0`, something else if `1`, and something else if it is `2`. However, that wouldn't look very elegant and would require us to memorize the values we associate with a particular thing. To solve these issues, we will instead create an **enumeration**. Enumerations, often referred to as enums, are a distinct type that we create, that is, they are themselves a collection of constant values. Place the following two lines after you enter the class:

   ```
   enum Menu{None, Pause, Options};
   private Menu currentMenu;
   ```

Notice how we are able to create a variable of the type Menu here; that's because we used the enum keyword to define a type called Menu, which can have one of the three values: Menu.None, Menu.Pause, and Menu.Options.

We will be using this value to determine whether we should show which menu we currently want to be at: the normal pause menu, the **Options** screen, or nothing when we enter each OnGUI call.

Under the hood, currentMenu is actually an integer with a value of 0 for Menu.None, 1 for Menu.Pause, and so on. However, it is much easier to read and understand what it is doing.

2. After this, we need to initialize the variable inside our Start function:

```
currentMenu = Menu.None;
```

The following screenshot shows the code:

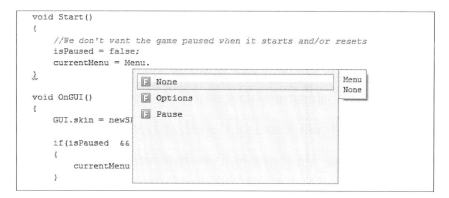

One of the neat things about using an enum is the fact that when you use it inside MonoDevelop, it will display all the possible options that you want to pick. Using this system, we will make it quite easy to add additional menus of your own!

3. After this, we will need to rewrite the OnGUI function to reflect our new state:

```
void OnGUI()
{
  GUI.skin = newSkin;

  if(isPaused  && currentMenu == Menu.None)
  {
    currentMenu = Menu.Pause;
  }
```

```
//Check if we are at a menu
if (currentMenu == Menu.None)
{
  Time.timeScale = 1.0f;
  return;
}

//We're at a menu, so let's pause the game
Time.timeScale = 0.0f;

switch (currentMenu)
{
  case Menu.Options:
    ShowOptionsMenu();
    break;
  case Menu.Pause:
    ShowPauseMenu();
    break;
}

}
```

The first change you'll notice is the fact that now we check to see if we are currently not at a menu and paused before going to the `Pause` menu. This will ensure we can go to any other menu that you'd want to go to and the game would still be paused.

Next, you'll see the other new aspect of C# that we'll talk about now: a `switch` statement:

```
int caseSwitch = 1;
switch (caseSwitch)
{
    case 1:
        print("Case 1");
        break;
    case 2:
        print("Case 2");
        break;
    default:
        print("Default case");
        break;
}
```

A `switch` statement (as seen in the preceding code) is used when we want to do something based on a number of single values, and doing something different based on the values (going to the default value if none of the other values are valid). These are commonly used with enumerations. Based on the value that `currentMenu` has, it will either return in the first `if` check or show the **Options** or **Pause** menu.

> Unlike some other programming languages, C# requires the end of the `switch` sections, including the final one, to be unreachable. That is, your code may not fall through into the next part of code. Typically, we solve this by adding a break to exit outside a `switch` statement.
>
> For more information about `switch` statements, check out http://msdn.microsoft.com/en-us/library/06tc147t.aspx.

4. Now, at this point, we need to write the `ShowOptionsMenu` function and update the `ShowPauseMenu` function to add access to the **Options** menu. Since both of these functions need to draw a window, the first thing I'm going to do is create a new function called `BuildWindow`:

```
void BuildWindow()
    {
        float windowX = ( Screen.width - windowWidth ) / 2;
        float windowY = ( Screen.height - windowHeight ) / 2;


        GUILayout.BeginArea(new Rect( windowX, windowY,
                                      windowWidth, windowHeight ));
    }
```

5. Next, we will need to rewrite the `ShowPauseMenu` function to add access to the **Options** menu:

```
void ShowPauseMenu()
    {
        BuildWindow ();

        GUILayout.BeginHorizontal();

        if (GUILayout.Button ("Resume"))
        {
            //resume the game
            isPaused = false;
```

```
        currentMenu = Menu.None;
    }

    if (GUILayout.Button ("Restart"))
    {
      Application.LoadLevel(Application.loadedLevelName);
    }

    GUILayout.EndHorizontal ();

    if (GUILayout.Button ("Options"))
    {
      currentMenu = Menu.Options;
    }
    GUILayout.BeginHorizontal ();

    if (GUILayout.Button ("Main Menu"))
    {
      Application.LoadLevel("Main_Menu");
    }

    if (GUILayout.Button ("Exit Game"))
    {
      // Only works when published
      Application.Quit ();
    }

    GUILayout.EndHorizontal ();

    GUILayout.EndArea ();
  }
```

6. Now, let's implement our new function, ShowOptionsMenu:

```
void ShowOptionsMenu ()
  {
    BuildWindow ();

    // Instead of the default blank background,
    // we will use what the GUISkin uses for the box
properties
    GUILayout.BeginVertical ("box");

    // Set our volume
    GUILayout.Label ("Master Volume - (" +
AudioListener.volume.ToString ("f2") + ")");
```

```
        AudioListener.volume = GUILayout.HorizontalSlider
        (AudioListener.volume, 0.0f, 1.0f);

        // Display and add the ability to change graphics
quality
int currentQuality = QualitySettings.GetQualityLevel ();
string qualityName = QualitySettings.names[currentQuality];
GUILayout.Label ("Quality - " + qualityName);


        GUILayout.BeginHorizontal();

        if (GUILayout.Button("Decrease"))
        {
          QualitySettings.DecreaseLevel();
        }
        if (GUILayout.Button("Increase"))
        {
          QualitySettings.IncreaseLevel();
        }

        GUILayout.EndHorizontal();

        if (GUILayout.Button ("Back"))
        {
          currentMenu = Menu.Pause;
        }

        GUILayout.EndVertical();

        GUILayout.EndArea ();
    }
```

If we go to the **Options** screen, then the first thing I do is create a vertical group passing in a parameter. This parameter is a string that tells the group to use that following type's properties for this group. Since we are using box, it looks at our GUISkin and grabs whatever background texture was used for it. Note that this is a texture provided to us by Unity, which you should feel free to replace on your own.

The first item that we add to the GUI is a label displaying the value of AudioListener.volume, the master volume of our scene. To do so, use the ToString function to convert the float to a string. The f2 parameter stands for fixed point 2. It rounds the number into a fixed-point value with two decimal places.

If you want to convert a float to an integer, you may consider using the `Mathf.Round` function, which will round a number to the nearest integer.

The next section has us using horizontal sliders. The `GUI.HorizontalSlider` and `GUI.VerticalSlider` functions are used to draw horizontal and vertical sliders respectively. This slider can be used to specify a number within a certain range. In the preceding example, we have a horizontal slider that we used for the volume of our game in the range of 0 to 1. `AudioListener.volume` is a static variable, so it will keep whatever value you have set for it as long as the game is going on.

The slider functions take the current value of the slider and the minimum and maximum values of the slider. The preceding example shows how to use a horizontal slider, but a vertical slider uses exactly the same parameters except the slider is drawn vertically instead of horizontally.

7. After this, we save all of our files and then go back into Unity and run the game, as shown in the following screenshot:

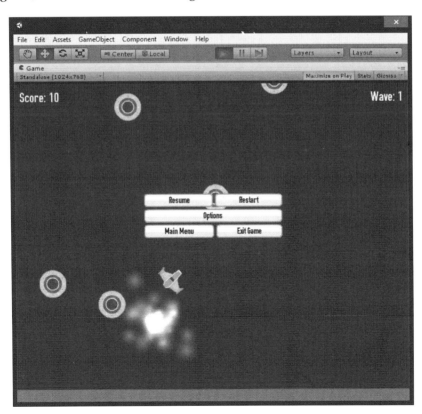

Over the course of this section, we've done two things. First of all we changed the pause menu to now have an additional **Options** menu.

And when we click on the **Options** button, we will see a separate menu that will allow users to modify the **Master Volume** value as well as the **Graphics Quality** value of their project. This is shown in the following screenshot:

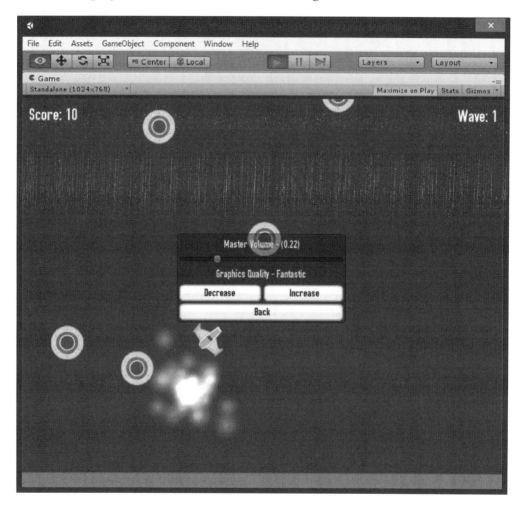

For more information on the UnityGUI system, there is a GUI scripting guide available at `http://docs.unity3d.com/Manual/GUIScriptingGuide.html`.

Summary

With that, we now have most of the commonly needed features that most games need to be completed. With the basis created here, you can easily add menus and features to make your game great! In the next chapter, we will start with a new project with more exciting things for us to work with
and explore even more of what Unity has to offer!

Challenges

For those of you who want to do more with this project, there are still plenty of things you can do, especially after finishing the rest of this book. Here are some ideas to get you thinking:

- Add a **Credits** screen to your main menu
- Add in three color sliders to customize your ship's color (`renderer.material.color`) with red, green, and blue values
- Add in **Music Volume** and **SFX Volume** sliders, and use those values to set the volume of sounds you play!
- Modify the `GUIStyle` parameter to reflect your own game!

3
Side-scrolling Platformer

At this point, we have a chance to work on a full game, but we've only used 2D so far. In this chapter, we will explore how we can use the concepts that we learned in 2D and use them with a 3D game with 2D gameplay.

As long as we have played games, there has been one particular genre that has stayed with us almost from the beginning, the platformer. Starting with *Donkey Kong* with the familiar content that we know, refined in *Super Mario Brothers*, given more action with *Mega Man*, taken faster with *Sonic the Hedgehog*, and used even today with games such as *Terraria*, *Super Meat Boy*, and *Child of Light*, there is something that draws us to this specific type of game, especially within the indie game community.

A platform game (known commonly as a platformer) consists of a player controlling a character that can move around a game environment with extensive jumping between platforms, hence the name.

Project overview

Over the course of this chapter, we will create a complete side-scrolling platformer project. We will learn the similarities between working in 2D and 3D and the differences, in particular when it comes to Physics.

Your objectives

This project will be split into a number of tasks. It will be a simple step-by-step process from beginning to end. Here is the outline of our tasks:

- Tile-based level creation
- Adding player functionality
- Adding collectables/power ups
- Designing the level layout and background

Prerequisites

As in *Chapter 1, 2D Twin-stick Shooter,* you will need Unity installed on your computer, but we will start a new project from scratch.

This chapter uses no graphical assets; however, the completed project and source files can be downloaded from the example code provided for this book on Packt's website (http://www.packtpub.com).

Setting up the project

At this point, I assume that you have a fresh install of Unity and have started it up:

1. With Unity started, go to **File | New Project**. Select a **Project Location** of your choice somewhere on your hard drive, and ensure that you have **Setup defaults for** set to 3D. Once completed, select **Create**. At this point, we will not need to import any packages, as we'll make everything from scratch. From there, if you see the **Welcome to Unity** pop up, feel free to close it out, as we won't be using it.

2. Create the following folders just as we described in the previous chapters:
    - Prefabs
    - Scenes
    - Scripts

Tile-based level creation

While our previous game worked by only needing to spawn enemies in the world, for most games with content, you'll typically have levels, each with its own environment. When building levels in games, there are some advantages to placing everything by hand, but if you're creating a game with many levels, that work will decrease your productivity. It's also important to note that the more assets you create for your game, the higher the cost.

With that in mind, it's a much better idea to create parts that can be reused to create games. If you've played older 2D games in the past, such as an adventure, RPG, or platforming games, you may have realized that there were a lot of places in the worlds that looked similar to each other, such as the trees, a wall, a chest, door, and so forth.

The reason they looked similar is due to the fact that they were using the same sprites. This is because they were truly tile-based games. A tile-based game is where the playing area consists of small rectangular, square, or hexagonal graphic images, referred to as tiles. Imagine a grid of blocks where every block is given a number or ID. Based on the ID, the game will determine how that grid is drawn and behaves when a player interacts with it.

An important thing to mention is that tile-based games are not a distinct genre; rather, the term refers to the technology a game engine uses for its visual representation. For example, most of the *Pokémon* series of games are top-down, role-playing video games, and the traditional *Mario* series of games are side-scrolling platformers, but both use a tile-based system for graphics. Tile-based engines allow developers to create large levels quickly with relatively few art assets, which is great as a programmer.

To show how easy it is to build, we will code a tile-based system for this project:

1. The first thing that we're going to want to do is actually create the blocks we'll be placing for the world. Let's first create a cube by selecting **GameObject** | **Create Other** | **Cube**.

2. We want this cube to have a collision so that our player can collide against it, but this time we will use a box collider. Check **Inspector** to confirm that it is there. If not, add this component by selecting **Component** | **Physics** | **Box Collider**.

   The box collider is the 3D equivalent of the box collider 2D component for 3D space.

3.   Rename the cube to `Wall` by selecting the top bar in **Inspector**, renaming it, and pressing *Enter*. Have a look at the following screenshot:

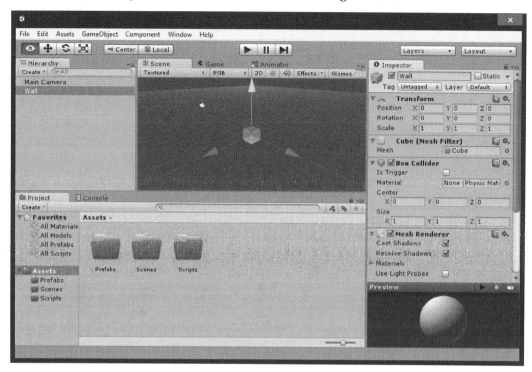

4.   In the **Project** tab, go to the **Prefabs** folder, and drag-and-drop the **Wall** object from **Hierarchy** into it. Once that is finished, select **Wall** in **Hierachy**, and then delete it by pressing the *Delete* key.

5.   Now, we will be spawning a large amount of objects into our world. It would be a good idea to have a parent object to store all of these objects to avoid cluttering our **Hierarchy**. To do this, let's create an empty game object by going to **GameObject** | **Create Empty**. From there, with the object selected, go to **Inspector**, set its name to `DynamicObjects`, and optionally, for neatness sake, set its **Position** to (0, 0, 0).

6.   The next thing we will do is create a game controller to hold the behavior to create our blocks. Create an empty game object with the name `_GameController`, and reset its **Position** to (0, 0, 0).

I put the _ before the actual name of the object in my projects, so it's always at the top of my hierarchy, and hence I have easy access to it. If this does not work, you can also drag-and-drop objects to change their place in the hierarchy.

7. Underneath the name, you'll see the **Tag** property. Change it from **Untagged** to **GameController**.

8. Next, with the game controller selected, go to the Inspector tab and then select **Add Component | New Script**. Once brought to the next menu, change the language to C#, and set the name of the script to `GameController`.

9. Select the newly created script, and move it to the `Assets\Scripts` folder. Go to `MonoDevelop` by double-clicking on the script file.

10. Inside the newly created code, we will first need to add two new variables for us to use: `level`, which will contain the data needed to create our level and `wall`, which will contain the block we want to spawn:

```
private int[][] level = new int[][]
{
  new int[]{1, 1, 1, 1, 1, 1, 1, 1, 1, 1, 1, 1, 1, 1, 1, 1, 1, 1},
  new int[]{1, 0, 0, 0, 0, 0, 0, 0, 0, 0, 0, 0, 0, 0, 0, 0, 0, 1},
  new int[]{1, 0, 0, 0, 0, 0, 0, 0, 0, 0, 0, 0, 0, 0, 0, 0, 0, 1},
  new int[]{1, 0, 0, 0, 0, 0, 0, 0, 0, 0, 0, 0, 0, 0, 0, 0, 0, 1},
  new int[]{1, 0, 0, 0, 0, 0, 0, 0, 0, 0, 0, 0, 0, 0, 1, 1, 1, 1},
  new int[]{1, 0, 0, 0, 0, 0, 0, 0, 0, 0, 0, 0, 0, 0, 1, 1, 1, 1},
  new int[]{1, 0, 0, 0, 0, 0, 0, 0, 1, 1, 1, 1, 1, 1, 1, 1, 1, 1},
  new int[]{1, 1, 1, 1, 0, 0, 0, 0, 0, 0, 0, 0, 0, 0, 0, 0, 0, 1},
  new int[]{1, 0, 0, 0, 0, 0, 0, 0, 0, 0, 0, 0, 0, 0, 0, 0, 0, 1},
  new int[]{1, 0, 0, 0, 0, 0, 0, 0, 0, 0, 0, 0, 0, 0, 0, 0, 0, 1},
  new int[]{1, 0, 0, 0, 0, 0, 0, 0, 0, 0, 0, 0, 0, 0, 0, 0, 0, 1},
  new int[]{1, 1, 1, 1, 1, 1, 1, 0, 0, 0, 0, 0, 0, 0, 0, 0, 0, 1},
  new int[]{1, 1, 1, 1, 1, 1, 1, 0, 0, 0, 1, 1, 1, 1, 0, 0, 0, 1},
  new int[]{1, 0, 0, 0, 0, 0, 0, 0, 0, 0, 1, 1, 1, 1, 0, 0, 0, 1},
  new int[]{1, 0, 0, 0, 0, 0, 0, 0, 0, 0, 0, 0, 0, 0, 0, 0, 0, 1},
  new int[]{1, 0, 0, 0, 0, 0, 0, 0, 0, 0, 0, 0, 0, 0, 0, 0, 1, 1},
  new int[]{1, 0, 0, 0, 0, 0, 0, 0, 0, 0, 0, 0, 0, 0, 0, 1, 1, 1},
  new int[]{1, 0, 0, 0, 0, 0, 0, 0, 0, 0, 0, 0, 0, 0, 1, 1, 1, 1},
  new int[]{1, 0, 0, 0, 0, 0, 0, 0, 0, 0, 0, 0, 0, 1, 1, 1, 1, 1},
  new int[]{1, 0, 0, 0, 0, 0, 0, 1, 1, 1, 1, 0, 0, 1, 1, 1, 1, 1},
  new int[]{1, 0, 0, 0, 0, 0, 0, 0, 0, 0, 0, 0, 1, 1, 1, 1, 1, 1},
  new int[]{1, 0, 0, 0, 1, 1, 0, 0, 0, 0, 0, 0, 1, 1, 1, 1, 1, 1},
  new int[]{1, 0, 0, 0, 1, 1, 0, 0, 0, 0, 0, 0, 1, 1, 1, 1, 1, 1},
  new int[]{1, 0, 0, 0, 1, 1, 0, 0, 0, 0, 0, 0, 1, 1, 1, 1, 1, 1},
  new int[]{1, 1, 1, 1, 1, 1, 1, 1, 1, 1, 1, 1, 1, 1, 1, 1, 1, 1}
};
public Transform wall;
```

The `wall` variable looks similar to things we've created before, but the `level` variable looks a bit different.

Working with arrays

The level variable is an array. We could create an integer for each place inside of our level, detailing what type is there; however, this is quite tedious, and we would have to remember each element's identifier. An array is a holder of multiple elements of the same type. To access an individual element of the array, we simply need to specify an index of where it is placed in between square brackets (the [and] characters). Arrays are played sequentially in memory, which means it's really easy to move between elements of them, and it's a very fast operation to access an individual element.

The level variable is actually a multidirectional array, which can be thought of as an array of an array of integers. We will use a multidirectional array, because it allows us to draw with numbers like a grid to place each of the elements in our level.

That being said, now we actually need to build the level. To do that, perform the following steps:

1. Let's create a function called `BuildLevel`:

```
void BuildLevel()
{
  // Get the DynamicObjects object that we created already in the
  // scene so we can make it our newly created objects' parent
  GameObject dynamicParent = GameObject.Find ("DynamicObjects");

  //Go through each element inside our level variable
  for (int yPos = 0; yPos < level.Length; yPos++)
  {
    for (int xPos = 0; xPos < (level[yPos]).Length; xPos++)
    {
      // Do nothing if the value is 0

      // If the value is 1, we want a wall
      if (level[yPos][xPos] == 1)
      {
        // Create the wall
        Transform newObject = Instantiate (wall, new Vector3 (xPos,
(level.Length - yPos), 0), Quaternion.identity) as Transform;

        // Set the object's parent to the DynamicObjects
        // variable so it doesn't clutter our Hierachy
        newObject.parent = dynamicParent.transform;
      }
    }
  }
}
```

The quaternion class is what is used for rotations inside of Unity. In this instance, `Quaternion.identity` stands for a matrix on rotation. For more information on quaternions, please check out `http://docs.unity3d.com/ScriptReference/Quaternion.html`.

As you can see, we access each of the arrays stored in the level by using `array[index]`, and for an index inside of that array, we use `array[index1][index2]`.

2. Next, we need to actually call this function. Do so in your `Start` function:

```
void Start ()
{
    BuildLevel ();
}
```

3. Save the script, and exit out to the Unity editor. When you get back, you should see under the `GameController` script that is there in the `wall` variable, which still needs a value for its variable. In order to assign the prefab we created previously, we'll need to go to the folder, and then drag-and-drop it into the box for the variable and then release the mouse. Have a look at the following screenshot:

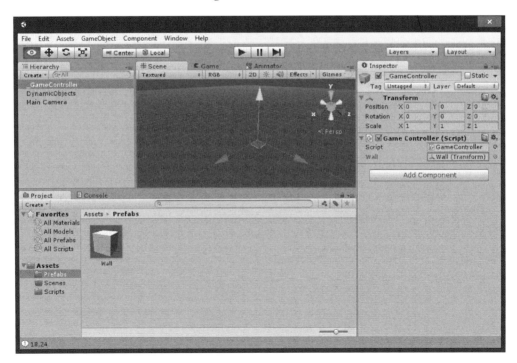

4. After this, click on the **Start** button to see the code execute:

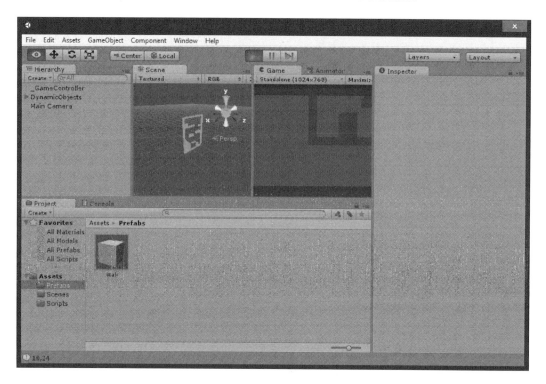

You may see a bit of the result in the **Game** screen that pops up, but if you click on the **Scene** tab, you'll see the level has been built for us!

You can drag-and-drop the **Scene** tab to share space with the **Game** tab if you want, as you can see in the preceding screenshot.

There are a number of other ways that you can use to modify your layout as well. Some of them are provided and will help your workflow.

To view them, you can either go to the **Window | Layouts** menu or select the right-most drop-down menu on the toolbar.

I personally use the **Default** layout for this book, but when I have two monitors, I like to spread things out with the **Game** tab on one monitor and everything else.

One of our technical editors prefers the 2 by 3 layout with a one-column Project tab (right-click the **Project** tab, and then select **One Column Layout**.

Creating our player

Having the basis of our world is great, but if we don't have a player, it doesn't matter how nice the level looks. In this section, we will create the actual player that will walk around and move in the world:

1. Let's first create a capsule by selecting **GameObject | Create Other | Capsule**. Have a look at the following screenshot:

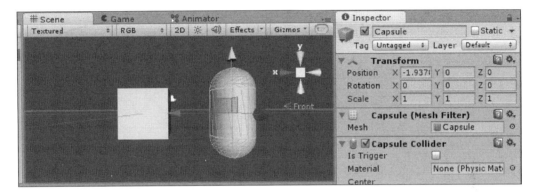

 If you are using Unity 4.6 or above, use the **GameObject | 3D Object | Capsule**

2. Right now, the capsule is too big to fit in our world because it is larger than our blocks. To easily fix this, we will set **Scale** of our capsule to (.4, .4, .4). Also, set **Position** to (1, 2, 0).

3. Now, we want our player to use gravity and forces, so we will need to add a rigid body component by going to **Component | Physics | Rigid Body**.

 The 2D and 3D Physics systems are not interchangeable. You'll need to choose one or the other when working on a project. We're using 3D right now, so you can have a good idea of what to look out for, and the differences between 2D and 3D.

4. Next, since we are creating 2D gameplay, we don't want our player to move in the **Z** axis, so under **Rigid Body**, open the **Constraints** box, and check **Z** in the **Freeze Position** variable. After that, check each axis for **Freeze Rotation**, as we do not want our character to change its rotation via **Rigid Body** (we'll rotate it via code). Have a look at the following screenshot:

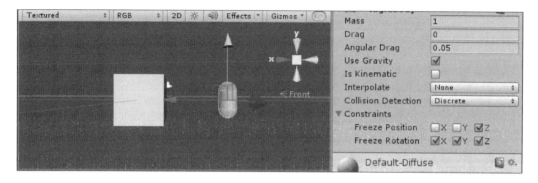

5. After this, all that's left is to create some custom functionality, which means another script. Create a new script file in the `Scripts` folder called `PlayerBehaviour`, and open it in `MonoDevelop`.

6. With the `PlayerBehaviour` script opened, let's first write down each of the issues we need to solve and make them functions. As programmers, it's our job to solve problems, and separating problems into smaller pieces will make it easier to solve, rather than trying to solve the entire thing all at once. Have a look at the following code:

```
void FixedUpdate ()
{
  // Move the player left and right
  Movement();

  // Sets the camera to center on the player's position.
  // Keeping the camera's original depth
  Camera.main.transform.position = new Vector3(transform.
position.x,
  transform.position.y,
  Camera.main.transform.position.z);
}
```

7. Next, we write the following code in the `Update` function:

```
void Update()
{
// Have the player jump if they press the jump button
  Jumping();
}
```

`Update()` is great and is called in every frame, but it's called at random times leading to more instant, but less constant, things, such as input. Instead of that, `FixedUpdate()` is a great function to use for things that need to happen consistently and for things like Physics (due to its fixed delta time). However, in a platformer, the player needs to feel a jump instantly, so that's why I put the `Jumping` function inside `Update`.

So, at this point, we have broken apart the player's behavior into two sections: their movement and their jumping.

8. Next, we need to declare some variables for us to use as follows:

```
// Force to apply when player jumps
public Vector2 jumpForce = new Vector2(0, 450);

// How fast we'll let the player move in the x axis
public float maxSpeed = 3.0f;

// A modifier to the force applied
public float speed = 50.0f;

// The force to apply that we will get for the player's movement
private float xMove;

// Set to true when the player can jump
private bool shouldJump;
```

9. I initialized the public data here, but the user can modify the numbers in **Inspector**. However, we still need to initialize the `private` variables in the `Start` function, as follows:

```
void Start ()
{
  shouldJump = false;
  xMove = 0.0f;
}
```

10. Now that we have the variables, we think we need to fill in the implementation for the `Movement` function now, as follows:

```
void Movement()
{
  //Get the player's movement (-1 for left, 1 for right, 0 for
  // none)
  xMove = Input.GetAxis("Horizontal");
```

```
if (xMove != 0)
{
  // Setting player horizontal movement
  float xSpeed = Mathf.Abs(xMove * rigidbody.velocity.x);

  if (xSpeed < maxSpeed)
  {
    Vector3 movementForce = new Vector3(1,0,0);
    movementForce *= xMove * speed;
    rigidbody.AddForce(movementForce);
  }

  // Check speed limit
  if (Mathf.Abs(rigidbody.velocity.x) > maxSpeed)
  {
    Vector2 newVelocity;

    newVelocity.x = Mathf.Sign(rigidbody.velocity.x) * maxSpeed;
    newVelocity.y = rigidbody.velocity.y;

    rigidbody.velocity = newVelocity;
  }
}
else
{
  // If we're not moving, get slightly slower
  Vector2 newVelocity = rigidbody.velocity;

  // Reduce the current speed by 10%
  newVelocity.x *= 0.9f;
  rigidbody.velocity = newVelocity;
}
}
```

In this section of code, we use a different way to get input from the player, the GetAxis function. GetAxis will return a value for directional movement. The value will be in the range -1 to 1 for keyboard and joystick input, so it can work on controllers or on various places on your keyboard. Unity already provides a few preset axes for us, which you can look at. We will go to these preset axes now.

11. Back in the Unity Editor, Access the **Input** properties by going to **Edit | Project Settings | Input**. Once there, extend the **Jump** tab. In **Alt Positive Button**, put in up. Have a look at the **Axes** and **Jump** tabs in the following screenshot:

 It's okay if there is an error shown in the console right now, as we haven't created the Jumping function yet.

12. Next, let's implement the Jumping function, as follows:

```
void Jumping()
{
  if(Input.GetButtonDown("Jump"))
  {
    shouldJump = true;
  }

  // If the player should jump
  if(shouldJump)
  {
```

```
        rigidbody.AddForce(jumpForce);
        shouldJump = false;
    }
}
```

Now, if we press space bar or the up arrow key, we will turn the `shouldJump` Boolean value to `true`. If it's `true`, then we'll apply `jumpForce` to our character.

13. With that completed, let's save our script and jump back into the Unity editor. Attach the newly created behavior to our player if you haven't done so already. Have a look at the following screenshot:

Great start! We now have a player in our world, and we're able to move around and jump. However, if you keep playing with it, you'll notice some of the issues this has: namely, the fact that you can always jump up as many times as you want, and if you hold a direction key hitting a wall, you'll stay stuck in the air. This could make for interesting game mechanics, but I'm going to assume this is not what you're looking for. In addition, all we see at this time is dark grey.

Let's solve those issues now. Perform the following steps:

1. Make sure you have exited the game by clicking on the play button again, and then create a directional light by going to **GameObject | Create Other | Directional Light**.

 Make sure you exit the game before making changes, otherwise you will lose everything that you've done.

If you go to the **Game** tab and play the game, you'll see immediately that the game changes for the better, graphics-wise. Have a look at the following screenshot:

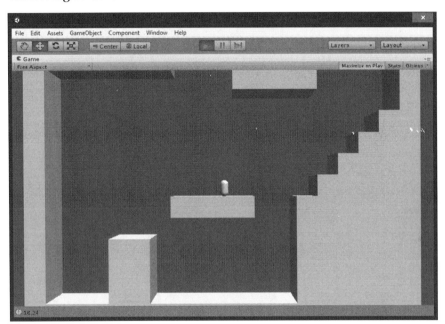

This is due to our inclusion of the directional light. You can think of a directional light like the sun in that no matter where you place it, it will affect objects. You may notice in **Inspector** that there are a number of properties that you can use to change the rotation of the light, the color, and how strong it is. Depending on the game, you may want to modify these properties accordingly. We'll be looking at it, and other light types, more closely in our next project.

2. Next, before we solve our movement issues, I wanted to show you a tool that you can use as a developer to help you when working on your own projects. Add the following function to your script:

```
void OnDrawGizmos()
{
  Debug.DrawLine(transform.position, transform.position +
  rigidbody.velocity, Color.red);
}
```

OnDrawGizmos is a function inherited by the MonoBehaviour class that will allow us to draw things appearing in the Scene view, and sure enough, you will not see anything in the Game view, but if you look at the **Scene** tab while the game is being played, you'll be able to see the velocity that our object is traveling at. Have a look at the following screenshot:

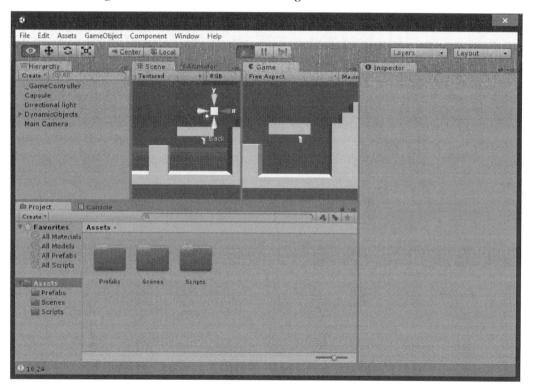

 Note that the **Game** tab needs to be active before Input registers any keys pressed, which is why I have both tabs open. You can also click on the **Gizmos** button on the right hand side of the **Game** tab in order to see the **Gizmos** during the game as well.

In this example, the red line shows that I'm jumping up and moving to the left-hand side. If you look at the **Scene** view when the player is walking, you'll see little bumps occurring. This isn't something we like to see, as we expect the collision to flow together. These bumps occur, because the moment we hit the edges of two separate boxes, the collision engine will try to push the player in different directions to prevent the collision from happening. After the collisions occur, the Physics engine will try to combine both of those forces into one, which causes these hiccups. We can fix this by telling Unity to spend some extra time doing the calculations.

3. Go into Unity's Physics properties by going to **Edit | Project Settings | Physics**. Change the **Min Penetration for Penalty** property to `0.0001`.

    The **Min Penetration for Penalty** property tells us how deep two objects are allowed to be penetrated by another before the collision solver pushes them apart.

4. Now there's the matter of being able to jump anytime we want. What we want to happen is if the player is on the ground, they can jump, but they cannot jump again until they are on the ground. This is to prevent the case of being able to jump while falling. So, to do this, we will need to introduce some new variables inside of our `PlayerBehaviour` script, as follows:

    ```
    private bool onGround;
    private float yPrevious;
    ```

5. Just like any `private` variables, we will need to initialize them in our `Start` function. Have a look at the following code:

    ```
    onGround = false;
    yPrevious = Mathf.Floor(transform.position.y);
    ```

6. Now, in our `Jumping` function, we just need to add the highlighted part of the following code:

    ```
    void Jumping()
    {
      if(Input.GetButtonDown("Jump"))
      {
        shouldJump = true;
      }

      // If the player should jump
      if(shouldJump && onGround)
      {
        rigidbody.AddForce(jumpForce);
        shouldJump = false;
      }
    }
    ```

7. In our `Update` function, we will add in a new function for us to check if we are grounded, as follows:

```
// Update is called once per frame
void Update ()
{
    // Check if we are on the ground
    CheckGrounded();

    // Have the player jump if they press the jump button
    Jumping();
}
```

8. Now, we just need to add in the code for `CheckGrounded`. Sadly, this isn't exactly a simple issue to solve without math, so we will actually need to use some linear algebra to solve the issue for us, as follows:

```
void CheckGrounded()
{
// Check if the player is hitting something from
// the center of the object (origin) to slightly below the
// bottom of it (distance)
    float distance = (GetComponent<CapsuleCollider>().height/2 *
    this.transform.localScale.y) + .01f;
    Vector3 floorDirection = transform.TransformDirection(-Vector3.
up);
    Vector3 origin = transform.position;

    if(!onGround)
    {
      // Check if there is something directly below us
      if (Physics.Raycast (origin, floorDirection, distance))
      {
        onGround = true;
      }
    }
    // If we are currently grounded, are we falling down or jumping?
    else if((Mathf.Floor(transform.position.y) != yPrevious))
    {
      onGround = false;
    }

    // Our current position will be our previous next frame
    yPrevious = Mathf.Floor(transform.position.y);
}
```

This function uses a `Raycast` function to cast an invisible line (ray) from origin in the direction of the floor for a certain distance, which is just slightly further than our player. If it finds an object colliding with this, it will return `true`, which will tell us that we are indeed on the ground.

In the game, we can leave the ground in two ways, by jumping or by falling down a platform; either way, we will change our `y` position. If that's the case, we are no longer on the ground, so `onGround` will be set to `false`. The `Floor` function will remove the decimal from a number to allow for some leeway for floating point error.

Now, our only issue resides in the fact that the player sticks to walls if they press into it. To solve this, perform the following steps:

1. We will simply not allow the player to move into a wall, by not adding a force if we're right next to a wall. Add the following bolded code to this section of code in the `Movement` function:

    ```
    // Movement()
    // if xMove != 0...
    if (xSpeed < maxSpeed)
    {
      Vector3 movementForce = new Vector3(1,0,0);
      movementForce *= xMove * speed;

      RaycastHit hit;
      if(!rigidbody.SweepTest(movementForce, out hit, 0.05f))
      {
        rigidbody.AddForce(movementForce);
      }
    }
    // Etc.
    ```

    The `SweepTest` function will check in the direction the rigid body is traveling, and if it sees something within a certain direction, it will get hit with the object that it has touched and return `true`. We want to stop the player from being able to move into the wall, so we will not add the force if that's the case.

2. Now, this works for the most part, except for when we are already along the wall, jumping up, and other fringe cases. To fix these issues when we touch a wall, we will do just as we solved the last problem. We will have a variable that will keep track if we touch a wall, as follows:

    ```
    private bool collidingWall;
    ```

3. After that, we need to initialize it in `Start`, as follows:

```
collidingWall = false;
```

4. After this, we will use the 3D collision detection functions to determine whether we're touching a wall, as follows:

```
// If we hit something and we're not grounded, it must be a wall
or // a ceiling.
   void OnCollisionEnter(Collision collision)
   {
     if (!onGround)
     {
       collidingWall = true;
     }
   }

   void OnCollisionExit(Collision collision)
   {
     collidingWall = false;
   }
```

You'll notice that the functions look quite similar to the 2D functions apart from… well, the word 2D.

5. Next, inside of your `Movement` function, add the following bolded code:

```
void Movement()
{
  //Get the player's movement (-1 for left, 1 for right, 0 for
  // none)
  xMove = Input.GetAxis("Horizontal");

  if(collidingWall && !onGround)
  {
    xMove = 0;
  }

  // Etc.
```

Now, if we collide against a wall, we will stop the player from applying a force.

6. Save the script, and go back to Unity. Refresh the scripts if needed, and hit the play button. Have a look at the following screenshot:

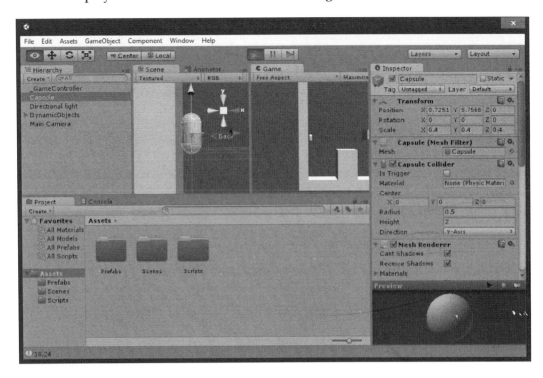

Now, our player can jump along walls, fall normally, and can only jump when he is on the ground! We now have the basis to complete a platformer game!

Creating collectibles

At this point, we have the basis of our game, but now, we need to add some gameplay to our world. Perhaps we will have it so that we need to collect all of the coins in the level, and then the goal will open:

1. Create a new particle system by going to **GameObject | Create Other | Particle System** (in case of Unity 4.6, go to **GameObject | Particle System**). Change the name of the object to `Collectible`. Next, we need to assign the object's tag to `Orb`. To do so, select **Tag | Add Tag**. Once in the **Tag** menu, assign **Element 0** as `Orb`, and press *Enter*. Select the **Collectible** game object in **Hierarchy** again, and then select **Tag** as `Orb`.

2. Under the **Shape** section, change the **Shape** variable to `Sphere` and the **Radius** to `0.01`.

3. Click on the downward-facing arrow on the right-hand side of **Start Lifetime**, and change the values to **Random Between Two Constants**. Change those values to 0 and .2. Do the same with **Start Speed** between 0 and 1. Make **Start Size** use random values between 0 and 1.5.

4. Under **Start Color**, change the value to yellow by clicking on the color to bring up the color select dialogue. Once there, set alpha (**A**) to 39. Have a look at the following screenshot:

5. Next, under **Emission**, set **Rate** to 100.

6. Now, add a sphere collider by selecting **Component | Physics | Sphere Collider**. Inside **Inspector**, trigger the **Is Trigger** Boolean to true, set **Center** to (0, 0, 0), and then set **Radius** to 0.4. Have a look at the following screenshot:

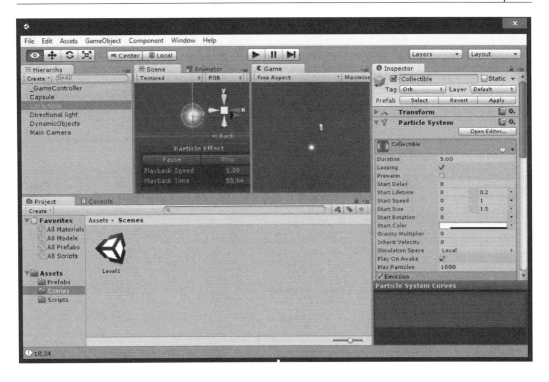

7. Finally, drag-and-drop the `Orb` object into the `Prefabs` section of the `Project` folder, and delete the object in **Hierarchy**.

8. Now, we need to modify our original build-level function to have support to add these collectibles as well to our level. While we're at it, let's make it so the level can spawn the player as well. Rename our player object to `Player`, and drag-and-drop it to the `Prefabs` folder as well, and delete it from the **Hierarchy** section as we will now learn how to spawn it via code.

9. Because we're writing a new function, we have some new variables to introduce in the `GameController` class:

```
public Transform player;
public Transform orb;
```

10. Then, change the build-level function, replacing what was inside of our for loops to:

```
void BuildLevel ()
{
  // Get the DynamicObjects object so we can make it our newly
  // created objects' parent
  GameObject dynamicParent = GameObject.Find ("DynamicObjects");
```

```
      // Go through each element inside our level variable
      for (int yPos = 0; yPos < level.Length; yPos++)
      {
        for (int xPos = 0; xPos < (level[yPos]).Length; xPos++)
        {
          Transform toCreate = null;
          switch(level[yPos][xPos])
          {
            case 0:
              //Do nothing because we don't want anything there.
              break;

            case 1:
              toCreate = wall;
              break;

            case 2:
              toCreate = player;
              break;

            case 3:
              toCreate = orb;
              break;

            default:
              print("Invalid number: "+(level[yPos][xPos]).ToString());
              break;
          }

          if(toCreate != null)
          {
            Transform newObject = Instantiate(toCreate, new
Vector3(xPos, (level.Length - yPos), 0), Quaternion.identity) as
Transform;

            // Set the object's parent to the DynamicObjects
            // variable so it doesn't clutter our Hierachy
            newObject.parent = dynamicParent.transform;
          }

        }
      }
    }
```

This is the first time you may have seen a switch statement. A **switch statement** can be thought of as a nice way to compare a single variable with a number of different values. In this case, the switch statement that we wrote in the preceding example could be rewritten as follows:

```
if(level[yPos][xPos] == 0)
{

}
else if(level[yPos][xPos] == 1)
{
  toCreate = wall;
}
else if(level[yPos][xPos] == 2)
{
  toCreate = player;
}
else if(level[yPos][xPos] == 3)
{
  toCreate = orb;
}
else
{
  print("Invalid number: "+ (level[yPos][xPos]).ToString());
}
```

But I'm sure you can tell, writing it as a switch statement is much nicer to look at and requires less code duplication, which is something we want to reduce as much as possible.

 For those of you with a programming background, you are required to put a `break` at the end of each case so that fall-throughs are not possible in C#.

11. After this, we need to modify our level array to actually have the collectibles and player in it. Replace one of the 0s in your level to a 2 to put the player there and add in some 3s for the player to collect. Mine looks like the following:

```
private int[][] level = new int[][]
{
  new int[]{1, 1, 1, 1, 1, 1, 1, 1, 1, 1, 1, 1, 1, 1, 1, 1, 1, 1},
  new int[]{1, 0, 0, 0, 0, 0, 0, 0, 0, 0, 0, 0, 0, 0, 0, 0, 0, 1},
  new int[]{1, 0, 0, 0, 0, 0, 0, 0, 0, 0, 0, 0, 0, 0, 0, 0, 0, 1},
  new int[]{1, 3, 0, 0, 0, 0, 0, 0, 0, 0, 3, 3, 3, 0, 0, 0, 0, 1},
  new int[]{1, 0, 0, 0, 0, 0, 0, 0, 0, 0, 0, 0, 0, 0, 1, 1, 1, 1},
```

```
new int[]{1, 0, 0, 0, 0, 0, 0, 0, 0, 0, 0, 0, 0, 0, 0, 1, 1, 1, 1},
new int[]{1, 0, 0, 0, 0, 0, 0, 0, 1, 1, 1, 1, 1, 1, 1, 1, 1, 1, 1},
new int[]{1, 1, 1, 1, 0, 0, 0, 0, 0, 0, 0, 0, 0, 0, 0, 0, 0, 0, 1},
new int[]{1, 0, 0, 0, 0, 0, 0, 0, 0, 0, 0, 0, 0, 0, 0, 0, 0, 0, 1},
new int[]{1, 0, 0, 0, 0, 0, 3, 0, 3, 0, 0, 0, 0, 0, 0, 0, 0, 0, 1},
new int[]{1, 0, 0, 0, 0, 0, 0, 0, 0, 0, 0, 0, 0, 0, 0, 0, 0, 0, 1},
new int[]{1, 1, 1, 1, 1, 1, 1, 0, 0, 0, 0, 0, 0, 0, 0, 0, 0, 0, 1},
new int[]{1, 1, 1, 1, 1, 1, 1, 0, 0, 0, 1, 1, 1, 1, 0, 0, 0, 0, 1},
new int[]{1, 0, 0, 0, 0, 0, 0, 0, 0, 0, 1, 1, 1, 1, 0, 0, 0, 3, 1},
new int[]{1, 0, 0, 0, 0, 0, 0, 0, 0, 0, 0, 0, 0, 0, 0, 0, 0, 0, 1},
new int[]{1, 0, 0, 0, 0, 0, 0, 0, 0, 0, 0, 0, 0, 0, 0, 0, 0, 1, 1},
new int[]{1, 0, 0, 0, 0, 0, 0, 0, 0, 0, 0, 0, 0, 0, 0, 0, 1, 1, 1},
new int[]{1, 0, 0, 0, 0, 0, 0, 0, 3, 0, 0, 0, 0, 0, 0, 1, 1, 1, 1},
new int[]{1, 0, 0, 0, 0, 0, 0, 0, 0, 0, 0, 0, 0, 0, 1, 1, 1, 1, 1},
new int[]{1, 0, 0, 0, 3, 0, 0, 1, 1, 1, 1, 0, 0, 1, 1, 1, 1, 1, 1},
new int[]{1, 0, 0, 0, 0, 0, 0, 0, 0, 0, 0, 0, 0, 1, 1, 1, 1, 1, 1},
new int[]{1, 0, 0, 0, 1, 1, 0, 0, 0, 0, 0, 0, 0, 1, 1, 1, 1, 1, 1},
new int[]{1, 0, 0, 0, 1, 1, 0, 0, 0, 0, 0, 0, 0, 1, 1, 1, 1, 1, 1},
new int[]{1, 0, 2, 0, 1, 1, 0, 0, 0, 0, 0, 0, 0, 1, 1, 1, 1, 1, 1},
new int[]{1, 1, 1, 1, 1, 1, 1, 1, 1, 1, 1, 1, 1, 1, 1, 1, 1, 1, 1}
};
```

12. Save your script, and exit back into the editor. Once there, select your `GameController` class, and then assign the `Player` and `Orb` variables with the appropriate prefabs. Finally, save your scene, and run the game. Have a look at the following screenshot:

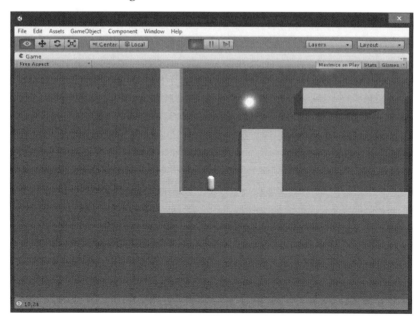

And there we go! Our player as well as collectibles are now spawning via our `BuildLevel` function. Lastly, let's make it so that we can actually collect them.

13. After we have the physical representation of the object done, let's now implement its functionality. Create a new script in our **Scripts** folder, which we will name `OrbBehaviour`. Open it up in `MonoDevelop` and fill it in with the following:

```
using UnityEngine;

public class OrbBehaviour : MonoBehaviour
{
  void OnTriggerEnter(Collider other)
  {
    Destroy(this.gameObject);
  }
}
```

14. Assign the `OrbBehavior` component to the `Orb` prefab. Save the scene, and then play the game. Have a look at the following screenshot:

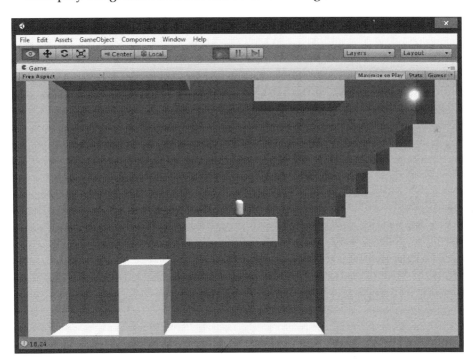

And with that we can now collect orbs, and they disappear when we touch them!

Keeping score

We now want to make it so that when we collect all of the orbs in the level, the goal will appear, and then you will win the game when you touch it:

1. Go back into MonoDevelop, and select the GameController class. Once there, add the following variables:

```
public static GameController _instance;
private int orbsCollected;
private int orbsTotal;
```

> While it may make more sense English-wise to use totalOrbs and collectedOrbs, programming-wise, putting the common word first means that when you start typing orbs, it will show both options for you when working with code completion in your own projects.

2. As normal, we will need to set these variables as well in the Start function after the BuildLevel function call, otherwise the Orb objects will not exist:

```
GameObject[] orbs;
orbs = GameObject.FindGameObjectsWithTag("Orb");

orbsCollected = 0;
orbsTotal = orbs.Length;
```

3. We will also want to initialize the _instance variable, but instead of using Start, we will use Awake, as follows:

```
void Awake()
{
  _instance = this;
}
```

Awake gets called before Start, which is important, because you have to initialize the _instance variable before you use it. This is known as a lazy singleton.

Singletons

As you work in Unity, you may find that you have certain managers, such as GameController, that we will only have one of. Rather than having to have other objects, store them as variables, or find them at runtime, we can use a design pattern called the **singleton pattern**. The gist of this is that there is one, and only one, object of this class that can be created. The version that I am using is the quickest way to get singleton-like behavior going.

Never use the `GameController._instance` variable inside another `Awake` function, as you are not guaranteed the order in which they'll be called. However, if you use it in `Start` or any of the other functions we talked about, you'll be okay because `Start` is guaranteed to be called after `Awake`.

1. As we collect orbs, we want to increase the value of our `orbsCollected` variable. Rather than just giving other things access to the variable, let's wrap this around a function so that we can do other things, such as updating the GUI later on. Have a look at the following code snippet, which will increment our `orbsCollected` variable by 1:

```
public void CollectedOrb()
{
  orbsCollected++;
}
```

In our `OrbBehaviour` script we call the function:

```
void OnTriggerEnter(Collider other)
{
  GameController._instance.CollectedOrb();
  Destroy(this.gameObject);
}
```

When you access the `_instance` variable, you get access to the public functions and variables that exist in the class.

2. With that completed, save the file and go back to the Unity Editor. Now that we have this data stored, let's display it on the screen so that players can see. Go to **GameObject | Create Other | GUIText**. Place it in the top-left corner of the screen (a position of 0, 1, 0 with an anchor of upper-left and alignment of left), and give the object the name `GUI - Score`.

 If you are using the Unity 4.6 beta or higher, simply create an empty game object, and add a `GUIText` component from **Component | Rendering | GUIText**.

3. Add one last variable to add to `GameController`, as follows:

```
public GUIText scoreText;
```

4. We need to initialize it in the `Start` function, as follows:

```
void Start()
{
  BuildLevel();
```

```
GameObject[] orbs;
orbs = GameObject.FindGameObjectsWithTag("Orb");

orbsCollected = 0;
orbsTotal = orbs.Length;

scoreText.text = "Orbs: " + orbsCollected + "/" + orbsTotal;
}
```

5. And now, because we have text displaying the orbs, we can now update our text accordingly. Have a look at the following screenshot:

```
public void CollectedOrb()
{
  orbsCollected++;
  scoreText.text = "Orbs: " + orbsCollected + "/" + orbsTotal;
}
```

6. With that, save the script, and then go back into the Unity editor. Once there, set our newly created variable with the GUI text object we created, and then click on the play button, as shown in the following screenshot:

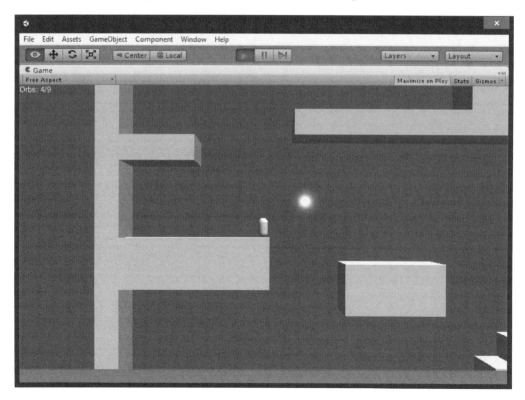

At this point, you can move around the level, and when you collect the orbs, they will now update the GUI, letting us know how many coins you collected and how many there are in total in the level. We're making great progress, and we almost have a full game; we just need one last thing, a way to win!

Winning the game

Now that we have the goals showing, we now need some way in order to complete the project. With that in mind, let's create our goal:

1. Create a new particle system by going into **GameObject | Create Other | Particle System** (in case of Unity 4.6, go to **GameObject | Particle System**). Change the name of the object to Goal.

2. Under the **Shape** section, change the **Shape** variable to Box, and change **Box X** to 1 and **Box Y** and **Box Z** to 0.

3. Click on the arrow on the right-hand side of **Start Lifetime**, and change the values to **Random Between Two Constants**. Change those values to 0 and 1. Do the same with **Start Speed** between 2 and 4. Make **Start Size** use random values between 0 and 0.5. Change **Start Color** to **Random Between Two Colors** using a green and purple color. Finally, uncheck the **Play On Awake** variable. Have a look at the following screenshot:

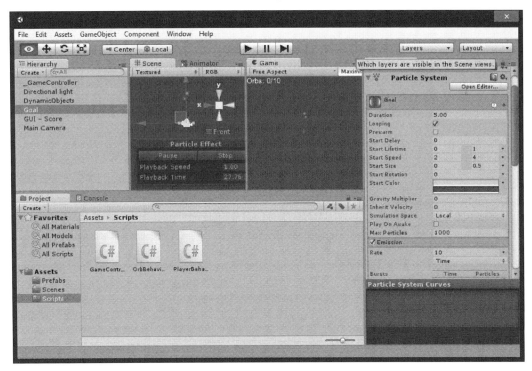

With that, you should have a nice stream of particles coming in for your new goal object!

4. Add in a box collider by selecting **Component | Physics | Box Collider**. Toggle the **Is Trigger** option to `true`, set **Center** to (`0`, `0`, `0`), and **Size** to (`1`, `1`, `1`).

5. Now that we have completed the goal's object, let's now have it spawn within our `BuildLevel` function in `GameController`. So, just as we did before, we drag-and-drop the object to our `Prefabs` folder and delete the original object. Then, we need to add two new variables for us to use, which are as follows:

```
public Transform goal;
private ParticleSystem goalPS;
```

6. After we add the new variables, add in the following in bold to `BuildLevel`:

```
void BuildLevel()
{
  // Get the DynamicObjects object so we can make it our newly
  // created objects' parent
  GameObject dynamicParent = GameObject.Find("DynamicObjects");


  //Go through each element inside our level variable
  for (int yPos = 0; yPos < level.Length; yPos++)
  {
    for (int xPos = 0; xPos < (level[yPos]).Length; xPos++)
    {
      Transform toCreate = null;
      switch(level[yPos][xPos])
      {
        case 0:
          //Do nothing because we don't want anything there.
          break;
        case 1:
          toCreate = wall;
          break;
        case 2:
          toCreate = player;
          break;
        case 3:
          toCreate = orb;
          break;
        case 4:
          toCreate = goal;
```

```
            break;
        default:
            print("Invalid number: " + (level[yPos][xPos]).
ToString());
            break;
        }

        if(toCreate != null)
        {
            Transform newObject = Instantiate(toCreate, new
Vector3(xPos, (level.Length - yPos), 0), Quaternion.identity) as
Transform;

            if(toCreate == goal)
            {
                goalPS = newObject.gameObject.
GetComponent<ParticleSystem>();
            }
            // Set the object's parent to the DynamicObjects
            // variable so it doesn't clutter our Hierachy
            newObject.parent = dynamicParent.transform;

        }


    }
  }
}
```

7. We also need to add in a 4 somewhere inside our level array, as follows:

```
private int[][] level = new int[][]
{
  new int[]{1, 1, 1, 1, 1, 1, 1, 1, 1, 1, 1, 1, 1, 1, 1, 1, 1, 1},
  new int[]{1, 0, 0, 0, 0, 0, 0, 0, 0, 0, 0, 0, 0, 0, 0, 0, 0, 1},
  new int[]{1, 0, 0, 0, 0, 0, 0, 0, 0, 0, 0, 0, 0, 0, 0, 0, 0, 1},
  new int[]{1, 3, 0, 0, 0, 0, 0, 0, 0, 0, 3, 3, 3, 0, 0, 0, 4, 0, 1},
  new int[]{1, 0, 0, 0, 0, 0, 0, 0, 0, 0, 0, 0, 0, 0, 1, 1, 1, 1},
  new int[]{1, 0, 0, 0, 0, 0, 0, 0, 0, 0, 0, 0, 0, 0, 1, 1, 1, 1},
  new int[]{1, 0, 0, 0, 0, 0, 0, 0, 1, 1, 1, 1, 1, 1, 1, 1, 1, 1},
  new int[]{1, 1, 1, 1, 0, 0, 0, 0, 0, 0, 0, 0, 0, 0, 0, 0, 0, 1},
  new int[]{1, 0, 0, 0, 0, 0, 0, 0, 0, 0, 0, 0, 0, 0, 0, 0, 0, 1},
  new int[]{1, 0, 0, 0, 0, 0, 3, 0, 3, 0, 0, 0, 0, 0, 0, 0, 0, 1},
  new int[]{1, 0, 0, 0, 0, 0, 0, 0, 0, 0, 0, 0, 0, 0, 0, 0, 0, 1},
  new int[]{1, 1, 1, 1, 1, 1, 1, 0, 0, 0, 0, 0, 0, 0, 0, 0, 0, 1},
  new int[]{1, 1, 1, 1, 1, 1, 1, 0, 0, 0, 1, 1, 1, 1, 0, 0, 0, 0, 1},
```

```
        new int[]{1, 0, 0, 0, 0, 0, 0, 0, 0, 0, 1, 1, 1, 1, 0, 0, 0, 3, 1},
        new int[]{1, 0, 0, 0, 0, 0, 0, 0, 0, 0, 0, 0, 0, 0, 0, 0, 0, 0, 1},
        new int[]{1, 0, 0, 0, 0, 0, 0, 0, 0, 0, 0, 0, 0, 0, 0, 0, 1, 1},
        new int[]{1, 0, 0, 0, 0, 0, 0, 0, 0, 0, 0, 0, 0, 0, 0, 0, 1, 1, 1},
        new int[]{1, 0, 0, 0, 0, 0, 0, 0, 3, 0, 0, 0, 0, 0, 0, 1, 1, 1, 1},
        new int[]{1, 0, 0, 0, 0, 0, 0, 0, 0, 0, 0, 0, 0, 0, 1, 1, 1, 1, 1},
        new int[]{1, 0, 0, 0, 3, 0, 0, 1, 1, 1, 1, 0, 0, 1, 1, 1, 1, 1, 1},
        new int[]{1, 0, 0, 0, 0, 0, 0, 0, 0, 0, 0, 0, 0, 1, 1, 1, 1, 1, 1},
        new int[]{1, 0, 0, 0, 1, 1, 0, 0, 0, 0, 0, 0, 0, 1, 1, 1, 1, 1, 1},
        new int[]{1, 0, 0, 0, 1, 1, 0, 0, 0, 0, 0, 0, 0, 1, 1, 1, 1, 1, 1},
        new int[]{1, 0, 2, 0, 1, 1, 0, 0, 0, 0, 0, 0, 0, 1, 1, 1, 1, 1, 1},
        new int[]{1, 1, 1, 1, 1, 1, 1, 1, 1, 1, 1, 1, 1, 1, 1, 1, 1, 1, 1}
    };
```

8. Next, in `UnityIinspector`, go in and assign the `Goal` object with your prefab of the game name.

9. With that done, we now need to go in and add in the ability to win. Go to the `CollectedOrb` function, and start our particle system when we get all of the orbs. Have a look at the following code:

```
public void CollectedOrb()
{
    orbsCollected++;
    scoreText.text = "Orbs: " + orbsCollected + "/" + orbsTotal;

    if(orbsCollected >= orbsTotal)
    {
        goalPS.Play();
    }
}
```

10. After that, we need to create the script for our goal. Create a new script in our **Scripts** folder, which we will name `GoalBehaviour`. Open it in `MonoDevelop`, and fill it in with the following:

```
using UnityEngine;

public class GoalBehaviour : MonoBehaviour
{
    ParticleSystem ps;
    void Start()
    {
        ps = GetComponent<ParticleSystem>();
    }
```

```
void OnTriggerEnter(Collider other)
{
  if(ps.isPlaying)
  {
    print("You Win!");
  }
}
}
```

11. Save the file, and attach it to the `Goal` prefab. With that all done, save the scene and hit the play button. Have a look at the following screenshot:

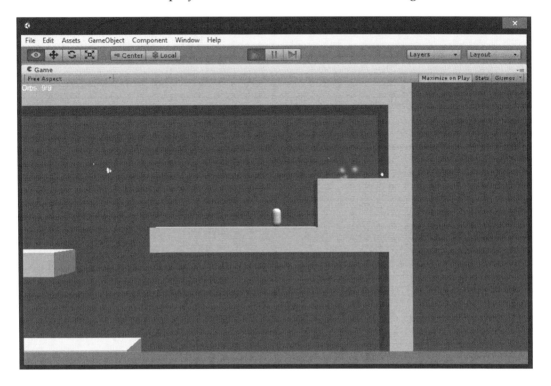

And with that, whenever we collect all of the coins we've placed in our level, the goal will appear, and then, when we touch it, the **Console** window will tell us that we've won!

Summary

With that, we now have all you need to get started building a side-scrolling platformer game on your own, adding in unique features and GUI as we discussed in the previous chapter. While doing so, we also gained an understanding of how working on 3D games is really not at all different than working with 2D. This will serve us greatly when we move on to the next chapter, where we will get started on a new game project!

Challenges

For those of you who want to do more with this project, there are still plenty of things you can do, especially after finishing the rest of this book. Here are some ideas to get your mind thinking:

- Add in sounds and music to the game, and customize the GUI in the ways we talked about earlier.

- Create levels of your own. Danny Calleri has created a really nice level editor called Toast Editor that you can run from your web browser to design levels graphically. To use it, go to `http://dannycalleri.github.io/toasteditor/index.html`. When exporting, use the C++ option, and replace the top line with our levels line, and add `new int []` to the beginning of every line in the array.

- Going one step further, instead of creating arrays for the levels, it is possible to load in text files in Unity so that you can load the levels from a file. For more information on text assets, see `http://docs.unity3d.com/Manual/class-TextAsset.html`.

- As it stands, when the player hits one of the orbs, they can jump again. Adding an additional parameter to the `Raycast` function with the tag of the object will solve the issue.

4
First Person Shooter Part 1 – Creating Exterior Environments

Now that we have experience working on all parts of the game in 2D and 3D, let's spend the next few chapters creating a full-featured game. We will be creating a first person shooter; however, instead of shooting a gun to damage our enemies, we will be shooting a picture in a survival horror environment; similar to the *Fatal Frame* series of games and the recent indie title *DreadOut*. To get started on our project, we're first going to look at creating our level or, in this case, our environments starting with the exterior.

In the game industry, there are two main roles in level creation: the environment artist and level designer.

An **environment artist** is a person who builds the assets that go into the environment. He/she uses tools such as 3ds Max or Maya to create the model, and then uses other tools such as Photoshop to create textures and normal maps.

The **level designer** is responsible for taking the assets that the environment artist has created and assembling them into an environment for players to enjoy. He/she designs the gameplay elements, creates the scripted events, and tests the gameplay. Typically, a level designer will create environments through a combination of scripting and using a tool that may or may not be in development as the game is being made. In our case, that tool is Unity.

One important thing to note is that most companies have their own definition for different roles. In some companies, a level designer may need to create assets and an environment artist may need to create a level layout. There are also some places that hire someone to just do lighting, or just to place meshes (called a mesher) because they're so good at it.

Project overview

In this chapter, we take on the role of an environment artist whose been tasked with creating an outdoor environment. We will use assets that I've placed in the example code as well as assets already provided to us by Unity for mesh placement. In addition to this, you will also learn some beginner-level design.

Your objectives

This project will be split into a number of tasks. It will be a simple step-by-step process from the beginning to end. Here is an outline of our tasks:

- Creating the exterior environment – Terrain
- Beautifying the environment – adding water, trees, and grass
- Building the atmosphere
- Designing the level layout and background

Prerequisites

As in *Chapter 1, 2D Twin-stick Shooter,* you will need Unity installed on your computer, but we will be starting a new project from scratch.

This chapter uses graphical assets that can be downloaded from the example code provided for this book on Packt's website:

`https://www.packtpub.com/books/content/support`

In addition, the completed project and source files are located there for you if you have any questions or need clarification.

The project setup

At this point, I assume you have a fresh installation of Unity and have started it. You can perform the following steps:

1. With Unity started, navigate to **File | New Project**.

2. Select a project location of your choice somewhere on your hard drive and ensure that you have **Setup defaults for** set to 3D.

3. Once completed, click on **Create**. Here, if you see the **Welcome to Unity** pop up, feel free to close it as we won't be using it.

Level design 101 – planning

Now just because we are going to be diving straight into Unity, I feel it's important to talk a little more about how level design is done in the gaming industry. While you may think a level designer will just jump into the editor and start playing, the truth is you normally would need to do a ton of planning ahead of time before you even open up your tool.

Generally, a level design begins with an idea. This can come from anything; maybe you saw a really cool building, or a photo on the Internet gave you a certain feeling; maybe you want to teach the player a new mechanic. Turning this idea into a level is what a level designer does. Taking all of these ideas, the level designer will create a level design document, which will outline exactly what you're trying to achieve with the entire level from start to end.

A **level design document** will describe everything inside the level; listing all of the possible encounters, puzzles, so on and so forth, which the player will need to complete as well as any side quests that the player will be able to achieve. To prepare for this, you should include as many references as you can with maps, images, and movies similar to what you're trying to achieve. If you're working with a team, making this document available on a website or wiki will be a great asset so that you know exactly what is being done in the level, what the team can use in their levels, and how difficult their encounters can be. Generally, you'll also want a top-down layout of your level done either on a computer or with a graph paper, with a line showing a player's general route for the level with encounters and missions planned out.

Of course, you don't want to be too tied down to your design document and it will change as you playtest and work on the level, but the documentation process will help solidify your ideas and give you a firm basis to work from.

For those of you interested in seeing some level design documents, feel free to check out *Adam Reynolds* (*Level Designer on Homefront* and *Call of Duty: World at War*) at `http://wiki.modsrepository.com/index.php?title=Level_Design:_Level_Design_Document_Example`.

If you want to learn more about level design, I'm a big fan of *Beginning Game Level Design, John Feil* (previously my teacher) *and Marc Scattergood, Cengage Learning PTR*. For more of an introduction to all of game design from scratch, check out *Level Up!: The Guide to Great Video Game Design, Scott Rogers, Wiley* and *The Art of Game Design, Jesse Schell, CRC Press.*

For some online resources, Scott has a neat GDC talk called *Everything I Learned About Level Design I Learned from Disneyland*, which can be found at `http://mrbossdesign.blogspot.com/2009/03/everything-i-learned-about-game-design.html`, and *World of Level Design* (`http://worldofleveldesign.com/`) is a good source for learning about level design, though it does not talk about Unity specifically.

Exterior environment – terrain

When creating exterior environments, we cannot use straight floors for the most part, unless you're creating a highly urbanized area. Our game takes place in a haunted house in the middle of nowhere, so we're going to create a natural landscape. In Unity, the best tool to use to create a natural landscape is the **Terrain** tool. Unity's terrain system lets us add landscapes, complete with bushes, trees, and fading materials to our game.

To show how easy it is to use the terrain tool, let's get started.

The first thing that we're going to want to do is actually create the terrain we'll be placing for the world. Let's first create a terrain by navigating to **GameObject | Create Other | Terrain**:

If you are using Unity 4.6 or later, navigate to **GameObject | Create General | Terrain** to create the Terrain.

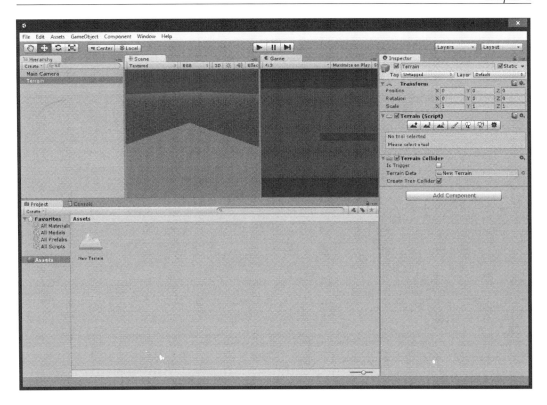

At this point, you should see the terrain. Right now, it's just a flat plane, but we'll be adding a lot to it to make it shine. If you look to the right with the **Terrain** object selected, you'll see the Terrain Editing tools, which can do the following (from left to right):

- **Raise/Lower Height**: This option will allow us to raise or lower the height of our terrain up to a certain radius to create hills, rivers, and more.

- **Paint Height**: If you already know the exact height that a part of your terrain needs to be, this option will allow you to paint a spot on that location.

- **Smooth Height**: This option averages out the area that it is in, and then attempts to smooth out areas and reduce the appearance of abrupt changes.

- **Paint Texture**: This option allows us to add textures to the surface of our terrain. One of the nice features of this is the ability to lay multiple textures on top of each other.

- **Place Trees**: This option allows us to paint objects in our environment, which will appear on the surface. Unity attempts to optimize these objects by billboarding distant trees so that we can have dense forests without a horrible frame rate.

- **Paint Details**: In addition to trees, we can also have small things such as rocks or grass covering the surface of our environment. We can use 2D images to represent individual clumps using bits of randomization to make it appear more natural.

- **Terrain Settings**: These are settings that will affect the overall properties of a particular terrain; options such as the size of the terrain and wind can be found here.

By default, the entire terrain is set to be at the bottom, but we want to have some ground above and below us; so first, with the terrain object selected, click on the second button to the left of the terrain component (the **Paint Height** mode). From here, set the **Height** value under **Settings** to 100 and then click on the **Flatten** button. At this point, you should notice the plane moving up, so now everything is above by default.

Next, we are going to add some interesting shapes to our world with some hills by *painting* on the surface. With the **Terrain** object selected, click on the first button to the left of our **Terrain** component (the **Raise/Lower Terrain** mode). Once this is completed, you should see a number of different brushes and shapes that you can select from.

Our use of terrain is to create hills in the background of our scene so that it does not seem like the world is completely flat.

Under the **Settings** area, change the **Brush Size** and **Opacity** values of your brush to **100** and left-click around the edges of the world to create some hills. You can increase the height of the current hills if you click on top of the previous hill. This is shown in the following screenshot:

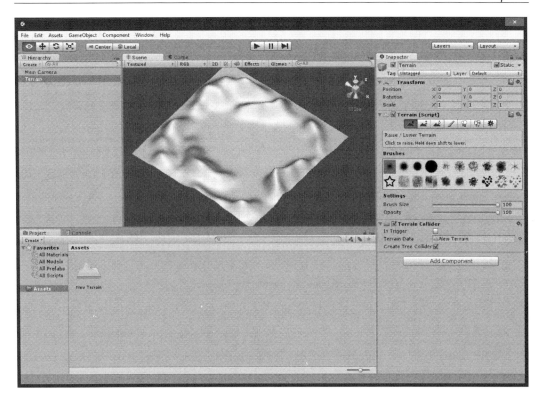

When creating hills, it's a good idea to look at multiple angles while you're building them, so you can make sure that none are too high or too short. Generally, you want to have taller hills as you go further back, otherwise you cannot see the smaller ones since they would be blocked.

In the **Scene** view, to move your camera around, you can use the toolbar in the top right corner or hold down the right mouse button and drag it in the direction you want the camera to move around in, pressing the *W*, *A*, *S*, and *D* keys to pan. In addition, you can hold down the middle mouse button and drag it to move the camera around. The mouse wheel can be scrolled to zoom in and out from where the camera is.

Even though you should plan out the level ahead of time on something like a piece of graph paper to plan out encounters, you will want to avoid making the level entirely from the preceding section, as the player will not actually see the game with a bird's eye view in the game at all (most likely). Referencing the map from the same perspective of your character will help ensure that the map looks great.

To see many different angles at one time, you can use a layout with multiple views of the scene, such as the 4 Split.

Once we have our land done, we now want to create some holes in the ground, which we will fill in with water later. This will provide a natural barrier to our world that players will know they cannot pass, so we will create a moat by first changing the **Brush Size** value to **50** and then holding down the *Shift* key, and left-clicking around the middle of our texture. In this case, it's okay to use the **Top** view; remember this will eventually be water to fill in lakes, rivers, and so on, as shown in the following screenshot:

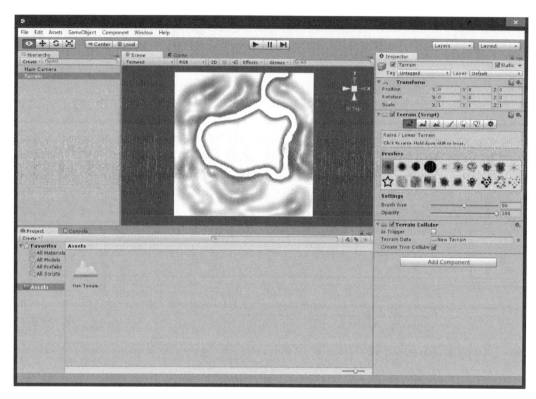

At this point, we have done what is referred to in the industry as "greyboxing", making the level in the engine in the simplest way possible but without artwork (also known as "whiteboxing" or "orangeboxing" depending on the company you're working for).

At this point in a traditional studio, you'd spend time playtesting the level and iterating on it before an artist or you takes the time to make it look great. However, for our purposes, we want to create a finished project as soon as possible. When doing your own games, be sure to play your level and have others play your level before you polish it.

For more information on greyboxing, check out `http://www.worldofleveldesign.com/categories/level_design_tutorials/art_of_blocking_in_your_map.php`.

For an example with images of a greybox to the final level, PC Gamer has a nice article available at `http://www.pcgamer.com/2014/03/18/building-crown-part-two-layout-design-textures-and-the-hammer-editor/`.

This is interesting enough, but being in an all-white world would be quite boring. Thankfully, it's very easy to add textures to everything. However, first we need to have some textures to paint onto the world and for this instance, we will make use of some of the free assets that Unity provides us with.

1. So, with that in mind, navigate to **Window | Asset Store**.

    The **Asset Store** option is home to a number of free and commercial assets that can be used with Unity to help you create your own projects created by both Unity and the community. While we will not be using any unofficial assets, the **Asset Store** option may help you in the future to save your time in programming or art asset creation.

2. An the top right corner, you'll see a search bar; type `terrain assets` and press *Enter*. Once there, the first asset you'll see is **Terrain Assets**, which is released by Unity Technologies for free. Left-click on it and then once at the menu, click on the **Download** button:

3. Once it finishes downloading, you should see the **Importing Package** dialog box pop up. If it doesn't pop up, click on the **Import** button where the **Download** button used to be:

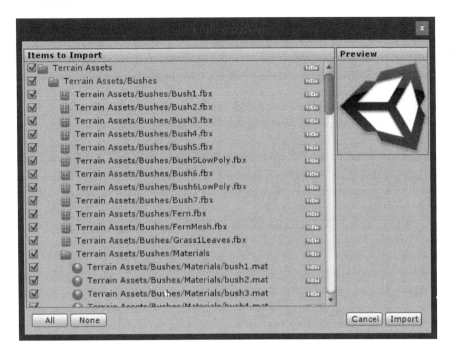

Generally, you'll only want to select the assets that you want to use and uncheck the others. However, since you're exploring the tools, we'll just click on the **Import** button to place them all.

4. Close the **Asset Store** screen; if it's still open, go back into our game view. You should notice the new **Terrain Assets** folder placed in our **Assets** folder. Double-click on it and then enter the **Textures** folder:

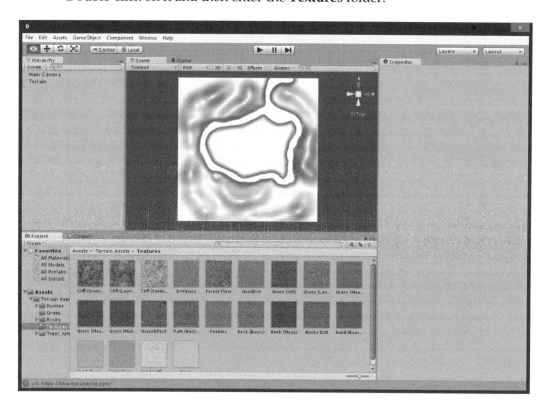

These will be the textures we will be placing in our environment.

5. Select the **Terrain** object and then click on the fourth button from the left to select the **Paint Texture** button. Here, you'll notice that it looks quite similar to the previous sections we've seen. However, there is a **Textures** section as well, but as of now, there is the information **No terrain textures defined** in this section. So let's fix that. Click on the **Edit Textures** button and then select **Add Texture**.

6. You'll see an **Add Terrain Texture** dialog pop up. Under the **Texture** variable, place the **Grass (Hill)** texture and then click on the **Add** button:

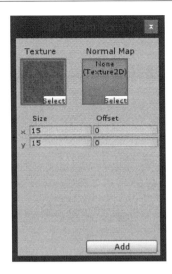

7. At this point, you should see the entire world change to green if you're far away. If you zoom in, you'll see that the entire terrain uses the **Grass (Hill)** texture now:

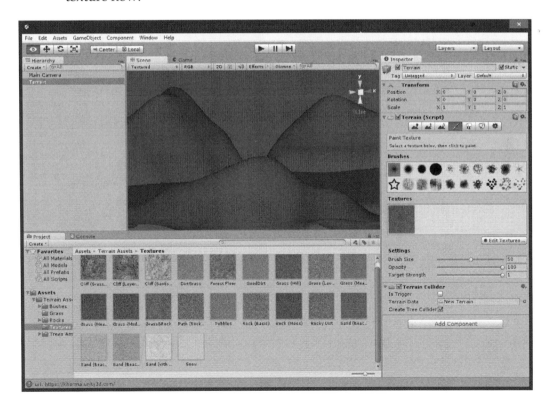

8. Now, we don't want the entire world to have grass. Next, we will add cliffs around the edges where the water is. To do this, add an additional texture by navigating to **Edit Textures...** | **Add Texture**. Select **Cliff (Layered Rock)** as the texture and then select **Add**. Now if you select the terrain, you should see two textures. With the **Cliff (Layered Rock)** texture selected, paint the edges of the water by clicking and holding the mouse, and modifying the **Brush Size** value as needed:

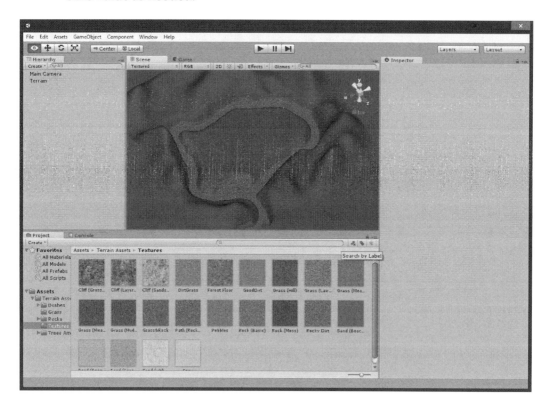

9. We now want to create a path for our player to follow, so we're going to create yet another texture this time using the **GoodDirt** material. Since this is a path the player may take, I'm going to change the **Brush Size** value to **8** and the **Opacity** value to **30**, and use the second brush from the left, which is slightly less faded. Once finished, I'm going to paint in some trails that the player can follow. One thing that you will want to try to do is make sure that the player shouldn't go too far before having to backtrack and reward the player for exploration. The following screenshot shows the path:

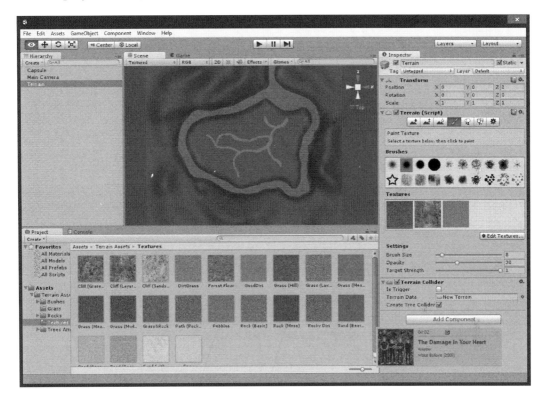

However, you'll notice that there are two problems with it currently. Firstly, it is too big to fit in with the world, and you can tell that it repeats.

10. To reduce the appearance of texture duplication, we can introduce new materials with a very soft opacity, which we place in patches in areas where there is just plain ground. For example, let's create a new texture with the **Grass (Meadow)** texture. Change the **Brush Size** value to **16** and the **Opacity** value to something really low, such as **6**, and then start painting the areas that look too static. Feel free to select the first brush again to have a smoother touch up.

11. Now, if we zoom into the world as if we were a character there, I can tell that the first grass texture is way too big for the environment but we can actually change that very easily. Double-click on the texture to change the **Size** value to (8,8). This will make the texture smaller before it duplicates. It's a good idea to have different textures with different sizes so that the seams of each texture aren't visible to others. The following screenshot shows the size options:

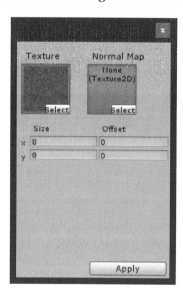

12. Do the same changes as in the preceding step for our **Dirt** texture as well, changing the **Size** option to `(8,8)`:

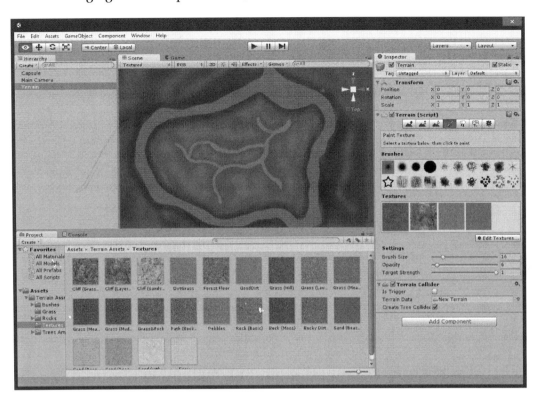

With this, we already have a level that looks pretty nice! However, that being said, it's just some hills. To really have a quality-looking title, we are going to need to do some additional work to beautify the environment.

Beautifying the environment – adding water, trees, and grass

We now have a base for our environment with the terrain, but we're still missing a lot of polish that can make the area stand out and look like a quality environment. Let's add some of those details now:

1. First, let's add water. This time we will use another asset from Unity, but we will not have to go to the Asset Store as it is included by default in our Unity installation. Navigate to **Assets** | **Import Package** | **Water (Basic)** and import all of the files included in the package.

2. We will be creating a level for the night time, so navigate to **Standard Assets | Water Basic** and drag-and-drop the **Nighttime Simple Water** prefab onto the scene. Once there, set the **Position** values to (1000,50, 1000) and the **Scale** values to (1000,1,1000):

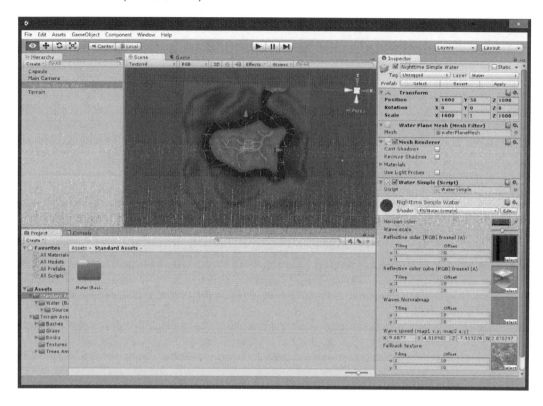

At this point, you want to repaint your cliff materials to reflect being next to the water better.

3. Next, let's add some trees to make this forest level come to life. Navigate to **Terrain Assets | Trees Ambient-Occlusion** and drag-and-drop a tree into your world (I'm using **ScotsPineTree**).

By default, these trees do not contain collision information, so our player could just walk through it. This is actually great for areas that the player will not reach as we can add more trees without having to do meaningless calculations, but we need to stop the player from walking into these. To do that, we're going to need to add a collider.

4. To do so, navigate to **Component | Physics | Capsule Collider** and then change the **Radius** value to 2.

> You have to use a Capsule Collider in order to have the collision carried over to the terrain.

5. After this, move our newly created tree into the `Assets` folder under the **Project** tab and change its name to `CollidingTree`. Then, delete the object from the **Hierarchy** view. With this finished, go back to our **Terrain** object and then click on the **Place Trees** mode button. Just like working with painting textures, there are no trees here by default, so navigate to **Edit Trees...** | **Add Tree**, add our `CollidingTree` object created earlier in this step, and then select **Add**.

6. Next, under the **Settings** section, change the **Tree Density** value to **15** and then with our new tree selected, paint the areas on the main island that do not have paths on them. Once you've finished with placing those trees, up the **Tree Density** value to **50** and then paint the areas that are far away from paths to make it less likely that players go that way.

7. You should also enable **Create Tree Collider** in the terrain's **Terrain Collider** component:

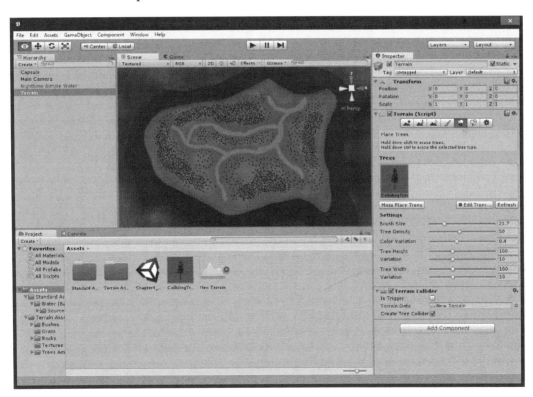

8. In our last step to create an environment, let's add some details. The mode next to the **Plant Trees** mode is **Paint Details**. Next, click on the **Edit Details...** button and select **Add Grass Texture**. Select the **Grass** texture for the **Detail Texture** option and then click on **Add**. In the terrain's **Settings** mode (the one on the far right), change the **Detail Distance** value to **250**, and then paint the grass where there isn't any dirt along the route in the **Paint Details** mode:

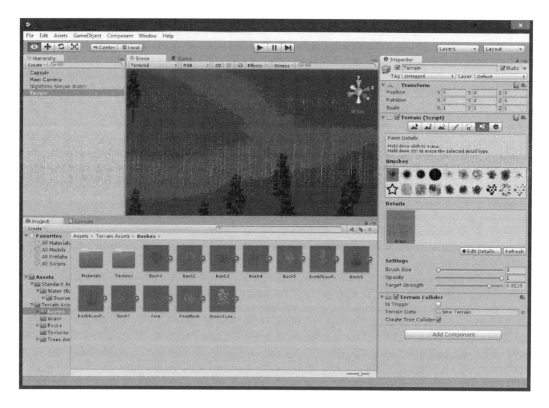

You may not see the results unless you zoom your camera in, which you can do by using the mouse wheel. Don't go too far in though, or the results may not show as well.

This aspect of level creation isn't very difficult, just time consuming. However, it's taking time to enter these details that really sets a game apart from the other games. Generally, you'll want to playtest and make sure your level is fun before performing these actions; but I feel it's important to have an idea of how to do it for your future projects.

9. Lastly, our current island is very flat, and while that's okay for cities, nature is random. Go back into the **Raise/Lower Height** tool and gently raise and lower some areas of the level to give the illusion of depth. Do note that your trees and grass will raise and fall with the changes that you make, as shown in the following screenshot:

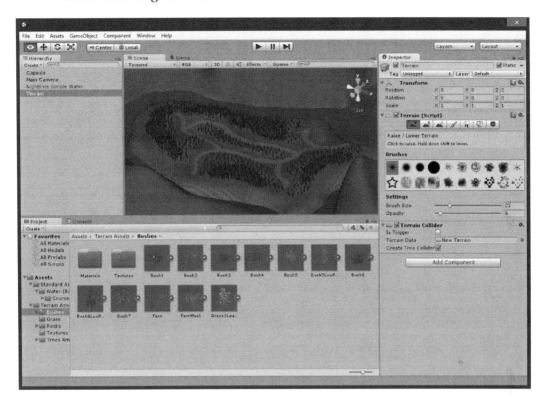

10. With this done, let's now add some details to the areas that the player will not be visiting, such as the outer hills. Go into the **Place Trees** mode and create another tree, but this time select the one without collision and then place it around the edges of the mountains, as shown in the following screenshot:

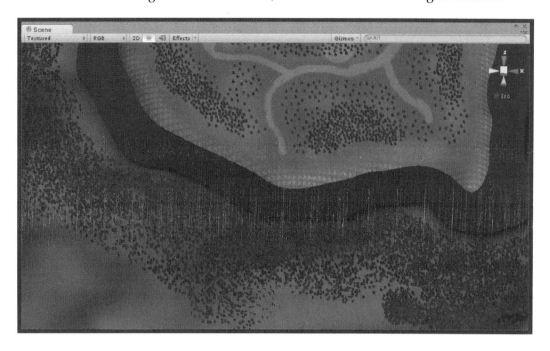

At this point, we have a nice exterior shape created with the terrain tools!

If you want to add even more detail to your levels, you can add additional trees and/or materials to the level area as long as it makes sense for them to be there.

For more information on the terrain engine that Unity has, please visit http://docs.unity3d.com/Manual/script-Terrain.html.

Creating our player

Now that we have the terrain and its details, it's hard to get a good picture of what the game looks like without being able to see what it looks like down on the surface, so next we will do just that. However, instead of creating our player from scratch as we've done previously, we will make use of the code that Unity has provided us. We will perform the following steps:

1. Start off by navigating to **Assets | Import Package | Character Controller**. When the **Importing Package** dialog comes up, we only need to import the files shown in the following screenshot:

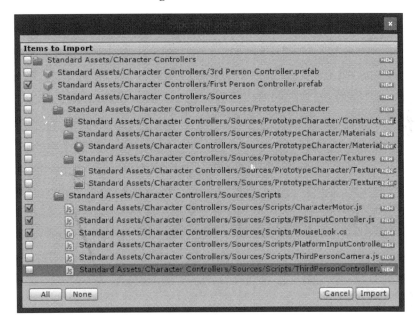

2. Now drag-and-drop the **First Person Controller** prefab under the **Prefabs** folder in our **Project** tab into your world, where you want the player to spawn, setting the **Y Position** value to above 100. If you see yourself fall through the world instead of hitting the ground when you spawn, then increase the **Y Position** value until you get there.

3. If you open up the **First Person Controller** object in the **Hierarchy** tab, you'll notice that it has a **Main Camera** object already, so delete the **Main Camera** object that already exists in the world.

4. Right now, if we played the game, you'd see that everything is dark because we don't have any light. For the purposes of demonstration, let's add a directional light by navigating to **GameObject | Create Other | Directional Light**.

If you are using Unity 4.6 or later, navigate to **GameObject | Create General | Terrain** to create the Terrain.

5. Save your scene and hit the **Play** button to drop into your level:

At this point, we have a playable level that we can explore and move around in!

Building the atmosphere

Now, the base of our world has been created; let's add some effects to make the game even more visually appealing and so it will start to fit in with the survival horror feel that we're going to be giving the game.

The first part of creating the atmosphere is to add something for the sky aside from the light blue color that we currently use by default. To fix this, we will be using a skybox. A skybox is a method to create backgrounds to make the area seem bigger than it really is, by putting an image in the areas that are currently being filled with the light blue color, not moving in the same way that the sky doesn't move to us because it's so far away.

The reason why we call a skybox a skybox is because it is made up of six textures that will be the inside of the box (one for each side of a cube). Game engines such as Unreal have skydomes, which are the same thing; but they are done with a hemisphere instead of a cube. We will perform the following steps to build the atmosphere:

1. To add in our skybox, we are going to navigate to **Assets | Import Package | Skyboxes**. We want our level to display the night, so we'll be using the **Starry Night Skybox**. Just select the **StarryNight Skybox.mat** file and textures inside the **Standard Assets/Skyboxes/Textures/StarryNight/** location, and then click on **Import**:

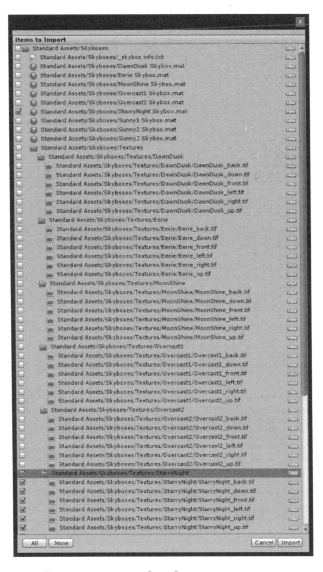

2. With this file imported, we need to navigate to **Edit | Render Settings** next. Once there, we need to set the **Skybox Material** option to the `Starry Night` skybox:

If you go into the game, you'll notice the level starting to look nicer already with the addition of the skybox, except for the fact that the sky says night while the world says it's daytime. Let's fix that now.

3. Switch to the **Game** tab so that you can see the changes we'll be making next. While still at the **RenderSettings** menu, let's turn on the **Fog** property by clicking on the checkbox with its name and changing the **Fog Color** value to a black color. You should notice that the surroundings are already turning very dark. Play around with the **Fog Density** value until you're comfortable with how much the player can see ahead of them; I used `0.005`.

Fog obscures far away objects, which adds to the atmosphere and saves the rendering power. The denser the fog, the more the game will feel like a horror game. The first game of the Silent Hill franchise used fog to make the game run at an acceptable frame rate due to a large 3D environment it had on early PlayStation hardware. Due to how well it spooked players, it continued to be used in later games even though they could render larger areas with the newer technology.

Let's add some lighting tweaks to make the environment that the player is walking in seem more like night.

4. Go into the **DirectionalLight** properties section and change the **Intensity** value to 0.05. You'll see the value get darker, as shown in the following screenshot:

 If for some reason, you'd like to make the world pitch black, you'll need to modify the **Ambient Light** property to black inside the **RenderSettings** section. By default, it is dark grey, which will show up even if there are no lights placed in the world.

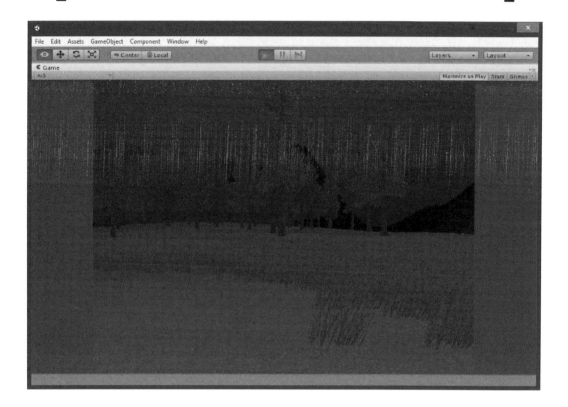

 In the preceding example, I increased the **Intensity** value to make it easier to see the world to make it easier for readers to follow, but in your project, you probably don't want the player to see so far out with such clarity.

With this, we now have a believable exterior area at night! Now that we have this basic knowledge, let's add a flashlight so the players can see where they are going.

Creating a flashlight

Now that our level looks like a dark night, we still want to give our players the ability to see what's in front of them with a flashlight. We will customize the **First Person Controller** object to fit our needs:

1. Create a spotlight by navigating to **GameObject | Create Other | Spotlight**. Once created, we are going to make the spotlight a child of the **First Person Controller** object's **Main Camera** object by dragging-and-dropping it on top of it.

2. Once a child, change the **Transform Position** value to (0, -.95, 0). Since positions are relative to your parent's position, this places the light slightly lower than the camera's center, just like a hand holding a flashlight. Now change the **Rotation** value to (0,0,0) or give it a slight diagonal effect across the scene if you don't want it to look like it's coming straight out:

3. Now, we want the flashlight to reach out into the distance. So we will change the **Range** value to 1000, and to make the light wider, we will change the **Spot Angle** value to 45. The effects are shown in the following screenshot:

 If you have Unity Pro, you can also give shadows to the world based on your lights by setting the **Shadow Type** property.

We now have a flashlight, so the player can focus on a particular area and not worry.

Walking / flashlight bobbing animation

Now the flashlight looks fine in a screenshot, but if you walk throughout the world, it will feel very static and unnatural. If a person is actually walking through the forest, there will be a slight bob as you walk, and if someone is actually holding a flash light, it won't be stable the entire time because your hand would move. We can solve both of these problems by writing yet another script. We perform the following steps:

1. Create a new folder called `Scripts`. Inside this folder, create a new C# script called `BobbingAnimation`.

2. Open the newly created script and use the following code inside it:

```
using UnityEngine;
using System.Collections;

/// <summary>
/// Allows the attached object to bob up and down through
/// movement or
/// by default.
/// </summary>
public class BobbingAnimation : MonoBehaviour
{
  /// <summary>
  /// The elapsed time.
  /// </summary>
  private float elapsedTime;

  /// <summary>
  /// The starting y offset from the parent.
  /// </summary>
  private float startingY;

  /// <summary>
  /// The controller.
  /// </summary>
  private CharacterController controller;

  /// <summary>
  /// How far up and down the object will travel
  /// </summary>
  public float magnitude = .2f;

  /// <summary>
  /// How often the object will move up and down
  /// </summary>
  public float frequency = 10;

  /// <summary>
  /// Do you always want the object to bob up and down or
  /// with movement?
  /// </summary>
  public bool alwaysBob = false;
```

```
/// <summary>
/// Start this instance.
/// </summary>
void Start ()
{
  startingY = transform.localPosition.y;
  controller = GetComponent<CharacterController> ();
}


/// <summary>
/// Update this instance.
/// </summary>
void Update ()
{
  // Only increment elapsedTime if you want the player to
  // bob, keeping it the same will keep it still
  if(alwaysBob)
  {
    elapsedTime += Time.deltaTime;
  }
  else
  {
    if((Input.GetAxis("Horizontal") != 0.0f) ||
(Input.GetAxis("Vertical")  != 0.0f) )
      elapsedTime += Time.deltaTime;
  }

  float yOffset = Mathf.Sin(elapsedTime * frequency) *
magnitude;

  //If we can't find the player controller or we're
  // jumping, we shouldn't be bobbing
  if(controller && !controller.isGrounded)
  {
    return;
  }

  //Set our position
  Vector3 pos = transform.position;

  pos.y = transform.parent.transform.position.y +
        startingY + yOffset;
```

```
        transform.position = pos;


    }
}
```

 The preceding code was prepared in the XML Comments style that I discussed earlier. For more information on that, check out *Chapter 1, 2D Twin-stick Shooter.*

The preceding code will tweak the object it's attached to so that it will bob up and down whenever the player is moving along the *x* or *y* axis. I've also added a variable called `alwaysBob`, which, when true, will make the object always bob.

Math is a game developer's best friend, and here we are using sin (pronounced sine). Taking the sin of an angle number gives you the ratio of the length of the opposite side of the angle to the length of the hypotenuse of a right-angled triangle.

If that didn't make any sense to you, don't worry. The neat feature of sin is that as the number it takes gets larger, it will continuously give us a value between 0 and 1 that will go up and down forever, giving us a smooth repetitive oscillation.

 For more information on sine waves, visit http://en.wikipedia.org/wiki/Sine_wave.

While we're using the sin just for the player's movement and the flashlight, this could be used in a lot of effects, such as having save points/portals bob up and down, or any kind of object you would want to have slight movement or some special FX.

3. Next, attach the `BobbingAnimation` component to the **Main Camera** object, leaving all the values with the defaults.

4. After this, attach the `BobbingAnimation` component to the spotlight as well. With the spotlight selected, turn the **Always Bob** option on and change the **Magnitude** value to `.05` and the **Frequency** value to `3`. The effects are shown in the following screenshot:

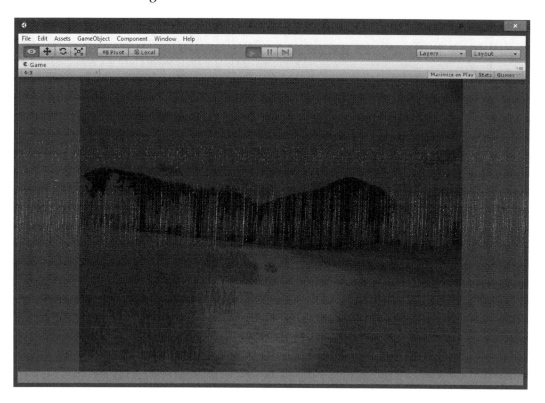

Summary

With this, we now have a great looking exterior level for our game! In addition, we covered a lot of features that exist in Unity for you to be able to use in your own future projects. With this in mind, you will learn how to build an interior environment in the next chapter!

Challenges

For those of you who want to do more with this project, there are still plenty of things you can do, especially after finishing the rest of this book. Here are some ideas to get you thinking:

- Add additional trees and textures to make the level appear even more realistic.

- Right now, the player can go down into the water and get stuck. Add a new trigger, so that whenever the player hits it, it will reset his/her position back to the starting position.

- Have someone play your game and see if they can navigate your environment to where you want to lead them.

- Once you learn how to create encounters, add some additional combat experiences in this level.

- Create collectibles that the player can collect in the level, in the same manner as the platformer project we did in *Chapter 3, Side-scrolling Platformer*, to reward the player travelling the map. Adding a light can help players know where to travel.

5
First Person Shooter Part 2 – Creating Interior Environments

Since nature is very chaotic, it makes sense to use tools such as terrain and placing objects with randomness to create a natural-looking environment. However, not all things are constructed like that. Man-made structures, such as office buildings, stone pillars, and floor tiles, are all made of pieces that look similar to one another. Rather than modeling out every single wall in your building, can't you use one you made before?

As you might remember in *Chapter 3, Side-scrolling Platformer*, we learned how we can use tiles to build a level using only a couple of different sprites, duplicating them as needed to create our environment. In this chapter, we will use the same line of thinking in a 3D environment using a method called modular level design.

Modular level design is a tool that AAA (pronounced triple A) developers (those working with the highest development budgets and promotion) have been using to create great-looking levels in the minimum amount of time possible. Breaking apart buildings into modules creates building blocks that can be placed next to one another, like building block pieces, to create an entire structure. This makes it much easier to create levels than just trying to model everything from scratch.

Project overview

Unlike the preceding chapter, where we worked as an environmental artist, here we take on the role of a level designer who has been tasked to create an interior environment using assets already provided to us by the environment artist. We will use already-provided assets as well as assets already provided to us by Unity for mesh placement.

Your objectives

This project will be split into a number of tasks. It will be a simple step-by-step process from beginning to end. Here is the outline of our tasks:

- Importing assets
- Creating tiles
- Placing tiles with grid snapping
- Creating and placing props
- Lightmapping quickstart prerequisites

In this chapter, we will continue from where the preceding chapter left off using the same project. You can continue with your previous project or pick up a copy along with the assets for this chapter from the example code provided for this book on Packt Publishing's website.

In addition, the completed project and source files are located there for you to check if you have any questions or need clarification.

Project setup

At this point, I have assumed that you have Unity started up and have our project from the previous chapter loaded. Now, perform the following steps:

1. With Unity started, open the project from the previous chapter.
2. Since we want to keep our projects nice and tidy, we are going to do some refining of our project's structure before starting with this project. Create the following folders:
   - Scenes
   - Terrains
   - Prefabs
   - Materials
3. Place the scene from the previous chapter in your Scenes folder.
4. Next, move the terrain object and Terrain Assets folder to the Terrains folder, so everything having to do with our terrains is in one place.
5. Place your tree prefab we made in the Prefabs folder.
6. Place the scripts from Standard Assets\Character Controllers\Sources\Scripts to your Scripts folder (optionally in a folder called Character).

7. Move the `First Person Controller` prefab to the `Prefabs` folder.

8. Move the `Skyboxes` and `Water` folders to the `Materials` folder, deleting the `Daylight Simple Water` prefab and moving the `Nighttime Simple Water` prefab to the `Prefabs` folder.

9. Finally, delete the `Standard Assets` folder now that there are no files inside it.

 Astute readers may notice that the `Water` folder has more content including a script inside it. Due to all of this being a part of implementing water in our exterior level, I decided to keep everything in one place; but all of this comes to personal choice.

10. Finally, if you are on our previous level, create a new scene by selecting **File | New Scene**.

Creating architecture overview

As a level designer, one of the most time-consuming parts of your job will be creating environments. There are many different ways out there to create levels. By default, Unity gives us some default meshes, such as a **Box**, **Sphere**, and **Cylinder**, and while it's technically possible to build a level in that way, it could get really tedious really quickly. Next, I'm going to quickly go through the most popular options to build levels for games made in Unity before we jump into building a level of our own.

3D modeling software

A lot of times, opening a 3D modeling software package and building architecture that way is what professional games studios will often do. This gives you maximum freedom in creating your environment and allows you to do exactly what you'd like to do. However, that requires you to be proficient in that tool, whether that be Maya, 3ds Max, Blender (which can be downloaded for free at `blender.org`), or some other tool. Then, you just need to export your models and import them into Unity.

Unity supports a lot of different formats for 3D models, but there are a lot of issues to consider. For some best practices, when it comes to creating art assets, please visit `http://blogs.unity3d.com/2011/09/02/art-assets-best-practice-guide/`.

Constructing geometry with brushes

Using **Constructive Solid Geometry** (CSG), commonly referred to as brushes, has been a long-existing way for games to have in-game level editors, which has led to people creating levels for them. Tools such as Unreal Engine 4, Hammer, Radiant, and other professional game engines make use of this building structure, making it quite easy for people to create and iterate through levels quickly through a process called white-boxing, as it's very easy to make changes to simple shapes. However, just like learning a modeling software tool, there can be a higher barrier to entry in using brushes to create your geometry, but for those creating certain types of games where you need to create a lot of different content, it can be a great tool.

Unity does not support building things like this by default, but there are several tools in the Unity Asset Store that allow you to do something like this. For example, sixbyseven studio has an extension called ProBuilder, which can add this functionality to Unity, making it very easy to build levels (it's what I use normally when building environments for 3D games in Unity). However, as an extension, you'll need to buy it either from them or through the Asset Store, as it is not free. You can find out more information about ProBuilder at http://www. protoolsforunity3d.com/probuilder/.

Modular tilesets

Another way to generate architecture is through the use of tiles that are created by an artist. You can use them to build your level. Similar to using LEGO pieces, we can use these tiles to snap together walls and other objects to create a building. With creative uses of tiles, you can create a large amount of content with just a minimal amount of assets. This is probably the easiest way to create a level at the expense of not being able to create unique-looking buildings since you only have a few pieces to work with.

Mix and match

Of course, it's also possible to use a mixture of the tools mentioned to get the advantages of certain ways of doing things. For example, you could use brushes to block out an area (which is why it is called greyboxing) and then use a group of tiles called a tileset to replace boxes with highly detailed models, which is what a lot of AAA studios do, using the boxes just for their collision. In addition, we could also place tiles initially and then add in props to break up the repetitiveness of levels, which is what we are going to do.

Importing assets

In this chapter, we are going to create an interior environment. This will be useful to know, because unlike a landscape, we can use straight floors and more structure as most houses are that way, and we will use models to build the environment!

To show how easy it is to use, let's get started. Perform the following steps:

1. Start off by going to the `Materials` folder in the `Project` tab, and create two new materials by selecting **Create | New Material**. Give one of the new materials the name `House` and the other, `Props`. Once you have that created go to your example code folder and move over the `2048_House_TEX.jpg` and `2048_Props_TEX.jpg` files. Once you've done that, apply that texture to the materials. Have a look at the following screenshot:

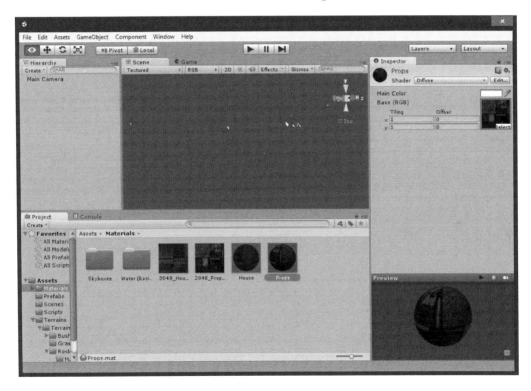

2.   Create a new folder in our `Assets` folder named `Models`.

Optionally, you can move the models from the `Terrain Assets` folder to here as well, but as we aren't using them anymore, I didn't.

John Espiritu has very kindly provided some models in modular pieces for us to work with. So, the next thing we will do is actually import those models.

For more info on John's stuff or to commission him yourself, check out `http://raynehaize.tumblr.com/` or `http://raynehaize.deviantart.com/`.

3.   With the `Models` folder selected, let's import the models by dragging-and-dropping the `Modular Pieces` and `Props` folders in it. Have a look at the following screenshot:

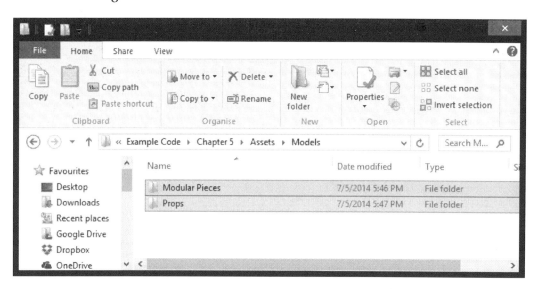

4. Back in Unity, move to the `Modular Pieces` folder in the `Project` tab. At this point, it should look somewhat as follows:

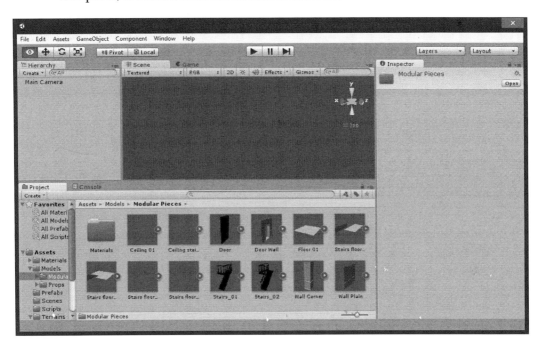

5. By default, Unity attempts to do some things automatically for us, which creates a lot of stuff we don't need for simple environment pieces like this. Select all the objects in this folder by selecting the `Ceiling 01` object, hold down the *Shift* key, and then select the `Wall Plain` object. This will bring you to **Model Importer**. Once you are in the **Inspector** tab, you will see three tabs you can select:

   ° **Model**: It contains settings to import the model. For information, check out `http://docs.unity3d.com/Manual/FBXImporter-Model.html`.

   ° **Rig**: It has settings that will either allow the model to support animation or not. For more information, check out `http://docs.unity3d.com/Manual/FBXImporter-Rig.html`.

   ° **Animations**: It has settings to import different animations from the model file. For more information, check out `http://docs.unity3d.com/Manual/FBXImporter-Animations.html`.

6. Inside the **Model** tab, change the **Scale Factor** to .025.

   The **Scale Factor** property allows you to apply a scalar to the model that you've imported. This is fine for this project, but generally, when working with animations, changing the scale factor may hurt your rig. So, be sure you have your artist create art at the correct scale.

7. Next, uncheck the **Import Models** option from the **Materials** section. After that, click on the **Apply** button.

   If left checked, Unity will have each object use its own material, which is intended to have its own texture. All of our pieces use the same texture, so there's no need to have multiple textures.

8. Select the **Rig** tab, change the **Animation Type** to None, and then click on **Apply**.

   If the object has animation, it will attempt to add an Avatar and more, which is unnecessary for this. Note that now the **Animations** tab will be grayed out, because we have no animations.

9. Delete the Materials folder inside the Modular Pieces folder.

When exporting an FBX file, it exports your model with UV coordinates but doesn't include the textures in the FBX file. You have to import your textures separately into Unity and add it to the material generated or assign it on your own.

As of this version of Unity, there is no way to have models not generate a material by default, hence our need to delete them. We will add materials to these models when we create their prefabs.

10. Repeat steps 5-8 with the `Props` folder as well. Once you finish, the folder should look like the following screenshot:

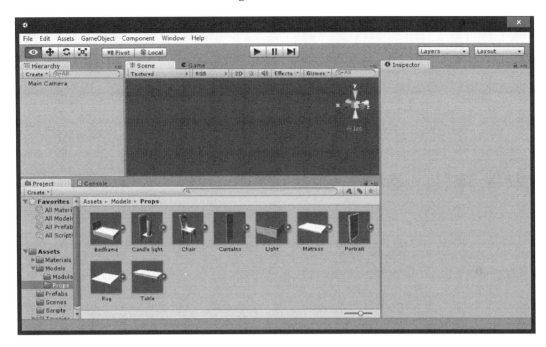

Now, we have our models in the project! This is a great first step, but it's useless unless it's actually in the game world. Let's get started with that now.

Creating tiles

Before we get started, it's a good idea to see how the object looks to us, so let's add in a temporary controller to give us an idea of what it looks like:

1. Go to the Prefabs folder, and drag-and-drop one of the modified **First Person Controller** prefabs that we made in the previous chapter into the **Scene** view. Once done, set **Position** to (0, 1, 0). Rather than setting each of the properties, we can easily do this by right-clicking on **Transform** and selecting **Reset Position** and then setting the **Y** position to 1. After this, in the **Character Motor** component, under the **Movement** section, set **Gravity** to 0 so that we do not fall for the time being (we will replace this controller later):

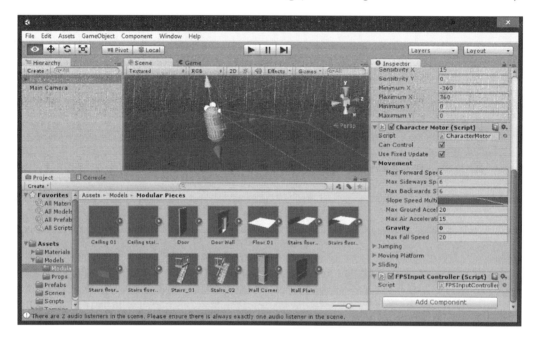

2. Right now, if you play the game, there will be a warning about having two audio listeners in the scene. This is due to having two main camera objects in our scene that contain audio listener components. Delete the one that is not part of our **First Person Controller** prefab by selecting the **Main Camera** object and then pressing the *Delete* key.

Now, in the upper-right corner of the scene view is the scene gizmo. This will display our current camera orientation, allow us to quickly modify the viewing angle, and switch from **Perspective** to **Isometric** mode easily, which will be great for us when placing objects in the world. (Note that in 2D mode, this gizmo won't be shown, so untoggle the 2D button on the **Scene** toolbar if that is the case.)

3. Click on the **Y** axis on the scene gizmo to switch our camera to an overhead view. Once there, go to the **Modular Pieces** folder, and then drag-and-drop the **Floor 01** object into our world, and change **Position** to (0, 0, 0) from the **Transform** section. Have a look at the following screenshot:

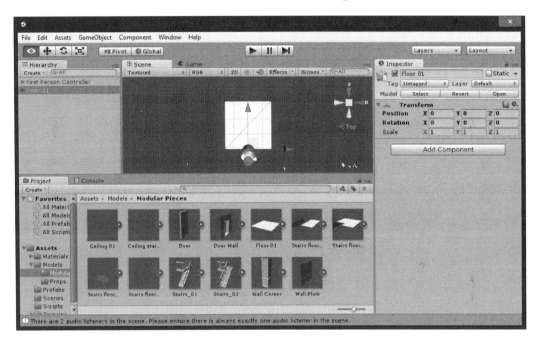

You'll notice that instead of the floor tile being in the center of the world when the position is reset, the bed is off on the Z axis. This is because the art files that the artist provided to us placed the pivot there, which you will see if the Gizmo Display Toggles are set to **Pivot**. Now, since we're going to be placing these objects as tiles, we want them to snap together as easily as possible. Generally, we want to place these pivots along one of the edges of the object. Some people prefer to place it on the center of the mesh, which you can easily do by changing the pivot toggle to **Center** by clicking on **Gizmo Display Toggle** to the right-hand side of the **Transform** widgets, but I don't like it, as it makes rotations and scaling more of a pain.

4. After this, open the **Floor 01** object to see the `Floor_01_Modular_pieces_grp` object and select it. This is the actual mesh we want to work with. With it selected, go to the **Mesh Renderer** component, and expand the **Materials** section. Then change **Element 0** to our house material either by dragging-and-dropping or clicking on the right-hand side circle button and then selecting it from the list shown. Finally, let's add in a box collider by going to **Component | Physics | Box Collider**.

   This collider is what the player will collide with in the world, so what you see will be what they will be walking into.

5. Now that we have the revised version created, rename the **Floor_01_Modular_pieces_grp** game object to `Floor`, and then drag-and-drop just that object as a prefab in the `Prefabs` folder; optionally, you can place the object in a new folder called `Modular Pieces`.

6. The floor may change to a really black color; this is because the material provided is a bit on the dark side. Let's create a new directional light to get a better view of the models by selecting **GameObject | Create Other | Directional Light**. Once it's created, set **Intensity** up to 2 and **X Rotation** to `130`. Have a look at the following screenshot:

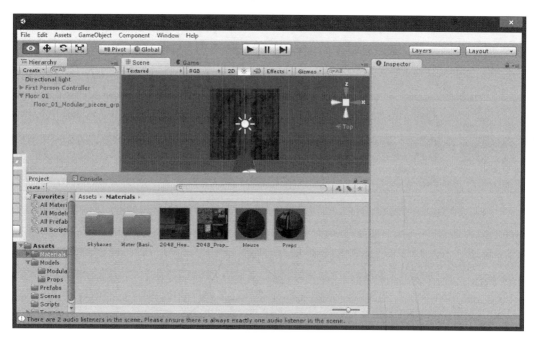

7. Now repeat steps 3-5 for the **Wall Plain** object. Next, move our player up in the **Z** axis to 1 so that it doesn't collide with the walls:

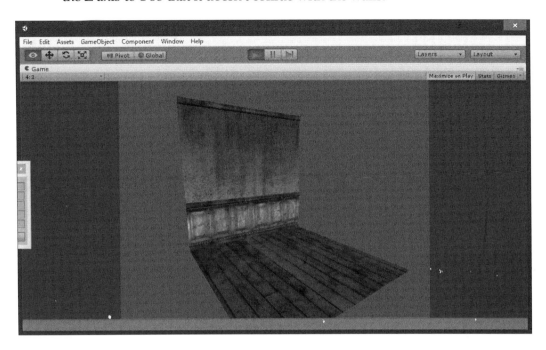

As you can see, the two pieces together are already starting to look like a room. Not too hard, right?

8. Delete those two prefabs, and now do the same steps for the other models in the `Modular Pieces` folders, thereby deleting them as they go on, using **Mesh Colliders** on the **Door Wall** and **Stairs** aspects.

> Everything besides the renaming and moving to the `Prefabs` folder can be done to all the objects by shift-clicking on them all to do each of the steps.

9. Now that we have the models for our environment fixed, let's assemble them into some tiles that we can place in the world. Create an empty game object, name it `Hallway`, and reset its position.

The pivot of an object is extremely important when doing modular level design. We want to make it extremely easy for us to duplicate objects and snap them together, so picking a part of the object that will tile well can save you a lot of time in the future.

For those interested in learning more about creating good modular game art, check out http://www.gamasutra.com/ view/feature/130885/creating_modular_game_art_ for_fast_.php.

10. Add a **Floor, Ceiling,** and **Wall** prefab to the object as children.

11. Duplicate the wall by pressing *Ctrl + D*, and then change **Position** of **Z** axis to 3.2 and **Rotation** of **Y** axis to 180. Have a look at the following screenshot:

This will act as our first building block, which we can use to create hallways by merely duplicating these **Hallway** objects.

12. Now, inside the project, add a folder to the `Prefabs` folder called `Tiles`. Make **Hallway** a prefab by dragging-and-dropping it in the `Tiles` folder. Have a look at the following screenshot:

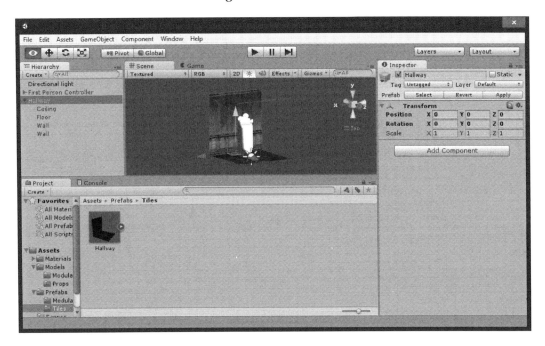

13. Delete one of the wall objects, and you'll notice that the object is no longer a prefab, as it's no longer colored blue. That is fine, because now we're going to create a doorway. Rename **Hallway** to `Hall Door`. Then add a **Door** object and a **Door Wall** object as children to the new **Hall Door** on the side that your wall object was previously at. Then, add **Hall Door** as a prefab in the `Tiles` folder.

You can make these doors functional later on, but for now, we are just building the environment.

14. Apart from these very simple tiles that we just made, we also want to create some rooms that are larger than one big tile, so next, we need to create nine additional prefab tiles that will look like the following screenshot:

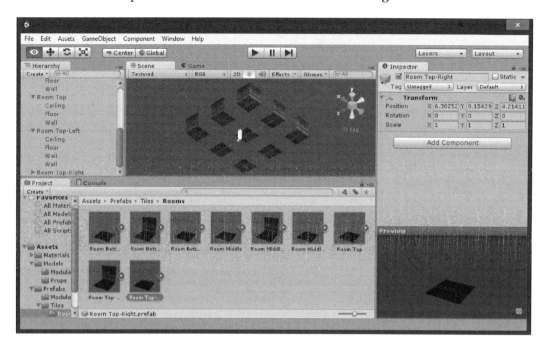

To name the objects, I went with the following convention:

- ◦ Room Top-Left
- ◦ Room Top-Middle
- ◦ Room Top-Right
- ◦ Room Middle-Left
- ◦ Room Middle
- ◦ Room Middle-Right
- ◦ Room Bottom-Left
- ◦ Room Bottom-Middle
- ◦ Room Bottom-Right

15. With these pieces, we can make rooms of whatever size we want! Delete the newly created prefabs from the hierarchy.

16. Finally, let's get the staircase built! Place two floors next to each other, one at **Position** (0, 0, 0) and the other at (-3.2, 0, 0). Next, add **Stairs 1**, **Stairs Floor 1**, and objects together, all at **Position** (0, 0, 0). Add **Stairs Floor 2** at **Position** (-3.2, 0, 0). Finally, add two walls on the first floor (one with 0.0 on **X** and one with -3.2) and two on the second floor (**Y** at 3.2). Once completed, you should have a staircase built, as shown in the following screenshot:

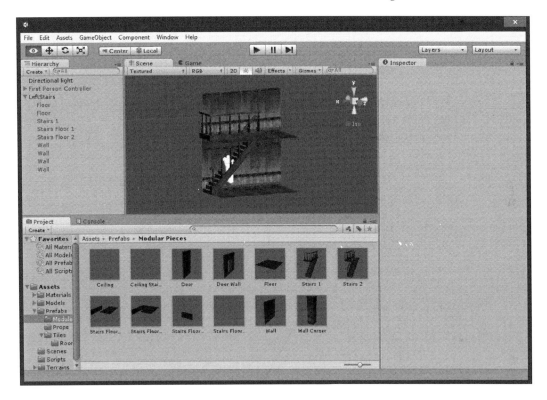

17. Create **GameObject** (empty), name it LeftStairs, and add all of those items as children of that top object. Then make the object a prefab inside the Prefabs\Tiles folder. Be sure to reset the position of **GameObject** by right-clicking on its **Transform** component and by selecting **Reset Position**.

18. Finally, the character controller by default won't be able to go upstairs like that correctly, as the stairs aren't a smooth surface. You will need to create another empty game object with a box collider (**Component | Physics | Box Collider**) to act as our stairs, so the player will glide above everything. This will require tweaking with the **Transform, Rotation**, and **Scale** tools to get them just right, but my options are set up in the following screenshot. Once you're finished, apply your changes to the prefab so that you can use it for others by clicking on **Apply** in the **Prefab** menu under the **Inspector** tab. Have a look at the following screenshot:

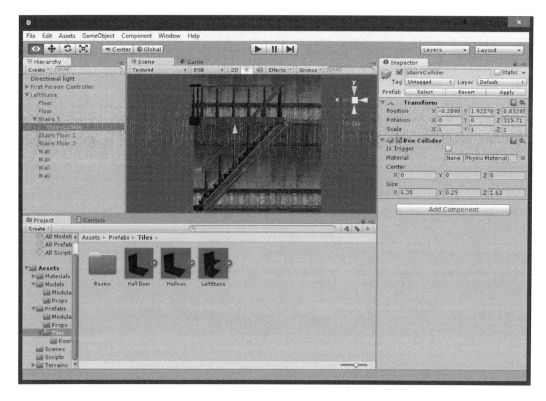

And with that we now have our tiles all set!

Placing tiles with grid snapping

Now that we have all of our tiles created, let's start building out our area:

1. Put a tile prefab in the world of your choice. Hold down the *Ctrl* key, and pull it in an axis' direction. You may have noticed a little snap that you wouldn't see when moving normally. This is due to unit snapping.

Grid snapping is a really useful tool when it comes to building stuff inside Unity. Instead of punching in numbers all the time when trying to set the positions of all of these tiles, we can just set our **Snap** size to be the size of our tiles 3.2 x 3.2 x 3.2.

  In addition to movement, we can also snap rotations and scaling.

2. Go to **Edit | Snap Settings**; we can change the value to snap easily by changing **Move** of **X** to 3.2 and **Move** of **Z** to 3.561, taking into account the wall's thickness.

3. Now that we have the snap settings working correctly, we will place a hallway to start our level and reset its **Position** property to (0, 0, 0).

4. Next, duplicate the mesh by hitting *Ctrl + D*, and then, holding *Ctrl*, drag the tile over to the right-hand side to continue the hallway.

5. After that I'm going to create a couple of other hallways and then place two **Hall Door** prefabs to fill out the area, as shown in the following screenshot:

6. Now, we need to create a few rooms. Open your rooms prefab and from the top viewport, place your middle piece in front of each doorway by first dragging it out, resetting its position, and then holding down *Ctrl* and snapping it there.

> Another way of placing assets in this way would be to place floors first wherever you want to create your layout and then spawning walls around the edges.

7. Next, use the correct **Room** tiles to fill out your rooms as you want them to look. Start with using your **Top Left**, **Top**, and **Right** prefabs. Have a look at the following screenshot:

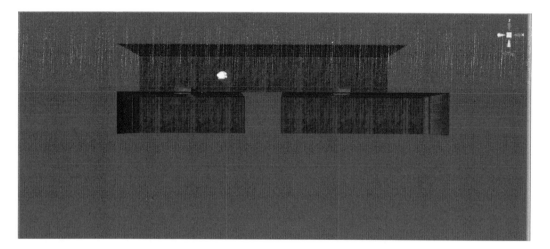

> Remember that once you place the object for the first time, all you need to do is duplicate, which should make it extremely quick to build (or prototype) levels.

Once we get over the wall, you'll remember that normal tiles are still 3.2, so modify **Move** of **Z** as needed to 3.2 or 3.6 accordingly. You can also assemble tiles by making use of the vertex snapping tool. Basically, you can take any vertex of a mesh, and with your mouse, place that vertex in the same position as a vertex from any other mesh.

8. Select the mesh you want to manipulate, and make sure the **Transform** tool is active. Press and hold *V* to enter the vertex snapping mode. Move your cursor over the vertex on the mesh you want to use as the pivot point. Hold down the left button once your cursor is over the desired vertex, and drag your mesh next to any other vertex on another mesh. You should see the object moving around via your input.

9. Release your mouse button and the *V* key when you are happy with the results. This should make it really easy to build out the rest of the rooms, but make sure you check at multiple angles to make sure the part is placed in the right area.

10. For the sake of trying it out, go to the **Hall Door** prefab inside the **Project** tab, and you should see a little button to the right of the image of the prefab. Once there, click on it to have all the children objects show up so that we can modify them. From there, select the **Door** object and uncheck the **Box Collider** component. This way, you can walk through the doors to see the rooms. Have a look at the following screenshot:

11. Using these same tools and a little trial and error, you can create a large amount of variety in your environments, such as the following:

12. Finally, create an empty game object, name it `Level 01`, and then assign all the rooms to it as children.

And there we go! We now know how to build out rooms using tiles and vertex snapping!

Creating and placing props

Now, it's great that we have a layout, but just a floor plan would get really boring really quickly in a first-person game. Luckily, we have a number of props that we can use to spice up the level a bit and add additional detail to our world. Perform the following steps:

1. First, let's move our **Level 1** object out of the way for now by making it a prefab and then deleting it from the **Hierarchy** tab.

2. Next, go to the `Props` folder, and select all of your models. Under the **Model** tab, check the **Generate Colliders** option, and click on **Apply**.

   This will create collisions for all the objects that we want to use. We didn't choose to generate colliders for the modular pieces, because we will generate them from scratch for our rooms.

3. Move the **Bedframe** object to your scene, and change the **Position** property of the object to (0, 0, 0) from the **Transform** section. To focus on the object, select it in **Hierarchy**, and then press the *F* key (this only works if the scene is selected). Alternatively, you can also double-click on it. You'll notice that in spite of being in the center of the world when the position is reset, the bed is off on the **X** axis, and that's again because of the art that we were provided with.

4. The first thing that we want to do is assign the **Props** material to all of these objects. We could do the same as before, but instead, I'm going to place each of the objects at (0, 0, 0), then select the actual mesh for all of them by holding down the *Ctrl* key (*Command* on Mac), selecting them, and then setting the material.

   You'll notice that the material fits really nicely with the models that were created. This is because the artist who created this used a UV map to tell the engine how to cut up the material and place it onto the faces that make up the object (the vertices). The texture that we have on the material is drawn in such a way that it has the appropriate part of the image at the right place. Setting up the UVs of an object is something that is done in a 3D modeling program, but when we load the model file, it contains this information. Have a look at the screenshot following the next information box.

 For more information on UV mapping, check out
`http://en.wikipedia.org/wiki/UV_mapping`.

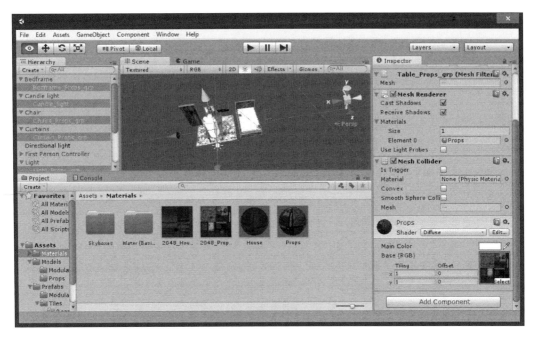

5. Just as we did with each of the modular pieces, make each of these a prefab inside a new `Props` folder, as shown in the following screenshot:

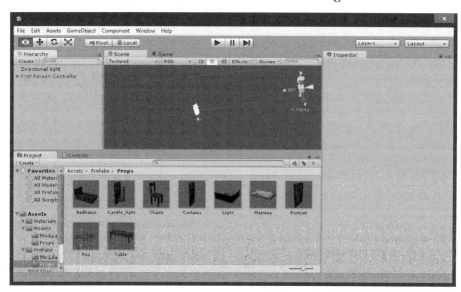

6. Now with that in mind, let's bring the **Level 01** prefab back to the level. Let's start off by adding the simplest of props to add, the chair. Drag-and-drop a chair object in your level; you should notice that it automatically gets placed on the floor at the right position, aside from the pivot looking quite out of place. Have a look at the following screenshot:

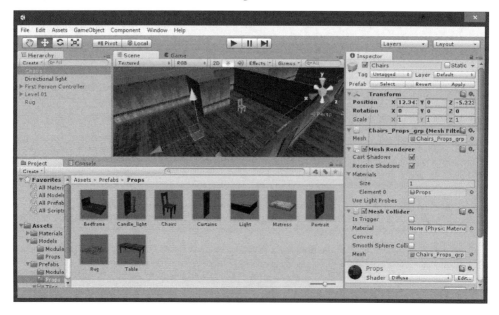

7. We could go back to our 3D modeling software to fix this problem, but perhaps you don't have access to the software, so let's fix the problem in Unity. Create a cube by going to **Game Object | Create Other | Cube**. (in case of Unity 4.6 or above, create a cube by going to **GameObject | 3D Objects | Cube**) Change the cube's **Position** property to (0, 0, 0) and **Scale** to (0, 0, 0). Then, we'll use **Vertex Snapping** to move the bottom of the chair's leg to be at (0, 0, 0), so it looks like it does in the following image. Feel free to hide other objects in the scene to make it easier to see by selecting them in **Hierarchy** and then toggling the check by their name in **Inspector**:

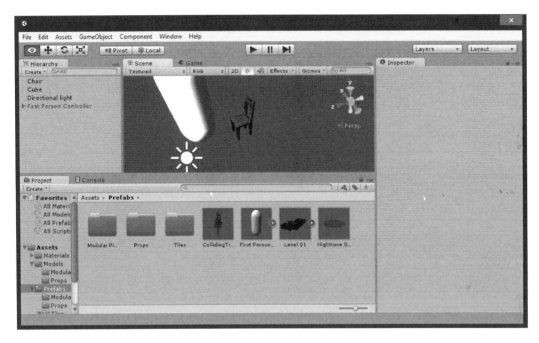

8. Once this is done, delete the **Cube** object, and create **GameObject** (empty) with the name `FixedChair`, and have the previous **Chair** be the child of our new one. After that, create a prefab named `FixedChair` in our `Prefabs\ Props` folder, and then delete it from **Hierarchy**.

9. After this, bring back our **Level 01** prefab, and now drop a chair in. As I'm sure you can see, it's much easier to place them now. Have a look at the following screenshot:

10. With this in mind, we can also use the **Rotation** tool to rotate the chairs a little bit and create some duplicates. The *E* key will switch to the **Rotation** tool:

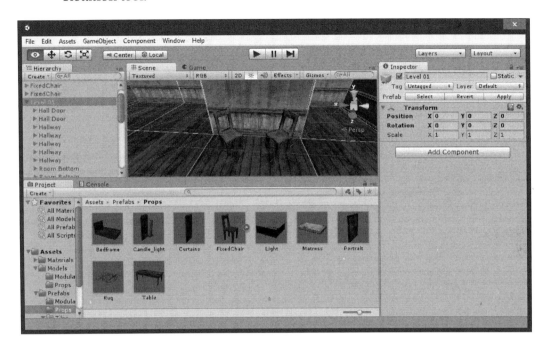

11. Now, we can continue with this with the other props as well, placing them how you feel would make the environment look more realistic.

12. Turning down the Direction Light's **Intensity** to .5, I got the following screenshot with some quick placement of objects:

13. Next, make sure all the newly added props are added to the **Level 01** prefab, and click on the **Apply** button to save all the changes we made.

    We now have a first story all fixed; let's now show how simple it is to create a second level.

14. Find a spot in your level that has an open space, and add in the **LeftStairs** object, adding in walls if needed to finish the space. After this, start placing tiles just as we did with Level 01.

A nice thing to keep in mind if you want to only focus on one level at a time, you can select the **Level 01** game object and click on the checkbox next to its name to disable everything about it, which will let you focus on just what you are doing with this level. In addition, we can use this in the future to also turn off and turn on levels to help with the frame rate if we have too many objects on the screen. Have a look at the following screenshot:

Lightmapping quickstart

Lightmapping is the process of baking or precalculating the lighting on a texture to static objects to make the game run faster and allow us to get the most out of our projects.

This generally isn't done as an optimization until you have your entire level finished, but I think this is probably the best place to talk about it. If you prefer to wait, come back to this section when you are done with your level, as doing a lightmapping pass can take a long time:

1. Go to **Edit | Render Settings**, and set **Ambient Light** to **Black,** as we want to have all the light to be from our lighting.

2. Next, we will need to select all of our model files in the `Models/Props` and `Models/Modular Pieces` folders (not the prefabs). From there, check **Generate Lightmap UVs** from the **Model** tab, and then click on the **Apply** button.

3. Lightmapping only works with static objects, that is, objects that will not be moving. That's our level stuff for sure, so select our **Level 01** parent object, and click on the **Static** option. It will ask if you want the change for the children as well, and you should click on **Yes, change children**. Have a look at the following screenshot:

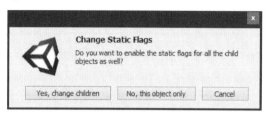

4. Next, go to **Window | Lightmapping**. This opens **Lightmapping Editor**, which we can use to bake our object, and more.

5. Once you're ready, click on the **Bake Scene** option. This may take a while on your larger projects. Once the process is completed, your scene will be ligtmapped. Have a look at the following screenshot:

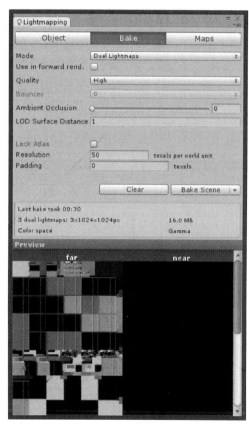

6. Let's see everything put together. Go back to the level we created in the previous chapter, *First Person Shooter Part 1 – Creating Exterior Environments*, and create a prefab of the controller with the **Flashlight** object named `Flashlight Controller`.

7. Go back to the interior level we just created, and replace the previously created controller with it.

8. Back in our level, select the **Main Camera** object of **Flashlight Controller**, and set **Background** to **Black**, and lower the magnitude of the **Bobbing Animation** component to `.1`.

To see it in action, let's take a look inside our game! Have a look at the following screenshot:

 For more information on lightmapping, check out `http://docs.unity3d.com/Documentation/Manual/` `LightmappingInDepth.html`.

Summary

And with that, we now have a great-looking interior level for our game! In addition, we covered a lot of features that exist in Unity for you to be able to use in your own future projects. With that in mind in the next chapter, we actually implement the mechanics we need to create a fully featured project!

Challenges

For those of you who want to do more with this project, there are still plenty of things you can do, especially after finishing the rest of this book. Here are some ideas to get your mind thinking:

- Create the layout for your game project. Try to create interesting areas, which you can use for encounters later on in the game.

- Place the props in interesting ways to break up repetition.

- Instead of having box colliders for every tile in our game, it would be much more efficient to just create box colliders for all the walls that are together.

- One of the major tools that level designers have is lighting. With it, we can create a mood or feeling in a place using the color, intensity, or even the lack of light. Players, in general, tend to follow lights, and you can use that as a level designer to help lead players along. Try using this in your level to lead players to the end of your level!

- Currently, the doors do not do anything. Add a trigger to the door (box collider with **Is Trigger** toggled), so when the player gets near a door, it will disappear. Once the player leaves the trigger, make it visible again. In addition, you can have a sound play when the door disappears to signify that the door has opened.

6
First Person Shooter
Part 3 – Implementing
Gameplay and AI

When I start teaching my game design students, one of the questions that I'll often hear is "What is a game?". Now, to some people, the card game *War* (`http://en.wikipedia.org/wiki/War_(card_game)`) is a game; however, the game is already determined before anyone actually plays the game since players have absolutely no interactions besides flipping cards.

Renowned game programmer and designer Sid Meier says that a game is "a series of interesting choices," and I really like that definition. At my alma mater and current employer DigiPen, we were taught that a video game was a real-time interactive simulation.

Having an environment is an excellent first step towards creating your game project; but, without anything to do but look around, this is a real-time simulation but it's not very interactive.

Project overview

In this chapter, we are going to be adding in that interactivity in the form of adding in enemies, shooting behaviors, and the gameplay to make our game truly shine. In addition, we'll also learn how to use an Xbox 360 Controller to accept input in our game as well.

Your objectives

This project will be split into a number of tasks. It will be a simple step-by-step process from beginning to end. Here is the outline of our tasks:

- Adding shooting behavior
- Creating an enemy
- Enemy movement
- Shooting/killing enemies
- Using Xbox 360 Controller Input
- Moving to other levels

In this chapter, we will continue where the last chapter left off using the same project. You may continue with your previous project or pick up a copy along with the assets for this chapter from the example code provided for this book on Packt's website at https://www.packtpub.com/books/content/support.

In addition, the completed project and source files are located there for you to check if you have any questions or need clarification.

Setting up the project

At this point, I assume that you have Unity started up and have our project from the previous chapter loaded. You can perform the following steps:

1. With Unity started, open the project from the previous chapter.

2. With that done, open our exterior environment from *Chapter 4, First Person Shooter Part 1 – Creating Exterior Environments*, by double-clicking on it in the **Scenes** folder.

Creating the shooting behavior

Now, with a traditional first person shooter, we shoot a bullet from a gun to damage enemies. However, we will create a camera that will shoot pictures to damage enemies. To show how easy it is to do, let's get started! Perform the following steps:

1. The first thing we need to do is go to the **FlashlightController** object we created earlier. So, with it selected, double-click on it to center the camera on it.

2. Our camera weapon is going to be another object, which will be a child of the **Main Camera** object. To do this, first select the **Main Camera** object that is located on our **FlashlightController** object and then navigate to **GameObject | Create Empty Child**. Also, in the **Inspector** section for this newly created object, confirm whether the object's position is 0, 0, 0. If it isn't, set it. Finally, name the object Photo Camera. Have a look at the following screenshot:

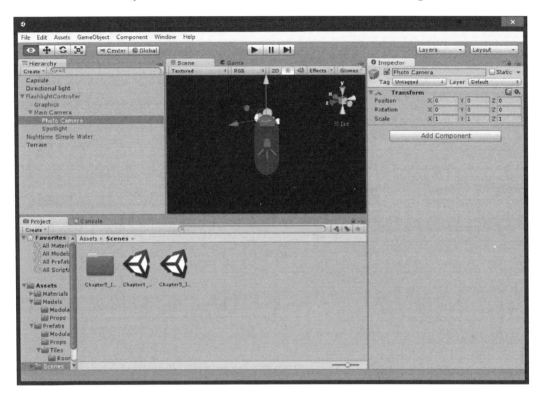

3. Next, add a camera component by clicking on the **Add Component** button at the bottom of the **Inspector** tab and then putting in the text Camera in the search bar before selecting it.

 Alternatively, you can just navigate to **Component | Add...** from the top bar to bring up the menu.

4. This camera will be zoomed in from the normal camera, so I'm going to change the **Field of View** value to 30.

5. We also want this camera to be on top of the previously created one, so we are going to change the **Depth** value to 1 (higher numbers put things in front of the other cameras).

6. That being said, we still want to see our previous camera as well in the background, so we're going to set the **Viewport Rect** values to put our new camera in the center of the screen at 75 percent of the size of the previous one. To do that, set the **X** and **Y** properties in the **Viewport Rect** option to .125 and the **W** and **H** properties to .75. To see the results of our work, check out the **Game** tab. Have a look at the following screenshot:

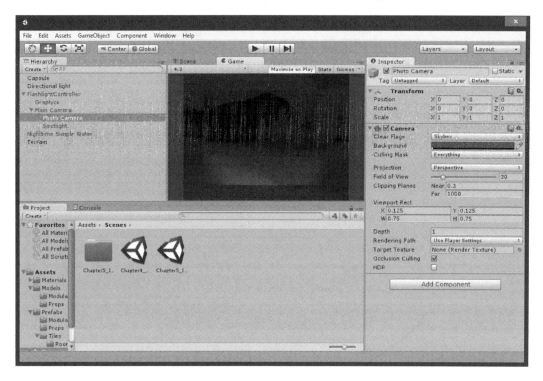

7. Now, in our game, this camera isn't just going to be a camera; it's also going to have a border around it. In this case, it'll be a cell phone. From the Chapter 6/Assets location, grab the phone.png file, and move it into the Materials folder inside your project browser.

8. Once it's imported, select it to bring up the properties in the **Inspector** tab. By default, in a 3D project, .png files will be imported with a **Texture Type** value of Texture. We want to change it to GUI (Editor \ Legacy), so click on **Apply**.

Depending on the version of Unity you are using, you will most likely see different things. In 4.3, you'll just see GUI. In 4.5, it'll look like the preceding screenshot. In 4.6, it will be Editor GUI and Legacy GUI.

9. Next, we need to add this texture to a custom GUI Skin to replace the default **Box** background, so let's go into the **Project** tab and navigate to **Create | GUI Skin** and name it `PhoneSkin`.

10. With the new GUI Skin selected, in the **Inspector** section, expand the **Box** property and, from there, expand the **Normal** selection, and change the **Background** property to the phone image, as you can see in the following screenshot:

11. Finally, we need to add this border to our **Photo Camera** object, so let's create a new C# script called `PhoneBorder`. Open the newly created script in MonoDevelop and put the following code in it. Have a look at the following code:

```
using UnityEngine;
using System.Collections;
```

```
// Code will run even if the game isn't playing
// so we can see it all the time in the Game tab.
[ExecuteInEditMode]
public class PhoneBorder : MonoBehaviour {
  public GUISkin phoneSkin;

    // How far to shift the image from the top left (in
    // pixels)
    public int xOffset = -30;
    public int yOffset = 0;

    // How far to extend the image from the bottom right (in
    // pixels)
    public int xExtend = 80;
    public int yExtend = 20;

    void OnGUI()
    {
      if(phoneSkin)
        GUI.skin = phoneSkin ;
      Camera cam = transform.camera;

      // Will create a box which will fill the screen above
      // our camera
      GUI.Box(new Rect(cam.pixelRect.x + xOffset,
                  (Screen.height - cam.pixelRect.yMax) +
                  yOffset,
                  cam.pixelWidth + xExtend,
                  cam.pixelHeight + yExtend), "") ;
    }
}
```

12. Now, save the script and exit back into the Unity Editor. Then, attach the PhoneBorder script to the phone camera object, and assign the phone skin variable to the GUI Skin we made in Step 10. You should now see the phone pop up, as shown in the following screenshot:

What this code basically does is render a box onto the screen that is positioned in the top-left corner of the camera, and is as large as the camera. The variables that we created for the offset extend and alter the image so that the camera we created is inside the phone. Take some time to modify the variables to see how each of them modifies the image. Have a look at the following screenshot:

13. Right now, I have the aspect ratio set to **4:3**, which we can see in the **Game** tab in the top-left corner just below the tab. This ratio is of the same size as old television sets and monitors, but the code we just created also works with widescreen monitors and makes the camera look much better. So, let's make the game use an aspect ratio of **16:9**. We can do that by clicking on the drop-down list beside **4:3** and then selecting **16:9**.

If you play the game at this point, the game should look something like the following screenshot:

Looks pretty good! But right now, the camera is always up there, and I only want to see it if the player right-clicks to zoom in.

14. So, with that in mind, let's create another C# script called `PhoneBehaviour` and open it inside MonoDevelop.

15. Place the following code into the `PhoneBehaviour` class as follows:

```
using UnityEngine;
using System.Collections;

public class PhoneBehaviour : MonoBehaviour {

    private PhoneBorder border;

    // Use this for initialization
    void Start ()
      {
```

```
      border = GetComponent<PhoneBorder> ();
    }

    // Update is called once per frame
    void Update ()
      {
        if (Input.GetMouseButton(1))
        {
          this.camera.enabled = true;
          border.enabled = true;
        }
        else
        {
          this.camera.enabled = false;
          border.enabled = false;
        }


      }
    }
```

Now, the camera will only come up whenever we hold down the right mouse button! Awesome! It's just like a sniper rifle in most FPS games.

Next, we want to add the ability to shoot our weapon and flash it on the screen whenever the camera is shot. To simulate this behavior, we will first create an image to be placed over our entire screen. We perform the following steps:

1. Just to make it easier to see things, let's first go to the **Photo Camera** object and disable the **Camera** and **Phone Border** scripts by unchecking their components from the **Inspector** menu.

2. Next, we will add a new GUI texture object by navigating to **GameObject | Create Other | GUITexture**. Let's rename this object Phone Flash.

 If you are using version 4.6 or later, you can create a GUI texture by navigating to **GameObject | Create General | GUITexture** or create an empty game object and add a GUITexture component.

3. Bring in the Flash.png image from our chapter's Assets folder into the Materials folder of our project browser, and change the GUI texture's **Texture** value to that.

4. Now, we need to set the image's width (**W**) and height (**H**) to the biggest resolution that you want to support; I'm using a value of `4000`. Next, set the **X** and **Y** positions to negative; halve the value (`-2000`) to center the image to your screen.

5. Click on the box beside the **Color** property, and change the **A** option (alpha) to `0`, so we can still see the rest of the world.

6. Next, go back into the `PhoneBehaviour` file, and add in the following variable:

```
public GameObject cameraFlash;
```

7. Now, a flash contains two parts: fading to white and then fading to a transparent color. The pieces of code doing both of these things are very similar, so we will create a helper function to do this for us, called `Fade`. Have a look at the following code:

```
IEnumerator Fade (float start, float end, float length,
                  GameObject currentObject)
{
    if (currentObject.guiTexture.color.a == start)
    {
      Color curColor;
      for (float i = 0.0f; i < 1.0f; i +=
Time.deltaTime*(1/length))
        {
            // Cannot modify the color property directly, so we
            // need to create a copy
            curColor = currentObject.guiTexture.color;

            // Do a linear interpolation of the value of the
            // transparency from the start
            // value to the end value in equal increments
            curColor.a = Mathf.Lerp(start, end, i);

            // Then we assign the copy to the original object
            currentObject.guiTexture.color = curColor;

            yield return null;
        }
        curColor = currentObject.guiTexture.color;

        // ensure the fade is completely finished (because
        // lerp doesn't always end on the exact value due to
        // rounding errors)
        curColor.a = end;
        currentObject.guiTexture.color = curColor;
    }
}
```

As you may recall from *Chapter 1, 2D Twin-stick Shooter*, we can use coroutines to pause functionality, yielding for a time and then resuming functionality. The IEnumerator class holds the current state of the program and tells us where to continue. The yield return here is asking us to stop the function now and resume after a period.

Since coroutines are just functions, we can also have parameters in them, just as in the preceding function. With this in mind, we can also nest them together in order to have complex interactions and use our abstracted functions in multiple ways to create interesting behaviors.

8. And then, we will call this function twice with our main function, CameraFlash, as follows:

```
IEnumerator CameraFlash()
{
    yield return StartCoroutine(Fade(0.0f, 0.8f, 0.2f,
cameraFlash));
    yield return StartCoroutine(Fade(0.8f, 0.0f, 0.2f,
cameraFlash));
    StopCoroutine ("CameraFlash");
}
```

 For more examples on how coroutines can be used, check out http://unitypatterns.com/introduction-to-coroutines/ and http://unitypatterns.com/scripting-with-coroutines/.

9. Finally, this function will never be called if we don't call it, so add the following highlighted code to our Update function:

```
void Update ()
  {

    if (Input.GetMouseButton(1))
    {
      // Flash the camera if I am aiming and I click
      if(Input.GetMouseButtonDown(0))
      {
        StartCoroutine(CameraFlash());
      }

      this.camera.enabled = true;
      border.enabled = true;
    }
```

```
    else
    {
        this.camera.enabled = false;
        border.enabled = false;
    }

}
```

10. Save the file and go back into the Unity Editor. Finally, back at the `Photo Camera` object, assign the `Phone Flash` object to the `Camera Flash` variable, and add a `GUILayer` component to the `Photo Camera` object by navigating to **Component | Rendering | GUILayer** (otherwise the flash won't show up on the actual camera).

11. Save the scene (*Ctrl + S*), and then click on the **Play** button and try out your new camera. Have a look at the following screenshot:

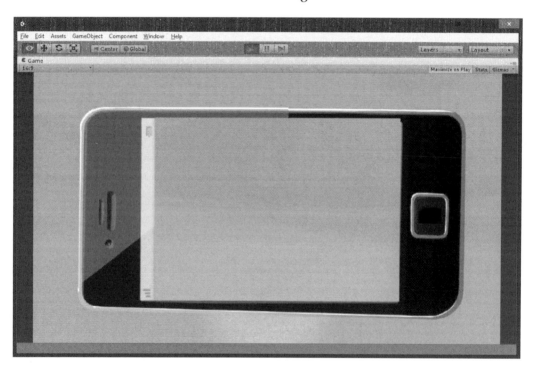

Looks like everything is in working order! We can look around with our camera, zoom in and out, and shoot pictures.

Creating an enemy

Now that we can take pictures, let's create an enemy to take pictures of! We will perform the following steps:

1. The first step to adding in an enemy is to import the assets required to use it. Inside our `Chapter 6\Assets\Ghost Model` location, you'll find a series of files.

2. First, let's create the material for our new mesh. To do this, go into either the `1024 Textures` or `2048 Textures` folder, and move the files into the `Materials` folder. Afterwards, navigate to **Create | Material**, and give it the name `GhostMaterial`. Change the **Shader** value to **Bumped Diffuse**, and move the `Ghost_Tex` file into the `Base` and `Ghost_TEX_NRM` file in the **Normalmap** selection. You'll get a warning indicating the texture isn't marked as a normal map; feel free to click on **Fix Now**, or go back into the file, and change its **Texture Type** value to `Normal map`. The following screenshot shows the Unity screen with these changes:

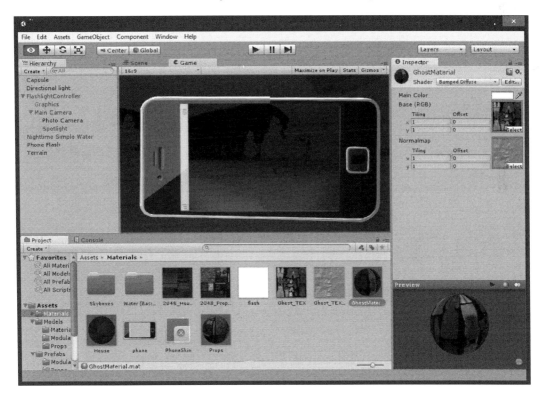

3. Now, move to the **Models** folder on the **Project** tab, and drag-and-drop the **Ghost_mesh.obj** file in there. Now, select the object to bring up its properties in the **Inspector** tab. Under **Scale Factor** in the **Model** tab, change the value to .10 to scale the object to 1/10th of its starting size. Then, check **Generate Colliders**, and uncheck the **Import Materials** option, making sure to hit **Apply**.

4. Under the **Rig** tab, change the **Animation Type** value to **None**, as this model doesn't have any animations, and then click on **Apply**.

5. Now, go somewhere in your world in the **Scene** view, and drag-and-drop the character onto the screen near your player and terrain. have a look at the following screenshot:

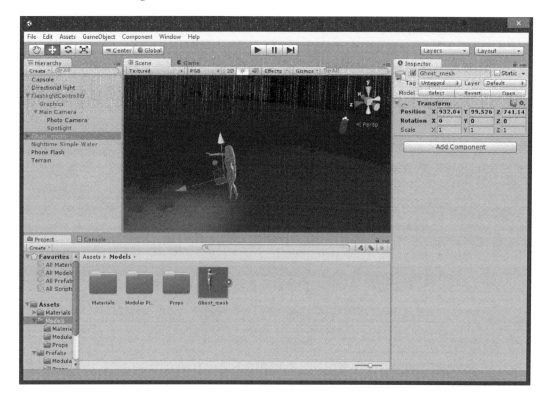

6. Right now, the mesh is just using the default material, so let's fix that. Expand the **Ghost_mesh** object, and select its child. In the **Inspector** tab, extend the **Mesh Renderer** tab, and change the material's **Element 0** property to our Ghost material, as shown in the following screenshot:

And now, the character has a material that makes it appear as an enemy much nicer. Spooky!

State machines 101

We oftentimes write code to provide the reactive or interactive parts within our simulation (or game world) — things such as when you're pressing a button or if you're walking or jumping. If you look at real life, you should notice that a lot of things are reactive systems in that same way, such as your mobile phone and toaster. Depending on the stimuli provided to these objects, the state of these objects may change. We describe something that can be in one of multiple states at a time as a state machine.

Almost every program that we write is or can be a state machine of some sort, because technically, the moment you write an `if` statement, you've created code that can be in one of at least two states. However, having a number of `switch` and `if` statements can quickly get out of hand, making it very hard for people to understand what your code is actually doing. As a programmer, we want to isolate problems and break them down into their simplest parts before jumping in to solve them.

There are different kinds of state machines, but for this first example, we are going to create a simple **Finite State Machine (FSM)**. When I say finite, it means that each of the states is already defined ahead of time. With a finite state machine, we can have different states in which we can process input differently depending on the state.

For example, if you are on a ladder, you can only move up and down and not to the sides.

Enemy movement

As spooky as the character is, right now, it is just a static mesh. It will not come to us to damage us, and we cannot damage it. Let's fix that next using the state machines we've just learned about! Perform the following steps:

1. Create a new script called `EnemyBehaviour`.

   We want our enemy to follow the player if they get too close to them; however, they will stay where they are if the player gets far enough away. Finally, if, for some reason, we defeat the enemy, they should no longer run this behavior, and we should kill them. The first step to creating a state machine is to extract the states that the object can be in. In this case, we have three states: `Idle`, `Following`, and `Death`. Just as we discussed in *Chapter 2, Creating GUIs*, using an enumeration is the best tool for the job here as well.

2. Add the following code to the top of the `EnemyBehaviour` class:

   ```
   public enum State
   {
     Idle,
     Follow,
     Die,
   }


   // The current state the player is in
   public State state;
   ```

   Now, depending on the value that the state is currently in, we can do different things. We could use something like the following code:

   ```
   void Update()
   {
       if(state == State.Idle)
       {
           //And so on
       }
       else if(state == State.Follow)
   ```

```
    {
        //And so on
    }
    //etc...
}
```

But, as I'm sure you can already see, this is incredibly messy. Also, what if we want to do something when we first enter the state? What about when you leave? To fix this issue, let's use a tool we covered earlier, the coroutine function, which we will have each of our states contain.

3. Next, we need to add in some additional variables we will use. Have a look at the following code:

```
    // The object the enemy wants to follow
    public Transform target;

    // How fast should the enemy move?
    public float moveSpeed = 3.0f;
    public float rotateSpeed = 3.0f;

    // How close should the enemy be before they follow?
    public float followRange = 10.0f;

    // How far should the target be before the enemy gives up
    // following?
    // Note: Needs to be >= followRange
    public float idleRange = 10.0f;
```

4. Now, we need to add in a coroutine function for each of the possible states, starting with the `Idle` state. Have a look at the following code:

```
    IEnumerator IdleState ()
    {
      //OnEnter
      Debug.Log("Idle: Enter");
      while (state == State.Idle)
      {
        //OnUpdate
        if(GetDistance() < followRange)
        {
          state = State.Follow;
        }

        yield return 0;
      }
```

```
    //OnEnd
    Debug.Log("Idle: Exit");
    GoToNextState();
  }
```

This state will continuously check whether the players are close enough to the target to start following it until its state is no longer `State.Idle`. You'll notice two functions we'll need to create later, `GetDistance` and `GoToNextState`, which we will implement after we finish the other states.

5. Continue with the `Following` state, as follows:

```
    IEnumerator FollowState ()
    {
      Debug.Log("Follow: Enter");
      while (state == State.Follow)
      {
        transform.position =
    Vector3.MoveTowards(transform.position,
                    target.position,
                    Time.deltaTime * moveSpeed);

        RotateTowardsTarget();

        if(GetDistance() > idleRange)
        {
          state = State.Idle;
        }

        yield return 0;
      }
      Debug.Log("Follow: Exit");
      GoToNextState();
    }
```

This state will move the enemy closer to the player while continuously checking if the target is far enough to go back to `Idle`. In addition to the other functions we talked about earlier, we also have a new function called `RotateTowardsTarget`, which we will also need to add in.

6. Finish off by adding in the `Die` state, as follows:

```
IEnumerator DieState ()
{
    Debug.Log("Die: Enter");

    Destroy (this.gameObject);
    yield return 0;
}
```

This state just destroys the object attached to it. Right now, there is no way to get here aside from us setting it in the **Inspector** tab, but it will be useful when we add in damage.

7. Now, we need to add in those functions we talked about earlier. First, let's add in `GetDistance` and `RotateTowardsTarget`, which are self-explanatory in terms of what they do. Have a look at the following code:

```
public float GetDistance()
{
    return (transform.position -
target.transform.position).magnitude;
}

private void RotateTowardsTarget()
{
    transform.rotation =
Quaternion.Slerp(transform.rotation,

Quaternion.LookRotation(target.position -
                        transform.position),
                        rotateSpeed * Time.deltaTime);
}
```

> The `Vector3` class also has a `Distance` function you can use.
> `Vector3.Distance(transform.position, target.transform.position);` will do the same thing as our `GetDistance` function does, but knowing the math behind things can be extremely helpful!

8. Now, we need to add in the ability to go to another state, as follows:

```
void GoToNextState ()
{
    // Find out the name of the function we want to call
    string methodName = state.ToString() + "State";

    // Searches this class for a function with the name of
    // state + State (for example: idleState)
    System.Reflection.MethodInfo info =
    GetType().GetMethod(methodName,
    System.Reflection.BindingFlags.NonPublic |
    System.Reflection.BindingFlags.Instance);
    StartCoroutine((IEnumerator)info.Invoke(this, null));
}
```

The preceding code is fairly advanced stuff, so it's okay if you do not fully understand it at a glance. For the preceding code, I could have written something like the Update example I wrote previously, calling the appropriate coroutine based on the state to go to.

Instead, this code will call the appropriate function with the name of the state plus the word State. The nice thing about this is that you can now write as many additional states as you want without having to modify this function. All you have to do is add an item to the State enumerator and then write a function for it with a proper name!

 For information on the GetMethod function and the different kinds of BindingFlags, you can visit http://msdn.microsoft.com/en-us/library/05eey4y9(v=vs.110).aspx.

9. Then, we need to start this whole state machine up with the following code:

```
void Start ()
{
    GoToNextState();
}
```

10. Finally, we need to save our file and exit back to the Unity Editor. Attach the **Enemy Behaviour** script to our **Ghost_mesh** object, and set the **Target** property to our **FlashlightController** object. Have a look at the following screenshot:

11. Save the scene and play the game. Have a look at the following screenshot:

As you can see now, you can follow the enemy's current state in the **Inspector** tab, and they will turn and move towards you whenever you get too close!

Advanced FSMs

This is a good introduction to state machines and what you can use them for, but there is a lot of additional information out there on their uses, such as an abstract version of a state machine at `http://playmedusa.com/blog/a-finite-state-machine-in-c-for-unity3d/`.

The Asset Store also features Playmaker, which is a fairly popular commercial add-on that creates state machines with a visual editor, making it very easy to add in states. For more information on Playmaker, check out `http://www.hutonggames.com/`.

Damaging and killing enemies

Now that we have enemies moving towards us, we need some way for them to be damaged and killed! Let's do that now by performing the following steps:

1. The first thing we need to do is make it easy to get a reference to all of our enemies, so let's add a tag by going to the **Inspector** tab and navigating to **Tag | Add Tag...**. Once the **Tag & Layer** menus come up, type in Enemy into **Element 0**. Then go back into the **Ghost_mesh** child object, add the **Enemy** tag to it, and rename the parent object to Ghost:

2. Next, let's dive back into MonoDevelop, edit our PhoneBehaviour script, and add the following code in bold to its Update function:

```
// Update is called once per frame
void Update () {
  if (Input.GetMouseButtonDown(0) &&
  Input.GetMouseButton(1))
  {
    StartCoroutine(CameraFlash());
```

```
        GameObject[] enemyList =
GameObject.FindGameObjectsWithTag("Enemy");

        foreach (GameObject enemy in enemyList)
        {
          if(enemy.renderer.isVisible)
          {
            EnemyBehaviour behaviour = enemy.transform.parent.
            gameObject.GetComponent<EnemyBehaviour>();
            behaviour.TakeDamage();
          }
        }
      }

      if (Input.GetMouseButton(1))
      {
        this.camera.enabled = true;
        border.enabled = true;
      }
      else
      {
        this.camera.enabled = false;
        border.enabled = false;
      }

    }
```

3. Now that we say there is a `TakeDamage` function in our `EnemyBehaviour` class, we need to add that in. Open the `EnemyBehaviour` class, and first, we need to create some variables as follows:

```
public float health = 100.0f;
private float currentHealth;
```

4. Next, we need to initialize `currentHealth`, so add the following code in bold to the `Start` function:

```
void Start ()
{
  GoToNextState();
  currentHealth = health;
}
```

5. Now, let's add in the `TakeDamage` function, as follows:

```
public void TakeDamage()
  {
    // The closer I am, the more damage I do
    float damageToDo = 100.0f - (GetDistance () * 5);

    if (damageToDo < 0)
      damageToDo = 0;
    if (damageToDo > health)
      damageToDo = health;

    currentHealth -= damageToDo;

    if(currentHealth <= 0)
    {
      state = State.Die;
    }
    else
    {
      // If we're not dead, now that we took a picture the
      // enemy knows where we are
      followRange = Mathf.Max(GetDistance(), followRange);
      state = State.Follow;
    }

    print ("Ow! - Current Health: " +
currentHealth.ToString());

  }
```

6. Now, save your scene and all the script files, and play the game! The following screenshot depicts the game screen:

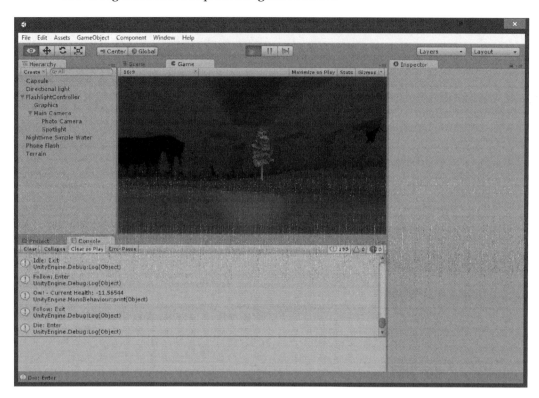

Now, the enemy will follow you when you take its picture and the closer you are to it, the more it will get damaged, which you can see by looking at the console!

Using controller input

One of the biggest advantages of using Unity as a game engine is the fact that you can support multiple platforms with minimal changes to your base game. In fact, right now, if you plug in an Xbox 360 Controller into your computer, restart Unity, and then try to play the game, you'll notice that the left-hand side joystick already moves the player, and if you press the Y button, you will jump into the air. However, some of the aspects don't work, so let's get them implemented.

Let's get started by performing the following steps:

1. The first thing that we're going to need to do is let Unity know that we want to work with some new input. So, to do that, we will need to navigate to **Edit | Project Settings | Input**. Have a look at the following screenshot:

2. Once there, we need to add four new axes to our project, the first being a new horizontal axis; so right-click on the **Mouse X** axis, and select **Duplicate Array Element**.

3. Extend the newly created **Mouse X** axes, and rename it to `360 Right Horizontal`. The controller output is never 100-percent correct, so we want to change the **Dead** value to `.05` so that any value between `-.05` and `.05` won't be counted.

4. Change the **Type** value to **Joystick Axis** and the **Axis** value to **4th axis (Joysticks)**.

5. Do the same for the **Mouse Y** axis with the name `360 Right Vertical` using the **5th axis (Joysticks)** option. Have a look at the following screenshot:

6. Now, we will need to alter the character controller's `MouseLook` script file, so double-click on it to open MonoDevelop. Once opened, add the following highlighted code to its `Update` function:

```
void Update ()
{
    if (axes == RotationAxes.MouseXAndY)
    {
        float rotationX = transform.localEulerAngles.y +
                        Input.GetAxis ("Mouse X") *
                        sensitivityX;

        rotationY += Input.GetAxis ("Mouse Y") * sensitivityY;
        rotationY = Mathf.Clamp (rotationY, minimumY,
                maximumY);

        transform.localEulerAngles = new Vector3 (-rotationY,
                        rotationX, 0);
```

```
    }
    else if (axes == RotationAxes.MouseX)
    {
      transform.Rotate(0, Input.GetAxis("Mouse X") *
                       sensitivityX, 0);
    }
    else
    {
      rotationY += Input.GetAxis("Mouse Y") * sensitivityY;
      rotationY = Mathf.Clamp (rotationY, minimumY,
                  maximumY);

      transform.localEulerAngles = new Vector3(-rotationY,
                                   transform.
                                   localEulerAngles.y, 0);
    }

    float rotationX360 = transform.localEulerAngles.y +
                         Input.GetAxis("360 Right
                         Horizontal") *
                         sensitivityX;

    rotationY -= Input.GetAxis("360 Right Vertical") *
                 sensitivityY;
    rotationY = Mathf.Clamp (rotationY, minimumY,
                maximumY);

    transform.localEulerAngles = new Vector3(-rotationY,
                                 rotationX360, 0);
}
```

This code will make the right joystick rotate the player's camera.

7. Now that we have that done, let's get the camera and shoot to work. To do that, we need to now open the `PhoneBehaviour` script. First of all, we're going to need to introduce a new variable to account for the fact that we want the player to have to release the right trigger before they can shoot again:

```
bool shotStarted = false;
```

8. Now, we will update the `Update` function to the following code. Note the changes in bold:

```
void Update ()
{
    if ((Input.GetMouseButton(1) ||
         Input.GetAxis("360 Left Trigger") > 0)
```

```
                && (Input.GetMouseButtonDown(0) ||
                (Input.GetAxis("360 Right Trigger") > 0
                && !shotStarted)))
        {
          shotStarted = true;
          StartCoroutine(CameraFlash());

          GameObject[] enemyList =
                      GameObject.FindGameObjectsWithTag("Enemy");

          foreach (GameObject enemy in enemyList)
          {
            if(enemy.renderer.isVisible)
            {
              EnemyBehaviour behaviour =
              enemy.transform.parent.gameObject.
  GetComponent<EnemyBehaviour>();
              behaviour.TakeDamage();
            }
          }
        }
        else if(Input.GetAxis("360 Right Trigger") == 0)
        {
          shotStarted = false;
        }

        if (Input.GetMouseButton(1) ||
        Input.GetAxis("360 Left Trigger") > 0)
        {
          this.camera.enabled = true;
          border.enabled = true;
        }
        else
        {
          this.camera.enabled = false;
          border.enabled = false;
        }

    }
```

9. Save your scripts, and start the game. Have a look at the following screenshot:

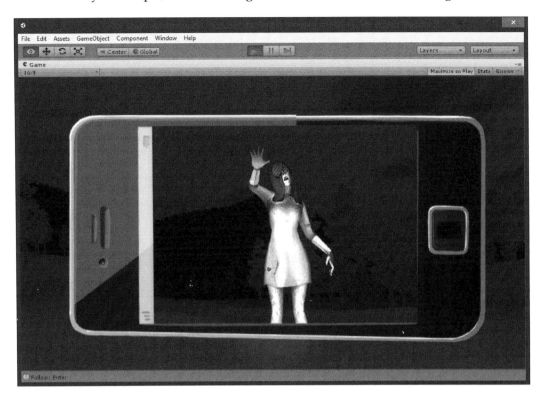

At this point, you should be able to play the project using an Xbox 360 Controller!

Now, depending on what platform you're running Unity on, there may be special things to take into consideration. For more information about using the Xbox 360 Controller, please visit `http://wiki.unity3d.com/index.php?title=Xbox360Controller`.

For those that don't want to deal with input too much and just want something that will standardize your input for common controllers, I hear good things about Gallant Games' InControl input manager, which you can find out more about from `http://www.gallantgames.com/incontrol`.

While not all the features are included, they have an open source version of most of the content at `http://github.com/pbhogan/InControl`; but if you use their tool, I recommend that you buy it to support further development.

Moving to other levels

Finally, let's see what we can do to make the changes we've made in this chapter show up in all of our levels. We perform the following steps:

1. We've been modifying a series of prefabs, so thankfully it's quite easy to update them for other levels. Select the **FlashlightController** object, and in the **Prefab** section, click on the **Apply** button to save our changes to the prefab.

2. The **Ghost** object, however, is just a model, so let's open the **Prefabs** folder in our project browser and drag-and-drop the object in there.

3. Move the **Phone Flash** object in as a prefab as well.

4. Now that we have everything set up, let's open our interior level.

5. Upon opening the level, you may notice that the other level already has the camera showing up if you look at the **Game** tab. Have a look at the following screenshot:

6. Don't start the level yet though! Next, add in the **Phone Flash** object by dragging-and-dropping it into the **Hierarchy** section. Then, open the **FlashlightController** object, go to the **Photo Camera** object, and set the **Camera Flash** object in your **Phone Behaviour** section to our **Phone Flash** object.

7. Then, you can drag-and-drop a **Ghost** prefab into the scene at a place of your choice and set the **Enemy Behaviour** object's **Target** property to the **FlashlightController** object.

8. After that, save the project and play the game. Have a look at the following screenshot:

Summary

And with that, we now have a great looking interior level for our game! In addition, we covered a lot of features that exist in Unity for you to be able to use in your own future projects. With that in mind, in the next chapter, we will actually implement the mechanics we need to create a fully featured project!

Challenges

For those of you who want to do more with this project, there are still plenty of things you can do, especially after finishing the rest of this book. Here are some ideas to get you thinking:

- Right now, the enemy will continue following you even if you're through a tree or a wall. Use the `Raycast` function we talked about in *Chapter 3, Side-scrolling Platformer*, to check a line from the player when the enemy collides with something. If it does, then set the enemy's state to `Idle`.

- If you're interested in adding in more complex AI behavior to your ghost, such as pathfinding, you can check out *Unity 4.x Game AI Programming, Aung Sithu Kyaw, Clifford Peters, and Thet Naing Swe, Packt Publishing*.

- Add sound effects to the ghost character so that the player knows when they are coming closer to the player, and add some tension to the game. Adding in other sound effects, such as those for taking a picture and walking around, can help create ambience as well. A good website to visit for sound effects is `https://www.freesound.org/`. However, you may need to edit them a bit to help make them fit the game better. To do that, I suggest Audacity, which you can download from `http://audacity.sourceforge.net/`.

- Add in multiple ghosts in the level to create interesting encounters for the player to work with.

- In addition, you could create additional ghosts, which can be faster and/or more aggressive. You could also use Unity's Culling Mask system to make the ghosts only visible if you have the camera out by putting the object on different layers (`http://docs.unity3d.com/Documentation/Components/Layers.html`). Then, you can set the culling mask for each camera to only display the layers that you want (`http://docs.unity3d.com/Documentation/Components/class-Camera.html`).

- In the last section, you saw that we set a couple of different objects to make sure the game worked correctly. That's the most efficient way performance-wise, but for convenience, you may want to get the objects through code with the `GameObject.Find` function. For more information about it, check out `http://docs.unity3d.com/ScriptReference/GameObject.Find.html`.

7
Creating Save Files in Unity

Now that we've created a series of projects in Unity, we have a firm foundation on what works and what doesn't. But right now, every time the game is over and you start again, you lose everything.

Project overview

In this chapter, we are going to add in functionality to some of our previously created games, adding in high scores and even an in-game level editor, which can be used for future projects.

Your objectives

This project will be split into a number of tasks. It will be a simple step-by-step process from beginning to end. Here is the outline of our tasks:

- Saving a high score
- Level editor – introduction
- Adding/removing walls at runtime
- Toggling editor, GUI, and selecting additional tiles
- Saving/loading levels to file

In this chapter, we will use projects that we created in the earlier chapters, specifically the projects from *Chapter 2, Creating GUIs*, and *Chapter 3, Side-scrolling Platformer*. You may continue with your previous projects or pick up a copy along with the assets for this chapter from the example code provided for this book on Packt Publishing's website (https://www.packtpub.com/books/content/support).

In addition, the completed project and source files are located there for you to check if you have any questions or need clarification.

Saving a high score

To begin with, let's look at one of the simplest ways to save/load data for individual pieces of simple data using the `PlayerPrefs` class.

The PlayerPrefs class

The `PlayerPrefs` class allows us to store small amounts of data on the end user's machine. Using `PlayerPrefs` is a great way to save data for user levels, the coordinates of where enemies are, or a high score so that when the user comes back to the game, it shows the highest score achieved over the course of all games played.

When I say small amounts of data, on the WebPlayer you can store only 1 MB of data, but this is the only limitation aside from hard drive space as of this writing.

The `PlayerPrefs` class can store the following types: `float`, `int`, and `string`. There are two key functions for each of the types `Get` and `Set` with the type added afterward (`GetFloat`, `SetString`, and so on).

The Set functions

The `Set` functions take in two parameters: the first being a string and the second of the type you're trying to set. This will save the value in the second parameter to the registry on your computer with the string as a reference for you to get the data back with the `Get` function. For example, creating a string and storing it will be somewhat like the following code:

```
void Start()
{
  string authorName = "John Doran";
  PlayerPrefs.SetString ("Author Name", authorName);
}
```

If there was a value previously saved with that variable, its name will be overwritten with the new value.

 To be sure that your variables do not get overwritten by other projects, it's important to make sure that you set **Product Name** and **Company Name** in **Project Settings**.

The Get functions

The Get functions will retrieve the value that it currently has set if there is one. If it cannot find a value (that variable doesn't exist yet), it will return 0 (for the int and float datatypes) or "" (for strings), or whatever you put in as the second parameter. So, as an example, I could write something like the following code:

```
void Start()
{
  // If the above code was ran, it would return "John Doran"
  // or whatever else was stored there. Otherwise, it will
  // return "Bob"
  print(PlayerPrefs.GetString("Author Name", "Bob"));
}
```

Then, if there already is a value assigned for Author Name, it will print out that, but otherwise, it will give you the value of Bob. This is great if you want to have a default value other than 0 or an empty string "".

Depending on what operating system you're currently using for this project or are porting to, the location of where the values are saved to are different.

Depending on what platform your game is running, the location of these values may be different. For those locations, or for more information on the PlayerPrefs class, check out http://docs.unity3d.com/ScriptReference/PlayerPrefs.html.

Now that we know how to use PlayerPrefs, let's see it in action by performing the following steps:

1. We are going to first open our **TwinstickShooter** project we created back in *Chapter 1, 2D Twin-stick Shooter*, and *Chapter 2, Creating GUIs*. Open your gameplay scene (in the example code, saved as *Chapter 2, Creating GUIs*). Have a look at the following screenshot:

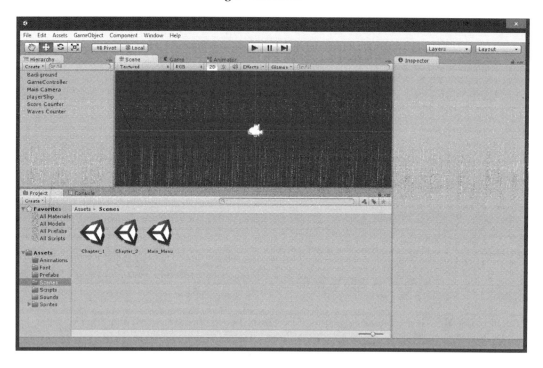

2. Since we want to add a high score, we'll need to add in a new GUI text object to display it. Switch to the **Game** tab so that we can see our GUI elements.

3. Go to the **Scene** tab if not there already, select **Waves Counter** that we created earlier, and duplicate it by pressing *Ctrl* + *D*. Rename this newly created object to High Score Counter. After that, change the **Position** property of **X** to .5 to center it. After this, change **Anchor** to Upper Center. Finally, just to have it look correct, change **Text** to High Score: 0. Have a look at the following screenshot:

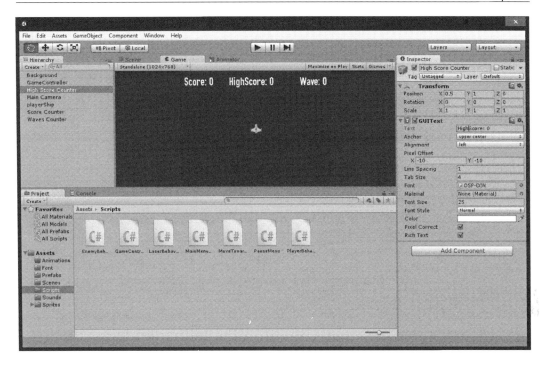

Again, while the text here is shown to us now, just like the score and lives, it is merely for our reference, as we will need to update the text via code.

4. Now, we will need to access our `GameController` class to make some modifications! From **Project** tab, open the `Scripts` folder, and double-click on the `GameController` file to open `MonoDevelop`.

5. The first thing we will do is add a new variable for our new text object, as follows:

```
public GUIText highScoreText;
```

6. The first thing we'll need to do is initialize the value in the text inside our `Start` function, so add in the following bolded code:

```
void Start ()
{
  StartCoroutine(SpawnEnemies());
  // Retrieves stored data if it exists from the
  // PlayerPrefs, otherwise 0
highScoreText.text = "High Score: " +
                     PlayerPrefs.GetInt("highScore").ToString();
}
```

7. Now, we need to update that value whenever we increase our score, so let's add the following bolded code to your `IncreaseScore` function:

```
public void IncreaseScore(int increase)
{
    score += increase;
    scoreText.text = "Score: " + score;

    if( score > PlayerPrefs.GetInt ("highScore"))
    {
        // Now we are saving the value to the disk for
        // retrieval later
        PlayerPrefs.SetInt ("highScore", score);
        highScoreText.text = "High Score: " + score.ToString();
    }
}
```

8. Next, go back to the Unity editor, and then select the **GameController** object in **Hierarchy**. Make sure that **Wave Text** is set to `Waves Counter` and **High Score Text** is set to `High Score Counter`. After that, play the game and gain some points, and then close the game. After that, play it again. Have a look at the following screenshot:

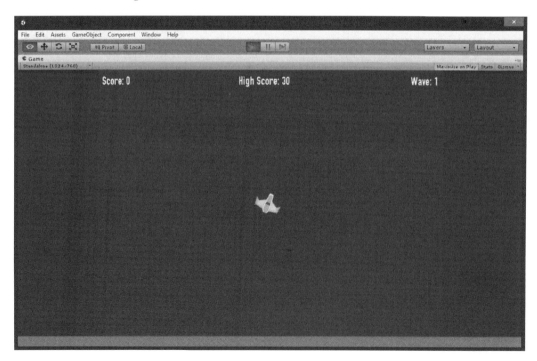

If all goes well, we should be able to notice that the high score has been saved and will stay even when we restart the game!

Level editor – introduction

Of course, there can come a time when you want to save things other than just `string`, `int`, or `float` variables. To deal with complex data types, there are more things that we can do. Perform the following steps:

1. We are going to first open up our **3D Platformer** project we created back in *Chapter 3, Side-scrolling Platformer*. Open your gameplay scene (in the example code saved as `Level1`) from the link described in the project setup.

2. As it currently stands, the ability to create our levels is inside our **GameController** script. For this project, however, we're going to extract that functionality and move it over to a new class. In **Project Browser**, go to the `Scripts` folder, and create a new C# script called `LevelEditor`. With that finished, open `MonoDevelop`.

3. Once in `MonoDevelop`, click on the `GameController.cs` file, and highlight the `level` variable. Cut it (*Ctrl + X*) and paste it (*Ctrl + V*) as a declaration in the `LevelEditor` class.

4. After this, remove the `BuildLevel` function from the file and stop it from being called in our `GameController` script's `Start` function. Instead of calling it here, we will be writing a new version for our new `LevelEditor` script.

   Next, we want access to our `goalPS` variable inside the `LevelEditor` class so that we have a reference to the particle system to turn to when we collect all the orbs, but right now, it's private. Now, I could set this variable as being `public` and be done with it, but instead, we're going to use another aspect of programming in C# called **properties**.

 If you decide to make something public but don't want to see it in **Inspector**, you can write code like the following:

```
[HideInInspector]
public ParticleSystem goalPS;
```

5. Add the following code after your `goalPS` variable declaration:

```
public ParticleSystem GoalPS
{
  get
  {
```

```
        return goalPS;
    }

    set
    {
        goalPS = value;
    }
}
```

This will allow us to access this newly created `GoalPS` variable to modify `goalPS` (our original one). The value that you see in the `set` function is a keyword that will be assigned.

Now, you may be asking why you should do this instead of making it `public`. There are two main reasons. First, we are allowed to use get and set just like a normal function. This will allow us to check the value of value before we actually assign something, which can be really useful if you want to make sure that a variable is within a certain range. Have a look at the following code:

```
private int health;
public int Health
{
    get
    {
        return health;
    }

    set
    {
        // Value can only be up to 100
        health = value % 100;
        if(health <= 0)
        print ("I'm dead");
    }
}
```

Also, by omitting either Get or Set, we can say that the variable cannot be changed outside of the class or accessed outside of the class.

For more information on properties, check out http://unity3d.com/learn/tutorials/modules/intermediate/scripting/properties.

Now that our level is no longer being created in the `GameController`, let's add the functionality back to our `LevelEditor`. Perform the following steps:

1. Add the following function:

```
void BuildLevel()
{

  //Go through each element inside our level variable
  for (int yPos = 0; yPos < level.Length; yPos++)
  {
    for (int xPos = 0; xPos < (level[yPos]).Length; xPos++)
    {
      CreateBlock(level[yPos][xPos], xPos, level.Length - yPos);
    }
  }
}
```

2. We haven't created the `CreateBlock` function, so right now it'll show up as being red, but before we add it in, we need to create some variables:

```
int xMin = 0;
int xMax = 0;
int yMin = 0;
int yMax = 0;

public List<Transform> tiles;

GameObject dynamicParent;
```

3. At this point, the `List` type will show up in red. This is because it doesn't know what we're talking about. Add the following line to our `using` statements up at the top of the file:

```
using System.Collections.Generic; // Lists
```

Lists

We used arrays previously in this book, which are containers for multiple copies of an object. One of the problems with arrays is the fact that you have to know how many you have before the game starts, and you cannot add or subtract from that number.

The list type is basically a dynamically sized array, which is to say that we can add and remove elements from it at any point that we want. It also gives us access to some nice helper functions such as IndexOf (which will return to us the index of an element in a list, something that can be really useful when using the index operator []).

 For more information on lists, check out http://unity3d.com/ learn/tutorials/modules/intermediate/scripting/ lists-and-dictionaries.

1. Now we need to actually create our CreateBlock function, as follows:

```
public void CreateBlock(int value, int xPos, int yPos)
{
   Transform toCreate = null;

   // We need to know the size of our level to save later
   if(xPos < xMin)
   {
      xMin = xPos;
   }
   if(xPos > xMax)
   {
      xMax = xPos;
   }

   if(yPos < yMin)
   {
      yMin = yPos;
   }
   if(yPos > yMax)
   {
      yMax = yPos;
   }

   //If value is set to 0, we don't want to spawn anything
   if(value != 0)
   {
      toCreate = tiles[value-1];
   }

   if(toCreate != null)
   {
      //Create the object we want to create
      Transform newObject = Instantiate(toCreate, new Vector3(xPos,
yPos,  0), Quaternion.identity) as Transform;

      //Give the new object the same name as ours
```

```
        newObject.name = toCreate.name;

        if(toCreate.name == "Goal")
        {
          // We want to have a reference to the particle system
          // for later
          GameController._instance.GoalPS = newObject.gameObject.
GetComponent<ParticleSystem>();

          // Move the particle system so it'll face up
          newObject.transform.Rotate(-90,0,0);
        }

        // Set the object's parent to the DynamicObjects
        // variable so it doesn't clutter our Hierarchy
        newObject.parent = dynamicParent.transform;
    }
}
```

2. Finally, we need to initialize all of these variables in our Start function, as follows:

```
public void Start()
{
    // Get the DynamicObjects object so we can make it our
    // newly created objects' parent
    dynamicParent = GameObject.Find("DynamicObjects");
    BuildLevel();

    enabled = false;
}
```

As we used previously, the GameObject.Find function looks within our scene to find an object with the name DynamicObjects. If it does not find the object, it will return null. It's always a good idea to make sure the value is not null, or you may be wondering why something in your code doesn't work when it's a spelling error or something of that sort. It's important to note that case is important and that DynamicObjects and dynamicObjects are different! If anything is different, it will not work:

```
    if(dynamicParent == null)
    {
      print("Object not found! Check spelling!");
    }
```

This function should be used only on seldom occasions, as it can be quite slow. For more info on GameObject.Find, check out http://docs. unity3d.com/ScriptReference/GameObject.Find.html.

3. Next, go back to **Inspector**, and attach the `LevelEditor` script to the **GameController** object by dragging the script file on top of it. Afterward, open up the **Tiles** variable, and change **Size** to 4. Then go to the `Prefabs` folder, and drag `Wall`, `Player`, `Collectible`, and `Goal` to the **Element 0**, **Element 1**, **Element 2**, and **Element 3** variables, respectively.

4. Finally, save your scene and play the game! Have a look at the following screenshot:

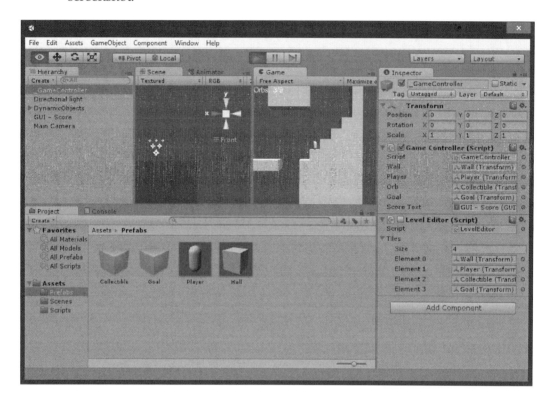

You'll notice that now, the class creates our level, and then turns itself off—a great start for our level editor!

Level editor – adding/removing walls at runtime

Now that our level editor will be able to load in this data, we now want to have a way to actually modify what we see onscreen. To do this, we'll need to create a GUI interface and functionality for our level editor.

1. The first thing we need to do is add a variable to keep track of what item we want to spawn:

```
//The object we are currently looking to spawn
Transform toCreate;
```

2. Now, we need to initialize this variable inside our `Start` function:

```
toCreate = tiles[0];
```

3. Next, we need to update our `Update` function and then explain how it's working, as follows:

```
void Update()
{
  // Left click - Create object
  if (Input.GetMouseButton(0) && GUIUtility.hotControl==0)
  {
    Vector3 mousePos = Input.mousePosition;

    //Set the position in the z axis to the opposite of the
    // camera's so that the position is on the world so
    // ScreenToWorldPoint will give us valid values.
    mousePos.z = Camera.main.transform.position.z * -1;

    Vector3 pos = Camera.main.ScreenToWorldPoint(mousePos);

    // Deal with the mouse being not exactly on a block
    int posX = Mathf.FloorToInt(pos.x +.5f);
    int posY = Mathf.FloorToInt(pos.y + .5f);

    // Convert from screenspace to worldspace using a Ray
    Ray ray = Camera.main.ScreenPointToRay(mousePos);

    // We need to check if there is an object already at
    // the position we're trying to create at
    RaycastHit hit = new RaycastHit();
```

```
              // If something within a distance of 100 in the
              // direction hits something hit will get the data of
              //the hit object.
              Physics.Raycast(ray, out hit, 100);

              if((hit.collider != null) && (hit.collider.name != "Player"))
              {
                //If it's the same, just keep the previous one
                if(toCreate.name != hit.collider.gameObject.name)
                {
                  CreateBlock(tiles.IndexOf(toCreate) + 1,
Mathf.FloorToInt(hit.collider.gameObject.transform.position.x),
Mathf.FloorToInt(hit.collider.gameObject.transform.position.y));

                  DestroyImmediate(hit.collider.gameObject);
                }
              }
              else
              {
                CreateBlock(tiles.IndexOf(toCreate) + 1, posX, posY);
              }
          }

          // Right clicking - Delete object
          if (Input.GetMouseButton(1) && GUIUtility.hotControl==0)
          {
            Ray ray = Camera.main.ScreenPointToRay(Input.mousePosition);

            RaycastHit hit = new RaycastHit();

            Physics.Raycast(ray, out hit, 100);

            // If we hit something other than the player, we
            // want to destroy it!
            if((hit.collider != null) && (hit.collider.name != "Player"))
            {
              Destroy(hit.collider.gameObject);
            }
          }
    }
```

You'll notice that we used something called `hotControl` when we were checking for input. The reason we did this was that whenever a player holds down a mouse button, it becomes "hot". No other controls are allowed to respond to mouse events while some control is "hot".

Once the user releases their mouse, `hotControl` gets set to `0` to indicate that other controls can respond to user input, which will be useful when we implement our GUI system, as we don't want to draw something when we're clicking on our mouse button.

 For more information on `GUIUtility.hotControl`, check out `http://docs.unity3d.com/ScriptReference/GUIUtility-hotControl.html`.

A lot of the stuff contained in this code is from reusing a lot of the aspects we learned earlier in the book, back when we did our platformer game. Yet, now we are using the same functions to work with the mouse position in the world and converting it to world space.

We use the `ScreenToWorldPoint` function to convert our mouse position from screenspace into world space with the Z position of the point being the units away from the camera we want the position to be. Since our world is at 0, we want the Z to be negative whatever the camera's Z position is.

 For more information on `ScreenToWorldPoint` check out `http://docs.unity3d.com/ScriptReference/Camera.ScreenToWorldPoint.html`.

We use this information to get the position we want to place the block at. Once we have this, we can just call `Instantiate` and create something; but, we also need to make sure we only have one object per tile, so we will use a raycast to determine if that area already has a block, and if it does, we will destroy it:

1. Now that we have all this set, let's save the file, and then exit back to the Unity editor and play the game.

2. If you select the GameController object, you'll notice that the checkbox next to the LevelEditor component is unchecked. This is because we disabled it in the Start function. We will enable it again in code later, but just for demonstration purposes, click on the check to activate it once again, and then in the Game tab, click on the screen, and right-click on areas in the level. Have a look at the following screenshot:

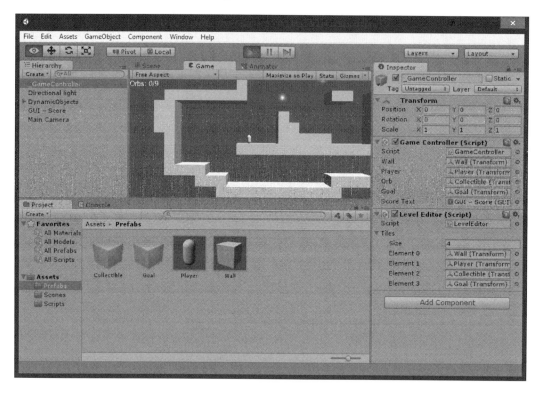

You'll notice that now we can draw walls anywhere within our scene and delete anything aside from our player!

Level editor – toggling editor, GUI, and selecting additional tiles

Now that we have the basic functionality in, it wouldn't be that enjoyable if all we could do was add and remove walls. We also want to be able to spawn collectibles and change the player's starting location. Let's work on that next:

1. Back in `MonoDevelop` in the `LevelEditor` class, we're going to want to first add in an `OnGUI` function to display the types of things we can create:

```
void OnGUI()
{
  GUILayout.BeginArea(new Rect(Screen.width - 110, 20, 100, 800));
  foreach(Transform item in tiles)
  {
    if (GUILayout.Button (item.name))
    {
      toCreate = item;

    }
  }
  GUILayout.EndArea();
}
```

2. Next, inside our `GameController` class, add the following code to our `Update` function (create the function as well if it doesn't exist in your current implementation, such as the example code):

```
void Update()
{
  if(Input.GetKeyDown("f2"))
  {
    this.gameObject.GetComponent<LevelEditor>().enabled = true;
  }
}
```

Now, if we move back to the game, and press the *F2* key, you'll see that a menu pops up, which we can then select items from. This works fine for the walls and the collectibles, but there's a bit of an issue with the player and the collectibles. Have a look at the following screenshot:

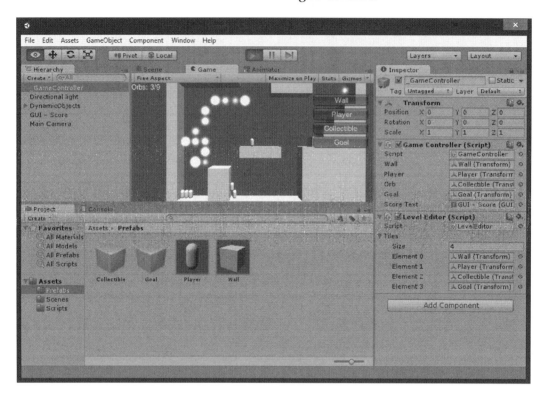

As you can see, we are spawning more players that all respond to player input, and the number of collectibles on our screen are not reflected properly in our text. We will solve both of these issues now. We will first create a new object called PlayerSpawner, which will act as the place where the player will start when the game starts, and make it such that we can only have one of them.

3. In **Project Browser**, select **Create | New Material**. Rename it to PlayerSpawn by clicking on the name of the material in the project browser, typing in the new name, and then pressing *Enter*.

4. With the PlayerSpawn object selected, set the **Shader** as **Transparent | Diffuse** so that we can make the material semitransparent. Then, change the **Main Color** property to a red color with a slight alpha. Have a look at the following screenshot:

If all goes well, it should look like the the following screenshot:

5. Now, let's create a cube to act as the visual representation of our level by going to **GameObject | Create Other | Cube**. Once the object is created, give it a name, PlayerSpawn. Switch to the **Scene** view if you haven't so that you can see the newly created object.

6. Under the **Mesh Renderer** component, set the **Materials | Element 0** property to our newly created PlayerSpawn material. Have a look at the following screenshot:

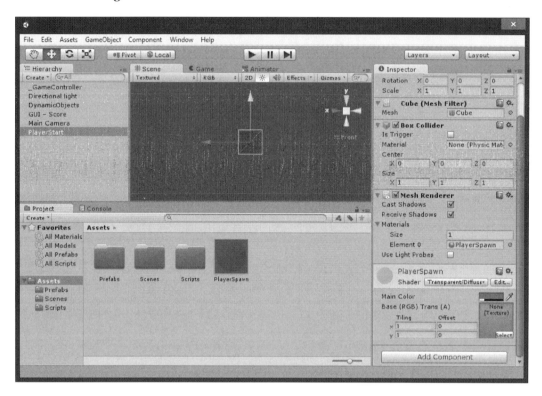

7. Next, go to the Scripts folder, and create a new C# script called PlayerStart. Once that's finished, open MonoDevelop, and use the following code:

```
using UnityEngine;
using System.Collections;

public class PlayerStart : MonoBehaviour
{
    //A reference to our player prefab
    public Transform player;
```

```
//Have we spawned yet?
public static bool spawned = false;

public static PlayerStart _instance;

// Use this for initialization
void Start ()
{
  // If another PlayerStart exists, this will replace it
  if(_instance != null)
    Destroy(_instance.gameObject);

  _instance = this;

  // Have we spawned yet? If not, spawn the player
  if(!spawned)
  {
    SpawnPlayer();
    spawned = true;
  }
}

void SpawnPlayer()
{
  Transform newObject = Instantiate(player,
                        this.transform.position,
                        Quaternion.identity) as Transform;

  newObject.name = "Player";
}

}
```

8. Back in the editor, attach our new component to the **PlayerStart** object in **Hierarchy**. Then, back in **Inspector**, set the **Player** variable to our `Player` prefab.

9. Lastly, in the **Box Collider** component, check the **Is Trigger** property.

10. Now, drag the `PlayerStart` object from **Hierarchy** to the `Prefabs` folder to make it a prefab. Then, delete the object from **Hierarchy**.

11. Next, select the _GameController object, and assign the PlayerStart prefab where you used to see the player in **Tiles | Element 1**. Save your scene, and play the game. Have a look at the following screenshot:

We can now select the **PlayerStart** object from the button and place it wherever we want, and there will always just be one. Also, once we have levels saving/loading, the code will properly spawn the player wherever the **PlayerStart** object is placed!

12. Now, to update the number of orbs we have in the level, we need to open **GameController** and add in a new function, as follows:

```
public void UpdateOrbTotals(bool reset = false)
{
  if (reset)
    orbsCollected = 0;

  GameObject[] orbs;
  orbs = GameObject.FindGameObjectsWithTag("Orb");
```

```
    orbsTotal = orbs.Length;

    scoreText.text = "Orbs: " + orbsCollected + "/" + orbsTotal;
}
```

13. Now that we have this function written, we need to call it every time we do something to modify our level. Go to the `LevelEditor` class, and add the following line to the end of our `Start` function:

```
GameController._instance.UpdateOrbTotals(true);
```

14. Then, inside the `Update` function, we'll need to add the following lines in bold:

```
void Update()
{
  // Left click - Create object
  if (Input.GetMouseButton(0) && GUIUtility.hotControl==0)
  {
    Vector3 mousePos = Input.mousePosition;

    //Set my position in the z axis to the opposite of mine.
    mousePos.z = Camera.main.transform.position.z * -1;

    Vector3 pos = Camera.main.ScreenToWorldPoint(mousePos);

    // Deal with the mouse being not exactly on a block
    int posX = Mathf.FloorToInt(pos.x +.5f);
    int posY = Mathf.FloorToInt(pos.y + .5f);

    // Convert from screenspace to worldspace using a Ray
    Ray ray = Camera.main.ScreenPointToRay(mousePos);

    // We need to check if there is an object already at
    //the position we're trying to create at
    RaycastHit hit = new RaycastHit();

    // If something within a distance of 100 in the
    //direction
    // hits something hit will get the data of the hit object.
    Physics.Raycast(ray, out hit, 100);

    if((hit.collider != null) && (hit.collider.name != "Player"))
    {
      //If it's the same, just keep the previous one
```

```
        if(toCreate.name != hit.collider.gameObject.name)
        {
            CreateBlock(tiles.IndexOf(toCreate) + 1, Mathf.
FloorToInt(hit.collider.gameObject.transform.position.x),
            Mathf.FloorToInt(hit.collider.gameObject.
                transform.position.y));

            DestroyImmediate(hit.collider.gameObject);
        }
    }
    else
    {
        CreateBlock(tiles.IndexOf(toCreate) + 1, posX, posY);
    }
    GameController._instance.UpdateOrbTotals();
}


// Right clicking - Delete object
if (Input.GetMouseButton(1) && GUIUtility.hotControl==0)
{
    Ray ray = Camera.main.ScreenPointToRay(Input.mousePosition);

    RaycastHit hit = new RaycastHit();

    Physics.Raycast(ray, out hit, 100);

    // If we hit something other than the player, we
    // want to destroy it!
    if((hit.collider != null) && (hit.collider.name != "Player"))
    {
        Destroy(hit.collider.gameObject);
    }
    GameController._instance.UpdateOrbTotals();
}

}
```

15. Save the file, save your project, and start the game. Press *F2* to open our menu and then draw. Have a look at the following screenshot:

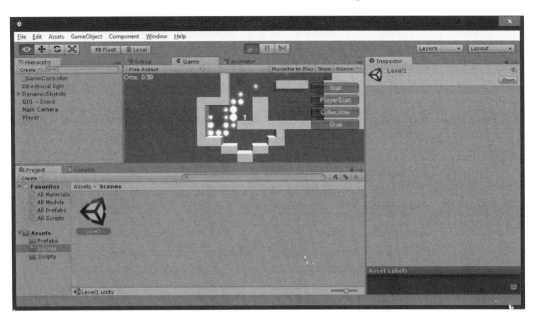

As you can see, we're now able to draw over the other object and place everything that we want for our level!

Level editor – saving/loading levels to file

Now that we have the groundwork all placed and ready, let's get to the real meat of the level editor: saving and loading! Perform the following steps:

1. Open our `LevelEditor` class in `MonoDevelop`. The first step will be to include some additional functionality at the beginning of our file:

```
//You must include these namespaces
//to use BinaryFormatter
using System;
using System.Runtime.Serialization.Formatters.Binary;
using System.IO;
```

2. The first thing we'll want to add is a variable, as follows:

```
string levelName = "Level1";
```

3. Now, we'll need to add the following code to the OnGUI function:

```
GUILayout.BeginArea(new Rect(10, 20, 100, 100));
levelName = GUILayout.TextField(levelName);
if (GUILayout.Button ("Save"))
{
  SaveLevel();
}
if (GUILayout.Button ("Load"))
{
  //If we have a file with the name typed in, load it!
  if(File.Exists(Application.persistentDataPath + "/" + levelName
+ ".lvl"))
  {
    LoadLevelFile(levelName);
    PlayerStart.spawned = false;

    // We need to wait one frame before UpdateOrbTotals
    // will work (Orbs need to have Tag assigned)
    StartCoroutine(LoadedUpdate());
  }
  else
  {
    levelName = "Error";
  }
}
if (GUILayout.Button ("Quit"))
{
  enabled = false;
}
GUILayout.EndArea();
```

4. We are missing some of these functions, so let's start with SaveLevel, as follows:

```
void SaveLevel()
{
  List<string> newLevel = new List<string>();

  for(int i = yMin; i <= yMax; i++)
  {
    string newRow = "";
    for(int j = xMin; j <= xMax; j++)
    {
      Vector3 pos = new Vector3(j, i, 0);
```

```
Ray ray = Camera.main.ScreenPointToRay(pos);
RaycastHit hit = new RaycastHit();

Physics.Raycast(ray, out hit, 100);
int l = 0;

// Will check if there is something hitting us within
// a distance of .1
Collider[] hitColliders = Physics.OverlapSphere(pos, 0.1f);

if(hitColliders.Length > 0)
{
  // Do we have a tile with the same name as this object?
  for(int k = 0; k < tiles.Count; k++)
  {
    // If so, let's save that to the string
    if(tiles[k].name == hitColliders[0].collider.gameObject.
name)
    {
      newRow += (k+1).ToString() + ",";
    }
  }
}
else
{
  newRow += "0,";
}
}
newRow += "\n";
newLevel.Add(newRow);
}
// Reverse the rows to make the final version rightside up
newLevel.Reverse();

string levelComplete = "";

foreach(string level in newLevel)
{
  levelComplete += level;
}
// This is the data we're going to be saving
print(levelComplete);
```

```
        //Save to a file
        BinaryFormatter bFormatter = new BinaryFormatter();
        FileStream file = File.Create(Application.persistentDataPath +
    "/"+ levelName + ".lvl");
        bFormatter.Serialize (file, levelComplete);
        file.Close ();

    }
```

To do this, we will go through the map, see what tiles are at a certain place, and add them to a string for each column using a list to store each of the rows. Then, we put them all together into a single string, which we could just store in `PlayerPrefs`.

However, instead of using the `PlayerPrefs` class as we did before, we will store our data in an actual file using the `FileStream` class.

FileStreams

To determine where to save our file, we will use the `Application.persistentDataPath` variable. This value will point to something differently, depending on what platform you're working with. For instance, on a Windows 8 computer, it will save to `C:\Users\YOUR_USER_NAME\AppData\LocalLow\COMPANY_NAME\PROJECT_NAME`. For more information, check out `http://docs.unity3d.com/ScriptReference/Application-persistentDataPath.html`.

For more information on `FileStreams`, check out the Microsoft Developers Network's page on it at `http://msdn.microsoft.com/en-us/library/system.io.filestream(v=vs.110).aspx`.

BinaryFormatter

But we don't want the file to be easy to read, so we'll use the `BinaryFormatter` class, which will convert our object into a byte array and be a stream of bytes, which will be much harder for potential hackers to read.

For more information on the `BinaryFormatter` class, check out the Microsoft Developers Network's page on it at `http://msdn.microsoft.com/en-us/library/system.runtime.serialization.formatters.binary.binaryformatter(v=vs.110).aspx`.

1. Now we need to add in the following functions to load the file that we'll be creating from the save functionality:

```
void LoadLevelFile(string level)
{
    // Destroy everything inside our currently level that's created
```

```
  // dynamically
  foreach(Transform child in dynamicParent.transform) {
    Destroy(child.gameObject);
  }

  BinaryFormatter bFormatter = new BinaryFormatter();
  FileStream file = File.OpenRead(Application.persistentDataPath +
"/"+ level + ".lvl");

  // Convert the file from a byte array into a string
  string levelData = bFormatter.Deserialize(file) as string;

  // We're done working with the file so we can close it
  file.Close ();

  LoadLevelFromString(levelData);

  // Set our text object to the current level.
  levelName = level;

  public void LoadLevelFromString(string content)
  {
    // Split our string by the new lines (enter)
    List <string> lines = new List <string> (content.Split
('\n'));
    // Place each block in order in the correct x and y position
    for(int i = 0; i < lines.Count; i++)
    {
      string[] blockIDs = lines[i].Split (',');
      for(int j = 0; j < blockIDs.Length - 1; j++)
      {
        CreateBlock(int.Parse(blockIDs[j]), j, lines.Count - i);
      }
    }
  }
```

2. Finally, we need to add in `LoadedUpdate` so that `Orbs` will be updated after they've been created, as follows:

```
IEnumerator LoadedUpdate()
{
  //returning 0 will make it wait 1 frame
  yield return 0;

  GameController._instance.UpdateOrbTotals(true);
}
```

3. Save the file, and exit to the editor. Save the project, and play the game! Have a look at the following screenshot:

As you can see, when we play the game you'll see a new menu appear on the left-hand side. We can now give a name to all of our files that we want, type in their name, hit **Save** to save it to a file, and then **Load** to load the data for the level if it exists! Finally, we can click on **Quit** to exit out of the editor whenever we want.

Have a look at the following screenshot:

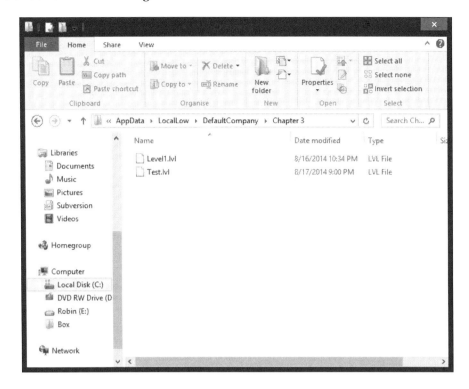

And as you can see here, the files are saved in our `Application.persistentDataPath` location!

Summary

And with that, we now have an in-game level editor and explored some of the various ways in which it's possible to save data inside Unity! This knowledge, plus exposure to the list class, should leave you ready to add additional functionality, such as this, to all of your projects!

Challenges

For those of you who want to do more with this project, there are still plenty of things you can do, especially after finishing the rest of this book. Here are some ideas to get your mind thinking:

- In the same way that we can only create one `PlayerStart`, change it so that we can only place one goal! In that same line of thinking, have the player start to be invisible when we are playing the game!

- In our first-person "shooter" game, save the player's **Position** and **Rotation** so that whenever you quit and resume the game, you start off where you were!

- Now that we have the new level editor working, change the system so that we start the game loading a level from a file instead of from the provided array!

- You may notice that at some places, collectibles are placed on top of one another. Now, this doesn't really hurt levels loaded, as when you save the level, it will only place one of them. However, should you want to fix this, you can just change the collider from a sphere collider to a box collider, as in the corners, it's not detecting that it's colliding.

- There are other additional ways to save files, such as using XML. For an example of this check out the Unity Wiki at `http://wiki.unity3d.com/index.php?title=Saving_and_Loading_Data:_XmlSerializer`.

8
Finishing Touches

We've come a long way, and now we have a series of completed projects! But, taking the time to get these projects out into the world is just as important. Playing the game in the editor is nice and all, but actually getting the game as its own standalone thing has a special feel to it that you can't duplicate in the editor.

And once you get the game published, you can just give someone a `.zip` file with your game, but you spent quality time on your project and want to give it the respect that it deserves.

People notice the polish that you put into your game and the little things, such as an installer, can help to get players into the mood of your project early on and see your game as a professional title.

Project overview

In this chapter, we're going to learn all about exporting our game from Unity and then creating an installer so that we can give it to all of our friends, family, and prospective customers!

Your objectives

This project will be split into a number of tasks. It will be a simple step-by-step process from beginning to end. Here is the outline of our tasks:

- Setting up the build settings
- Customizing your exported project via the player settings
- Building an installer for Windows

In this chapter, we will be using one of the projects that we created in the previous chapters, specifically the `Twinstick Shooter` project that we worked on in *Chapter 1, 2D Twin-stick Shooter, Chapter 2, Creating GUIs,* and *Chapter 7, Creating Save Files in Unity.* You may continue with your previous projects or pick up a copy along with the assets for this chapter from the example code provided for this book on Packt Publishing's website at `https://www.packtpub.com/books/content/support`.

In addition, the complete project and source files are located there for you to check if you have any questions or need clarification.

Setting up the build settings

There are many times during development that you may want to see what your game looks like if you build it outside of the editor. It can give you a sense of accomplishment; I know, I felt that way the first time I pushed a build to a console devkit. Whether it's for PC, Mac, Linux, web player, mobile, or console, we all have to go through the same menu, the **Build Settings** menu. We perform the following steps:

1. We are going to first open our `Twinstick Shooter` project that we created back in *Chapter 1, 2D Twin-stick Shooter, Chapter 2, Creating GUIs,* and *Chapter 7, Creating Save Files in Unity.* Open up your main menu scene (in the example code, it is saved as `Main_Menu`). Have a look at the following screenshot:

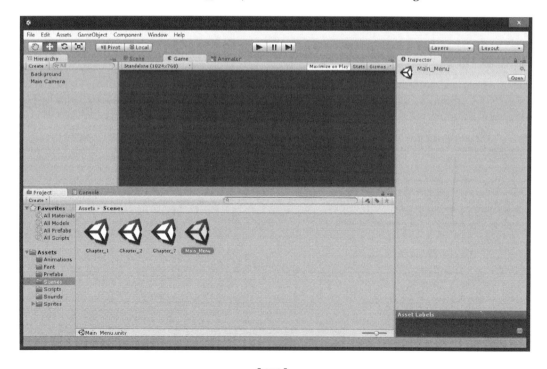

2. To access our **Build Settings** menu, we will need to navigate to **File | Build Settings** from the top menu (or press *Ctrl + Shift + B*). Have a look at the following screenshot:

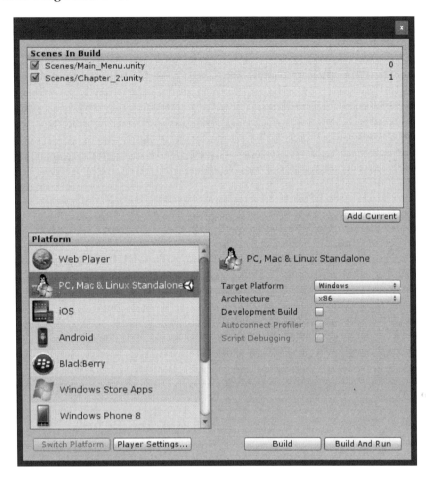

3. If you have been following thoroughly from *Chapter 2, Creating GUIs*, you should see two icons in the **Scenes In Build** section. If you have not, click on the **Add Current** button.

Another way to add levels to your build is to just drag-and-drop them from the project browser. It's also important to note that you can also drag them around to order them however you want. The level that is at index 0 will be the one that the game starts with.

4. Now, we are going to use the map that we created in *Chapter 7, Creating Save Files in Unity*, so left-click on the **Chapter_2** scene, and press the *Delete* key to remove it.

5. Then open the **Chapter_7** map, go back to the **Build Settings** menu, and click on **Add Current** again; alternatively, you can drag-and-drop the scene files as well.

6. Finally, we no longer want to open up the **Chapter_2** level, so open up our `MainMenuGUI.cs` script in MonoDevelop, and change the 2 to 7 in the `LoadLevel` function call.

 For future projects, you may make a string variable to hold the name of the level for the button to go to, and just change it inside the **Inspector** tab.

7. Once you're ready, select a platform from the bottom-left corner menu. The Unity logo shows which one you're currently compiling for. We're going to compile for Windows now, so if it is currently not set to **PC, Mac & Linux Standalone**, select that, and click on the **Switch Platform** button.

8. Once you have all this set up, click on the **Build** button. Once this is done, it will ask you for a name and a location to put the game in. I'm going to name it `TwinstickShooter` and put it in an `Export` folder located in the same directory as the `Assets` and `Library` folder. Afterward, hit **Save**. Have a look at the following screenshot:

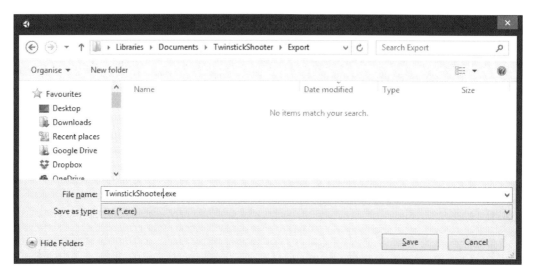

9. You may need to wait a bit, but as soon as it finishes, it will open up the folder with your new game. Have a look at the following screenshot:

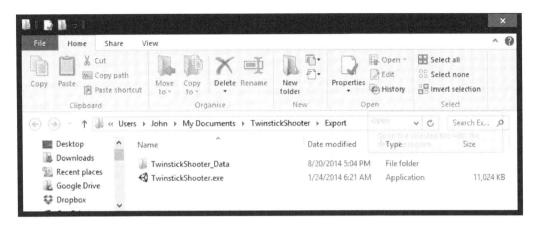

When building for Windows, you should get something like the preceding screenshot. We have the executable, but we also have a data folder that contains all the assets for our application (right now called `TwinstickShooter_Data`). You must include the data folder with your game, or it will not run. This is a slight pain, but later on in this chapter, we will create an installer so that we can put it on a computer without any hassle.

If you build for Mac, it will bundle the app and data all together, so once you export it, all you need to give people is the application.

If you are interested in submitting your Mac game to the Mac App Store, there is a nice tutorial about doing just that at `http://www.conlanrios.com/2013/12/signing-unity-game-for-mac-app-store.html`.

If you double-click on the `.exe` file to run the game, you'll be brought to the following startup menu, as shown in the following screenshot:

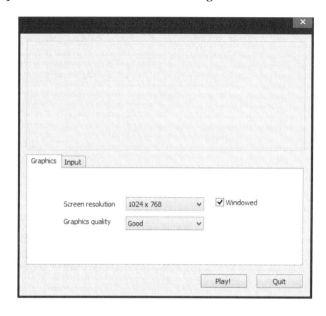

This will allow players to customize their **Screen Resolution** values as well as other options, such as what buttons to use for input. I personally feel this menu makes projects look more unprofessional, so I'll be teaching you how to remove this as well.

Anyway, once we click on the **Play!** button, we'll be taken to the proper game screen, as shown in the following screenshot:

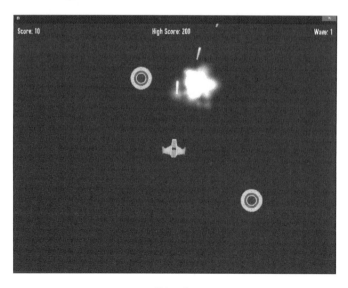

And it's working great. We can work at any resolution that we choose, and all the menus are functioning as well!

 For more information on publishing and specific things to look out for, check out the following link:

`http://docs.unity3d.com/Manual/PublishingBuilds.html`

Customizing your exported project via the player settings

Now that we know what happens by default, let's take some time to customize the project to make it look as nice as possible. The **PlayerSettings** section is where we can define different parameters for each platform that we want to put the game onto. We perform the following steps:

1. To open the player settings, you can either click on the **Player Settings...** button from the **Build Settings** menu or navigate to **Edit** | **Project Settings** | **Player**. Have a look at the following screenshot:

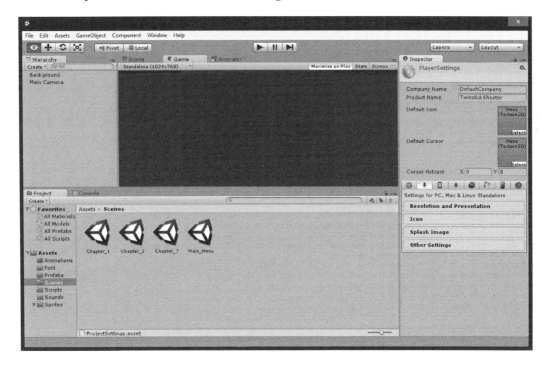

The player settings are actually shown in the **Inspector** tab. There are some key properties at the top, which are cross-platform, which means that they will apply to all platforms (or rather, that they will be the defaults that you can later override).

2. Now, in the Example Code folder, you'll find a cursor_hand image. Drag-and-drop that image to the **Assets/Sprites** location of the project browser. Once there, select the image, and in the **Inspector** tab, change the **Texture Type** value to Cursor.

3. Then, in the **PlayerSettings** section, drag-and-drop the **cursor_hand** image into the **Default Cursor** property and the **playerShip** image into the **Default Icon** property. Have a look at the following screenshot:

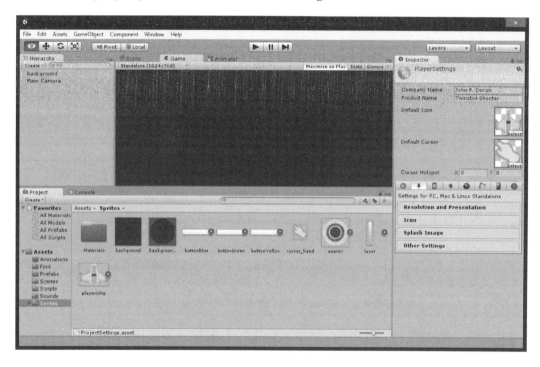

 If you want your game to have multiple cursors or change cursors at runtime, the Cursor.SetCursor function will be quite helpful. For more information on that, check out http://docs.unity3d.com/ScriptReference/Cursor.SetCursor.html.

4. On your computer, in the `Example Code` folder, move the `ConfigBanner` image into the `Sprites` folder. Then, under **PlayerSettings**, click on the **Splash Image** section to open the **Config Dialog Banner** property, which you should set to our newly imported image.

 If you want to create a config dialog banner of your own, make sure you make the image 432 x 200 pixels in size or smaller.

5. Next, you'll need to decide whether you want to display the display resolution dialog or not. If you want to keep it, skip this step. Otherwise, open up the **Resolution and Presentation** section, and under **Standalone Player Options**, set the **Display Resolution Dialog** value to `Disabled`.

6. With that finished, navigate to **File | Save Project**, and build the game once more, overwriting the previously created one! Depending on your choice, you'll see the menu shown in the following screenshot:

Or just jump straight into the game. Have a look at the following screenshot:

The game already looks much better and more polished than before! There are a number of other things that you can do, such as restrict the kind of aspect ratios your game runs or resolutions, or force windowed, or fullscreen. I leave it to you to play around and get your project as nice as possible before moving onward!

 For more information on the properties for all the different platforms that are available, check out http://docs.unity3d.com/Manual/ class-PlayerSettings.html.

Building an installer for Windows

Just as I mentioned previously, having a separate Data folder with our .exe file is somewhat of a pain. Rather than give people a .zip file and hope they extract it all and then keep everything in the same folder, I will have the process be automatic and give the person an opportunity to have it installed just like a professional game. With that in mind, I'm going to go over a free way to create a Windows installer, as follows:

1. The first thing we need to do is get our setup program. For our demonstration, I will be using Jordan Russell's Inno Setup software. Go to http://jrsoftware.org/isinfo.php, and click on the **Download Inno Setup** link. Have a look at the following screenshot:

2. From there, click on the **Stable Release** button, and select the **isetup-5.5.5.exe**
   file. Once it's finished, double-click on the executable to open it, clicking on
   the **Run** button. If it shows a security warning message, click on **Yes** to allow
   the changes to take place. Have a look at the following screenshot:

3. From there, run through the installation, making sure to uncheck the **Install Inno Setup Preprocessor** option since we won't be using it. Upon finishing this task, make sure that **Launch Inno Setup** is checked, and then click on the **Finish** button.

4. When you open the program, it will look somewhat like the following screenshot:

5. From there, choose **Create a new script file using the Script Wizard** and then click on **OK**.

6. From there, click on the **Next** button, and you'll come to the **Application Information** section. Fill in your information, and then click on **Next**. Have a look at the following screenshot:

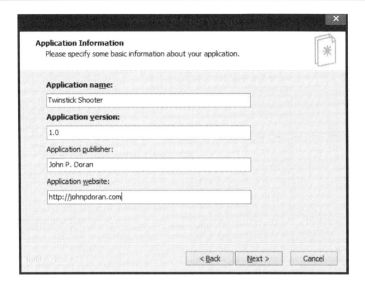

7. Next, you'll come to some information about the application folder. In general, you will not want to change this information, so I will click on **Next**.

8. From here, we'll be brought to the **Application Files** section where we need to specify the files we want to install. Under the **Application main executable file:** section, click on **Browse** to go to the location of your `Export` folder, where the `.exe` file is present, select it, and click on **Open**. Have a look at the following screenshot:

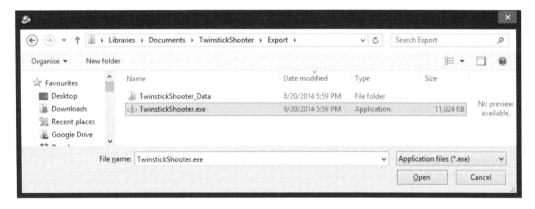

9. Now, we need to add in the data folder. Click on the **Add Folder...** button, select the data folder, and then click on **OK**. Have a look at the following screenshot:

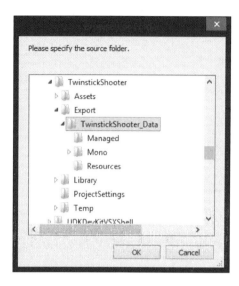

10. It will then ask if files in subfolders should be included as well. Select **Yes**. Then, select the folder in the **Other Applications file** section, and click on the **Edit** button. From there, set the **Destination subfolder** property to the same name as your data folder, click on **OK**, and then click on **Next**. Have a look at the following screenshot:

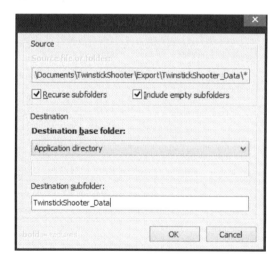

11. In the next menu, check whichever options you want, and then click on **Next**. Have a look at the following screenshot:

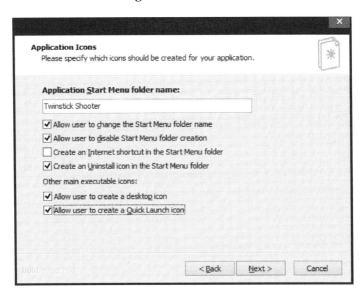

12. Now, you'll have an option to include a license file, such as EULA or whatever your publisher may require, and any personal stuff you want to tell your users before or after installation. The program accepts .txt and .rtf files. Once you're ready, click on the **Next** button. Have a look at the following screenshot:

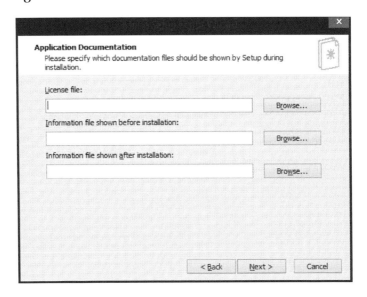

13. Next, they'll allow you to specify what languages you want the installation to work for. I'll just go for English, but you can add more. Afterward, click on **Next**.

14. Finally, we need to set where we want the setup to be placed as well as the icon for it or a password. I created a new folder on my desktop called `TwinstickSetup` and used it. Then, click on **Next**, as shown in the following screenshot:

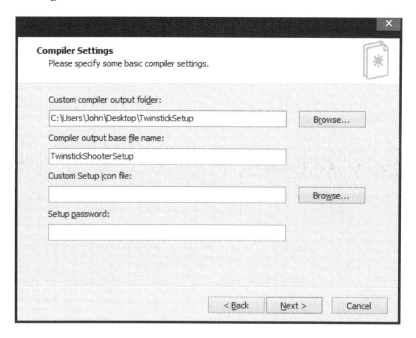

 If you want to include a custom icon but don't have a `.ico` file, you can use the `http://www.icoconverter.com/` link.

15. Next, you'll be brought to the successfully completed script wizard screen. After this, click on **Finish**. Have a look at the following screenshot:

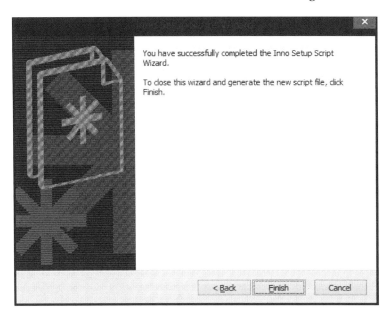

16. Now, it will ask you if you want to compile the script. Select **Yes**. It'll also ask you if you want to save your script. You'll also want to say **Yes**, and I saved it to the same folder as my exporting folder. It'll take a minute or two, but as soon as you see **Finished** in the console window, it should be ready. Have a look at the following screenshot:

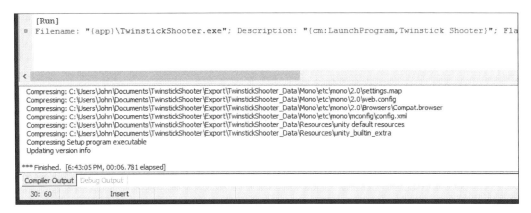

17. If you go to the same place as your `Export` folder, you should see your installer, as shown in the following screenshot:

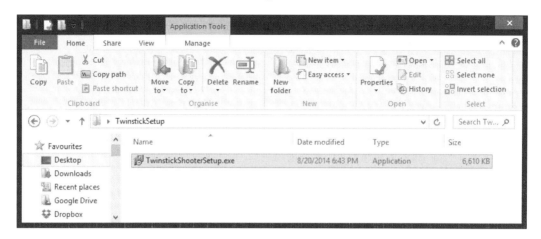

18. If you run it, it'll look somewhat like the following screenshot:

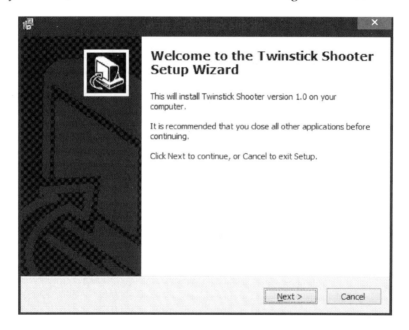

And with that, we now have a working installer for our game!

Summary

And with that, our game has been compiled with the possibility of running on multiple platforms (including the Web), and we have learned how to create an installer for Windows! This information will serve you quite well when you create projects of your own to get them out to as many people as possible!

Challenges

For those of you who want to do more with this project, there are still plenty of things you can do, especially after finishing the rest of this book. Here are some ideas to get your mind thinking:

- There are still a number of things you can do with Inno Setup. You may wish to do more things, such as change the image on the right-hand side of the installer welcome screen. For more information on that, check out the documentation for Inno Setup at `http://jrsoftware.org/ishelp/`.

- Now that you know how to export to PC, Mac, and Linux, you can try exporting your game to Android as well! You'll need to have the Android SDK and a few other things to take into consideration, but it's not too bad at all. For more information on doing Android development, check out `http://docs.unity3d.com/Manual/android-GettingStarted.html`.

- You may also be interested in getting your game onto iOS. For information on iOS, check out `http://docs.unity3d.com/Manual/iphone-GettingStarted.html`.

9
Creating GUIs Part 2 – Unity's New GUI System

Since the release of Unity 4.6, there are now some additional UI tools that have been added to make elements much more visual and easy to place, letting you know exactly what you're going to get.

Everything that we did in *Chapter 2*, *Creating GUIs*, is still quite relevant and works completely for now, and for the foreseeable future. In this chapter, we are going to see how to create some new elements using these new tools so that you can compare and contrast when it's a good idea to use one or the other.

The new UI is actually created inside our scene. We've learned how to create UI elements by calling code several times a frame during the `OnGUI` loop. The old UI system is still great to know, as it is still the backbone of the UI system, and will for the foreseeable future still be the means by which you can extend Unity's editor.

However, the new UI system uses a lot of the new things that were added when Unity added in their native 2D tools, and it is great for the more visually inclined to see exactly what they're going to get in their final project.

Project overview

In this chapter, we will do some of the cool things that we can do with Unity's new GUI system.

Your objectives

This project will be split into a number of tasks. It will be a simple step-by-step process from beginning to end. Here is the outline of our tasks:

- Creating health bars
- Adding in text
- Working with buttons and anchors

In this chapter, we will use one of the projects we created in the previous chapters, specifically the First Person Shooter project that we worked on in *Chapter 4, First Person Shooter Part 1 – Creating Exterior Environments, Chapter 5, First Person Shooter Part 2 – Creating Interior Environments*, and *Chapter 6, First Person Shooter Part 3 – Implementing Gameplay and AI*. You can continue with your previous projects or pick up a copy along with the assets for this chapter from the example code provided for this book on Packt's website at `https://www.packtpub.com/books/content/support`.

In addition, the completed project and source files are located here for you to check, if you have any questions or need clarification.

Project setup

For this chapter, you will need to use Unity 4.6 or later. At the time of writing, Unity 4.6 is available in beta, which can be downloaded from `http://unity3d.com/unity/beta/4.6`. Specifically, I used Unity 4.6 Beta 17.

Though I have experienced no problems with the Unity 4.6 Beta version, it's recommended that you do not use it for content you plan to ship soon, and it can be used for testing purposes only, but the steps that I take in this chapter should carry over when 4.6 is officially released.

That being said, I do recommend installing both the stable version of Unity and the Beta version. However, if you just run the Unity Beta installer, it will overwrite your previous version. For information on installing multiple versions of Unity, check out `http://docs.unity3d.com/Manual/InstallingMultipleVersionsofUnity.html`.

Creating health bars

One of the advantages that the new UI system has over the previous one is the fact that you can place UI elements in either 2D or 3D as an overlay to the screen, just as we did before or as part of the game world itself. With that in mind, I thought a good first thing to implement would be health bars above our enemy's heads from our shooter project that we worked on in *Chapter 4, First Person Shooter Part 1 – Creating Exterior Environments, Chapter 5, First Person Shooter Part 2 – Creating Interior Environments*, and *Chapter 6, First Person Shooter Part 3 – Implementing Gameplay and AI*. We perform the following steps:

1. We are going to first open our first person shooter project we created back in *Chapter 4, First Person Shooter Part 1 – Creating Exterior Environments, Chapter 5, First Person Shooter Part 2 – Creating Interior Environments*, and *Chapter 6, First Person Shooter Part 3 – Implementing Gameplay and AI*. Open up your exterior scene (in the example code, saved as `Chapter4_Exterior`). Once loaded, double-click on the **Ghost** object in order to center it on the screen. For visibility's sake, toggle the lighting off by clicking on the sun icon to the right of the 2D option under the **Scene** tab. Have a look at the following screenshot:

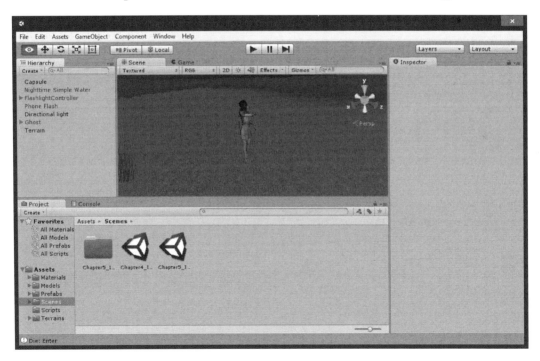

2. The first thing we need to do to add UI elements using the new UI system is create a canvas. To do that, navigate to **GameObject | UI | Canvas**. Have a look at the following screenshot:

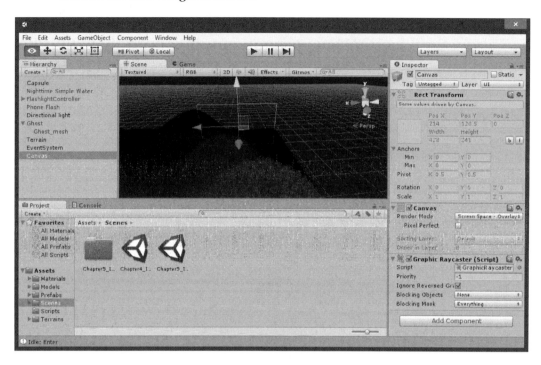

You can think of the canvas as a holder for how a group of UI elements will be rendered. It's possible to have more than one canvas in a scene but to have an element of the new UI, you will have to place it onto a canvas.

 If you try to create a UI element, one doesn't already exist, one will be created for you automatically, and the element will be placed as a child.

When we create a **Canvas** object, we are given a new module called **Rect** that replaces the **Transform** module we've been used to. This allows us to scale, rotate, and modify the UI using one tool, which is the newly created one on the right-hand side, next to the scaling tool in the top-left corner.

 For more information on the **Rect** component, check out the tutorial video at http://unity3d.com/learn/tutorials/modules/beginner/ui/rect-transform.

3. Double-click on the **Canvas** object in the **Hierarchy** tab so that we can see the whole object. Now, one of the first things you'll probably notice is that the canvas is really, really big. That's because the size of the canvas is based on the size of what's displayed on the **Game** tab, because the **Render Mode** property is set to **Screen Space – Overlay** by default.

4. Change the **Render Mode** property to **World Space**, because we want it to be in the game world. You should notice now that the **Rect Transform** properties are no longer greyed out, showing us that now we are allowed to modify them. Have a look at the following screenshot:

Instead of just being placed in front of everything, this mode changes our canvas to be an actual object in the world, which we can place wherever we want but can still interact with. It's like a television or computer monitor in our game world, onto which the elements we place in the canvas will be printed.

5. Since it's in the world now, we're going to want to adjust the size of our **Rect** module to handle just the content that we want in the world. In this instance, change the **Width** property to `130` and the **Height** property to `20`.

> You should change the width and height to fit everything in your UI. In this instance, we are just going to have a scrollbar and some text, so I know the size of it is 130 x 20. This value can be modified at anytime as long as the **Render Mode** property is set to **World Space**.

6. We want to place the health bar above our enemies' heads, so we should make this canvas a child of the **Ghost** object. To do that, click and hold the **Canvas** object in the **Hierarchy** tab, and drop it on top of the **Ghost** object.

7. As we already know, children of an object have a position that is based on the parent. So, with that in mind, we're going to use a trick to place the canvas directly on the enemy. To do that, right-click on the **Rect Transform** component on the **Canvas** object, and then select **Reset Position**. Have a look at the following screenshot:

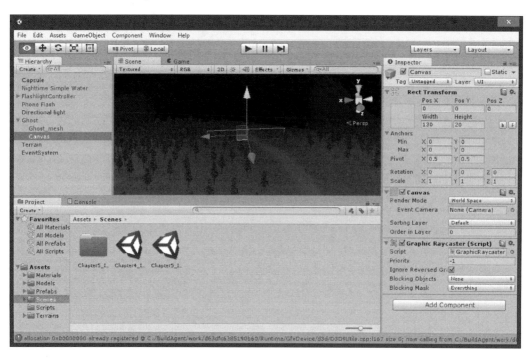

8. We're getting there, but the object is still way too big for what we want to do. But we don't want to modify the width and height. In this instance, making use of the **Scale** property would be a great solution. Change the **Scale** property to `.010` in all of the axes. If you double-click, you'll see that the object is now placed at the bottom of our enemy. Have a look at the following screenshot:

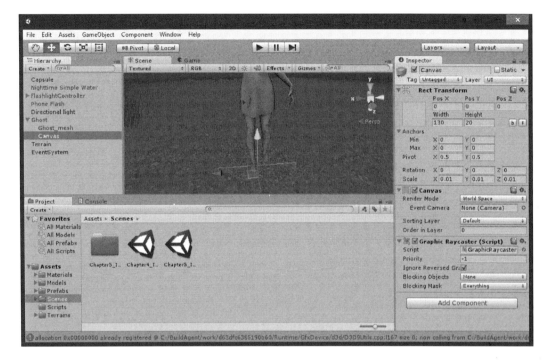

9. Now that we have this, let's use the translate tool and move the canvas so that it's over our enemy's head, or you can just change the **Pos Y** property to 2.5. Have a look at the following screenshot:

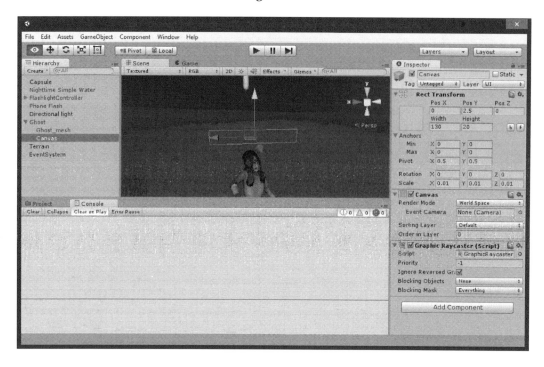

10. This looks pretty nice, but let's add in something so that we can actually see it. For our purposes, we are going to use a slider as the basis of our lifebar. To do that, with the **Canvas** object selected, navigate to **GameObject | UI | Slider**, as shown in the following screenshot.

A **slider** is a graphic with a handle that the user can drag to change a value between a minimum value and a maximum value. In this instance, we are using a slider for its display purpose rather than the interaction that it offers, but let's first see what it does. Have a look at the following screenshot:

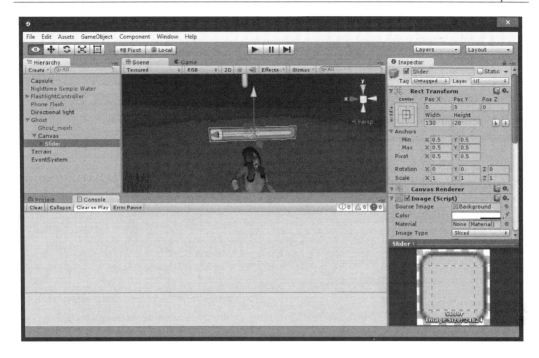

Now, if you play the game, you'll notice that we can jump into the game and actually change the slider. Have a look at the following screenshot:

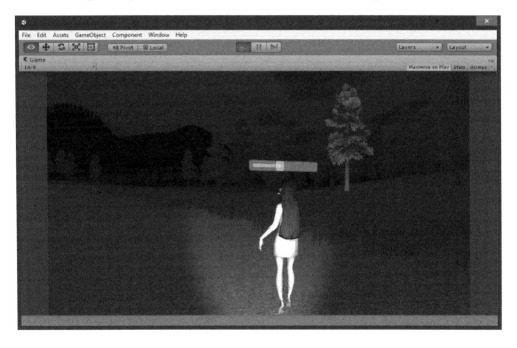

Now, this is really cool if you want to actually create menus in your world like in the Dead Space series, but we don't really want the player to change that, as we'll be setting it in the code.

11. Expand the **Slider** object in the **Hierarchy** tab to see the **Fill Area** and **Handle Slide Area** objects. Delete the **Handle Slide Area** object, as we won't need it.

12. After that, expand the **Fill Area** object, and select the **Fill** object. From there, set the **Color** property on the **Image** component to a green color to make it look more like a health bar:

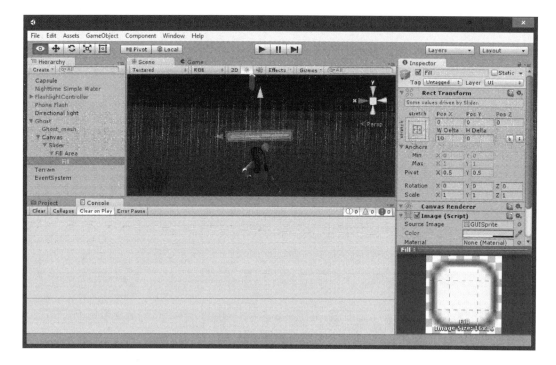

13. Now, back in the **Slider** object in the **Slider** component, uncheck the **Interactable** property. Now, the object will not be able to receive the mouse clicks to change its value.

14. We now have the objects created, but there's no interaction as of yet. With that in mind, we're going to need to jump into some code, specifically in our `EnemyBehaviour` script. Open it in `MonoDevelop`.

15. From there, the first thing we're going to need to do is add a new item to the top of the code in our `using` section, as follows:

```
using UnityEngine.UI;
```

16. After this, we also need to add a new variable, as follows:

```
// Reference for drawing the healthbar
public Slider healthBar;
```

17. Now, we need to add a new function, which we will call whenever this needs to be updated:

```
private void UpdateHealthbar()
{
    healthBar.value = currentHealth/health;
}
```

In this example, the `value` property of the health bar is a value from `0` to `1`, which is how much of the slider should be filled in.

18. Now, we need to add a call to this function in both the `Start` and `TakeDamage` functions:

```
UpdateHealthbar();
```

19. Next, save your file, move back to Unity, and assign the **Slider** object to the **Health Bar** property. Have a look at the following screenshot:

20. After this, save your scene, and click on the play icon! The following
    screenshot comes up:

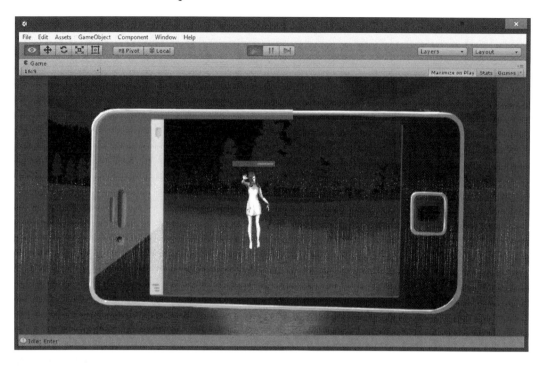

The health bar works, and we now have an easy way to tell how well our shots are
damaging enemies!

Adding in text

In addition to placing the health bar, to get some experience using text, let's use that
as well:

1. With the **Canvas** object selected, create a text object by navigating to
   GameObject | UI | Text.

2. Now, it may be hard to see it being added at first, so let's first change the color of the text. Select the **Text** object, and go to its **Text** component. Once there, change the **Color** property to white:

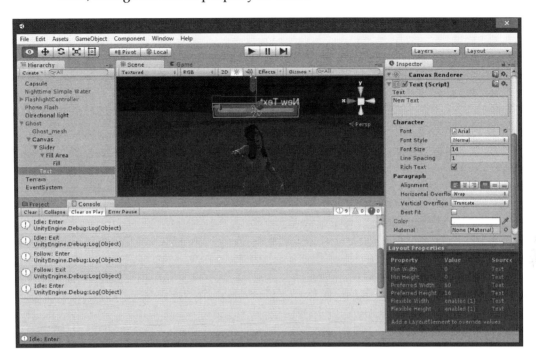

 In the new UI system, objects are drawn in order, which means that if the text object was before the slider, the slider would cover the text. However, you can drag objects into whichever order you want.

3. At this point, you'll notice that the text is actually backwards. Fixing this is very simple; just change the **Rect Transform** module on it to have a **Y Rotation** value of 180.

 Make sure this is done on the **Text** object, or your health will go down from right to left rather than left to right.

4. For our purposes, we will have this be displayed in the center of our object. To do this, we can just set the **Alignment** property to the center, both vertically and horizontally, as shown in the following screenshot:

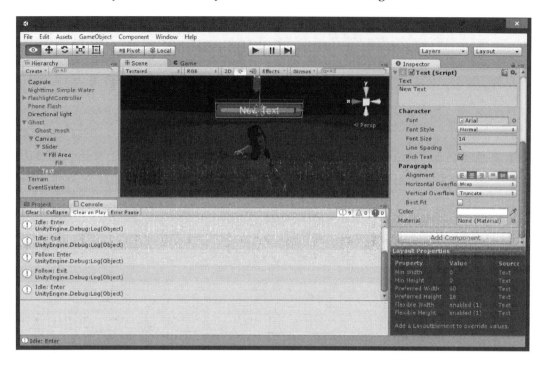

5. You can modify the **Text** property of the **Text** component, and it will change what is being displayed, which is great to prototype things out before we set them in the code. For example, right now, I can change the value to 100/100, as shown in the screenshot following the next paragraph of text.

   This is a great start, but there are still two problems that we will need to solve. First, the text isn't being updated when the health changes. Secondly, when we start the game and go towards the enemy, the health shows up backwards, and when the character moves, we have to watch the UI turn with the enemy.

Thankfully, we can fix this by turning the canvas to always face the player, which is similar to how a billboard works in the particle and terrain placement systems.

6. Open up our `EnemyBehaviour` script once again in `MonoDevelop`. First, we need to create a new variable for our text:

```
// Reference to the textbox
  public Text healthText;
```

7. Now, add the following line to the end of the `TakeDamage` function:

```
healthText.text = ((int)currentHealth).ToString() + "/" +
  health.ToString();
```

8. Finally, we need to have the canvas always face us. To do that, we will add in the `Update` function, as follows:

```
public void Update()
{
// Going to move the Canvas so that it moves both the
//slider and the text
```

```
healthBar.transform.parent.GetComponent<RectTransform>().Lo
okAt(
Camera.main.gameObject.transform
);
}
```

To use the **Rect Transform** component, you can cast the transform, as shown in the following information box:

```
(RectTransform)transform;
```

Or you can call `GetComponent` for the relevant component, as follows:

```
GetComponent<RectTransform>;
```

9. Save your script, and go back to the Unity editor. Once there, assign the **Health Text** property to the `Text` object. Finally, hit the **Apply** button under **Prefab** so that our other ghosts can have this added functionality as well.

10. Save your scene, and play the game! The following screenshot comes up:

At this point, we now have the health bar working exactly the way we want to and can see that setting the text object is almost exactly the same as doing it with the old GUI tools!

Working with buttons and anchors

Now that we have the health bars working, let's tackle something similar to what we did before, in creating a simple HUD with a reset button. We'll also learn how to make our things look great at any resolution. We will need to perform the following steps:

1. Let's start off with creating yet another canvas by navigating to **GameObject | UI | Canvas**. In this case, we want this canvas to cover our entire screen no matter which camera we are using, so this time we will keep the **Render Mode** property at **Screen Space – Overlay**. In order to differentiate from our last one, I will rename the canvas game object to HUD.

2. With the **HUD** object selected, next we will create a button by navigating to **GameObject | UI | Button**.

   If we just play the game now, you'll notice that the button will appear, but it will seem like it's not anywhere in particular.

3. For this example, I want to place this button in the top-left corner of my screen. Double-click on the **Button** object to center the camera on it. Once you've done that, right-click on the camera gizmo in the top-right corner, and set it to use the **Back** camera option. Have a look at the following screenshot:

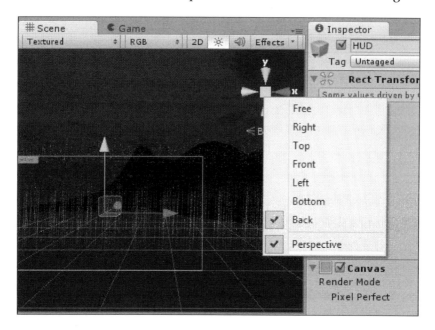

4. With that done, to the right of the scale tool on the toolbar, you'll see a new option of the **Rect** tool. With it selected, click inside the button (but not on the blue circle), and drag it over to the top-left corner. Have a look at the following screenshot:

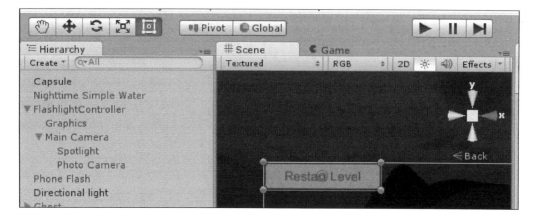

The **Rect** tool works almost exactly like 2D tools, so you can scale, move, and rotate the elements all in one tool instead of moving through others.

The following screenshot shows the working of the **Rect** tool:

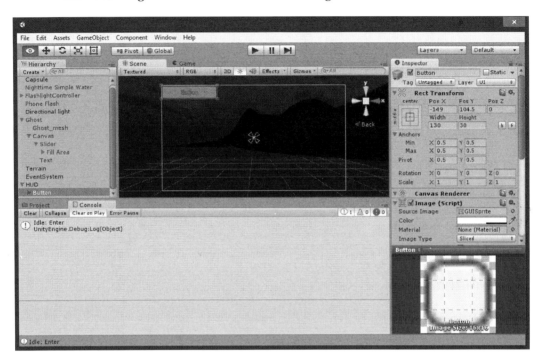

5. This shows that you want the button there, and if you switch to the **Game** tab, it will look like it's working correctly. But if you click on the play button and change the resolution, you'll see that the button doesn't move. Have a look at the following screenshot:

6. To fix this, we will need to use anchors. Anchors work similarly to how we moved the older GUI system's elements, except that if you click on the little box in the center, you'll have some helpful graphics to help you see what values to set the pivots and anchors to. So, click on the anchor box, and select the top-left corner anchor. Have a look at the following screenshot:

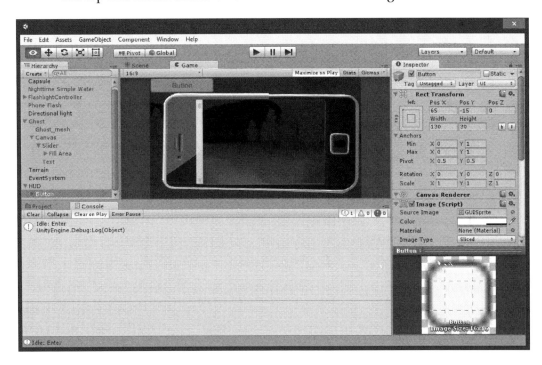

 If you hold down the *Alt* key while selecting an anchor, it will automatically move your object as well.

7.   Now, let's change the button's text by expanding the **Button** object and selecting the **Text** object inside. Once inside, change the **Text** value to `Restart Level`. Have a look at the screenshot following the next information box:

 You do not have to have the **Text** object if your button doesn't need it. In fact, you can also include images or any other UI element to be part of your image.

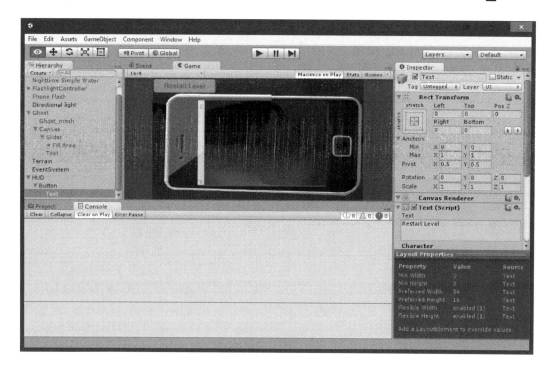

Finally, we need to actually implement the action.

As you may have noticed, when we created a canvas, there was another game object that was created called **EventSystem**. When the game starts, it will look at these input modules and decide how to handle different types of inputs.

The **EventSystem** game object will determine when events are triggered, such as the `OnClick` event, which is called when we press and release our mouse over the button we just created (which is different from how the old GUI system worked).

For more information on the **EventSystem** game object, check out `http://unity3d.com/learn/tutorials/modules/beginner/ui/ui-events-and-event-triggers`.

If you select our **Button** object, you'll see a list of actions at the bottom that will be executed when the button is clicked on, without having to write any additional code to do so.

You can add additional events to be triggered from the UI by adding an Event Trigger component.

We perform the following steps:

1. Click on the **+** button on the **OnClick** section of the **Button** component to add a new action to be called when the button is clicked on. Here, we'll see some options allowing us to pick an object and then call a function that is on that object.

2. We currently don't have a reset function to call, so let's add that in really quickly. Go to the `Scripts` folder, and create a new C# script called `Events`. Then open it up in `MonoDevelop`.

3. Once in `MonoDevelop`, replace the file with the following code:

```
using UnityEngine;
using System.Collections;

public class Events : MonoBehaviour
{

    // Restarts the current level
    public void RestartLevel ()
    {
        Application.LoadLevel(Application.loadedLevel);
    }

}
```

4. Save the file, and attach the script onto the **FlashlightController** object.

5. After this, go back to the **Button** object, and drag-and-drop the
    FlashlightController object into the left-hand side of the **OnClick**
    section. Once there, click on the right-hand side, and navigate to
    Events | RestartLevel. Have a look at the screenshot following the
    next information box:

In addition to calling functions, you can also modify
properties in this way as long as they are of the basic types.

6. Save your scene, and then hit play to take a look at what we've done:

Now, when we hit the **Restart Level** button, the level will restart! Excellent!

 For more information on the UI buttons, such as how to add animations between states, please visit http://unity3d.com/ learn/tutorials/modules/beginner/ui/ui-button.

We still have a bit left to do. You see, this looks nice now; but if we were to use a really large screen (or a retina display), the button will be extremely small. Have a look at the following screenshot:

To solve this, we can use the **ReferenceResolution** component for the canvas we'd like to scale.

7. With the **HUD** canvas selected, add in a reference resolution by navigating to **Component | Layout | Reference Resolution**.

8. Save your scene once more, and play the game again! The following screenshot shows the game screen:

Now, the canvas will scale appropriately based on the resolution provided!

Summary

And now, we have a solid foundation that we can expand upon to build things using the new Unity GUI system. I could write an entire book on how to create user interfaces, but in the meantime, I have some additional resources that may be beneficial as you go on from here! At this point, we also have all the knowledge we need to create a wide array of various gameplay projects from here on! You've worked in 2D and 3D; you've built levels in many different ways; you've programmed three complete games; and on top of that, you've learned about both of Unity's UI systems, one of which isn't even out yet! This may be the end of the book; but it's only the start of your Unity journey!

Additional resources

As this is still in beta, there are not too many official resources that have been written about the UI system as of this writing, but there are some video lessons that are available at `http://unity3d.com/learn/tutorials/modules/beginner/ui`.

However, the Unity forums have a very active community, including Unity developers, who are happy to answer questions that developers may have. There is a specific place to ask about the new UI system at `http://forum.unity3d.com/forums/developer-preview-4-6-beta.60/`.

There is also a set of example projects, which have a number of examples showing how to use some of the aspects of the system at `http://forum.unity3d.com/threads/ui-example-project.263418/#post-1744107`.

For those interested in seeing some additional things to make your life easier when working with Unity 4.6, there is an excellent thread on the Unity forums with some additional resources at `http://forum.unity3d.com/threads/scripts-useful-4-6-scripts-collection.264161/`.

Challenges

For those of you who want to do more with this project, there are still plenty of things you can do, especially after finishing the rest of this book. Here are some ideas to get your mind thinking:

- Redo the UI that we did in *Chapter 2, Creating GUIs*, using the new UI system to note the similarities and differences between them.

- Create a second button below the current one we created. Rather than positioning it by hand, use the **Vertical Layout Group** component. Spend time in the in-progress script reference (`http://docs.unity3d.com/460/Documentation/ScriptReference/index.html`) and manual (`http://docs.unity3d.com/460/Documentation/Manual/`) for the latest version of the documentation in progress.

> These links may expire once 4.6 is released. If that's the case, remove the /460 section, and they should work fine to get a better foundation at all of the new components created for the new UI system!

Index

About Packt Publishing

Packt, pronounced 'packed', published its first book "*Mastering phpMyAdmin for Effective MySQL Management*" in April 2004 and subsequently continued to specialize in publishing highly focused books on specific technologies and solutions.

Our books and publications share the experiences of your fellow IT professionals in adapting and customizing today's systems, applications, and frameworks. Our solution based books give you the knowledge and power to customize the software and technologies you're using to get the job done. Packt books are more specific and less general than the IT books you have seen in the past. Our unique business model allows us to bring you more focused information, giving you more of what you need to know, and less of what you don't.

Packt is a modern, yet unique publishing company, which focuses on producing quality, cutting-edge books for communities of developers, administrators, and newbies alike. For more information, please visit our website: www.packtpub.com.

Writing for Packt

We welcome all inquiries from people who are interested in authoring. Book proposals should be sent to author@packtpub.com. If your book idea is still at an early stage and you would like to discuss it first before writing a formal book proposal, contact us; one of our commissioning editors will get in touch with you.

We're not just looking for published authors; if you have strong technical skills but no writing experience, our experienced editors can help you develop a writing career, or simply get some additional reward for your expertise.

PUBLISHING

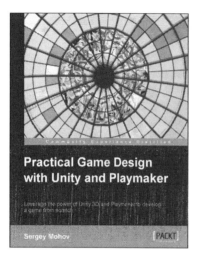

Practical Game Design with Unity and Playmaker

ISBN: 978-1-84969-810-8   Paperback: 122 pages

Leverage the power of Unity 3D and Playmaker to develop a game from scratch

1.   Create artificial intelligence for a game using Playmaker.

2.   Learn how to integrate a game with external APIs (Kongregate).

3.   Learn how to quickly develop games in Unity and Playmaker.

4.   A step-by-step game development tutorial using AI scripting, external APIs, and Multiplayer implementation.

Unity 4.x Cookbook

ISBN: 978-1-84969-042-3   Paperback: 386 pages

Over 100 recipes to spice up your Unity skills

1.   A wide range of topics are covered, ranging in complexity, offering something for every Unity 4 game developer.

2.   Every recipe provides step-by-step instructions, followed by an explanation of how it all works, and alternative approaches or refinements.

3.   Book developed with the latest version of Unity (4.x).

Please check **www.PacktPub.com** for information on our titles

Unity Android Game Development by Example Beginner's Guide

ISBN: 978-1-84969-201-4   Paperback: 320 pages

Learn how to create exciting games using Unity 3D for Android with the help of hands-on examples

1. Enter the increasingly popular mobile market and create games using Unity 3D and Android.

2. Learn optimization techniques for efficient mobile games.

3. Clear, step-by-step instructions for creating a complete mobile game experience.

Unity Multiplayer Games

ISBN: 978-1-84969-232-8   Paperback: 242 pages

Build engaging, fully functional, multiplayer games with Unity engine

1. Create a variety of multiplayer games and apps in the Unity 4 game engine, still maintaining compatibility with Unity 3.

2. Employ the most popular networking middleware options for Unity games.

3. Packed with ideas, inspiration, and advice for your own game design and development.

Please check **www.PacktPub.com** for information on our titles

10697017R00176

Printed in Great Britain
by Amazon.co.uk, Ltd.,
Marston Gate.